שלום רב ל... א ... ...

My best wishes ...
Melani ... Doves
for good health and ...
Israel ...

ArtScroll History Series®

Rabbi Nosson Scherman / Rabbi Meir Zlotowitz

General Editors

Destined

Published by
Mesorah Publications, ltd

to Survive

Uplifting stories
from the worst of times

by Israel I. Cohen

Portions translated from Yiddish by Rabbi Shmuel Yaakov Klein
Edited by Gitta Cohen Shafran

Introduction by Herman Wouk

FIRST EDITION
First Impression ... August 2001

Published and Distributed by
MESORAH PUBLICATIONS, LTD.
4401 Second Avenue / Brooklyn, N.Y 11232

Distributed in Europe by
LEHMANNS
Unit E, Viking Industrial Park
Rolling Mill Road
Jarow, Tyne & Wear, NE32 3DP
England

Distributed in Israel by
SIFRIATI / A. GITLER — BOOKS
6 Hayarkon Street
Bnei Brak 51127

Distributed in Australia and New Zealand by
GOLDS WORLDS OF JUDAICA
3-13 William Street
Balaclava, Melbourne 3183
Victoria, Australia

Distributed in South Africa by
KOLLEL BOOKSHOP
Shop 8A Norwood Hypermarket
Norwood 2196, Johannesburg, South Africa

ISBN:
1-57819-792-9 (hard cover)
1-57819-793-7 (paperback)

Typography by CompuScribe at ArtScroll Studios, Ltd.

Printed in the United States of America by Noble Book Press Corp.
Bound by Sefercraft, Quality Bookbinders, Ltd., Brooklyn N.Y. 11232

ACKNOWLEDGMENT

I would like to thank the Julius Kuhl Family Foundation, especially our family friend George Kuhl, for his encouragement, true friendship and financial support in bringing this book to print. May it be in memory of his beloved parents and brother, of blessed memory:

לז״נ

יחיאל בן יצחק אייזיק קוהל ע״ה

זוג׳ פרומעט בת ר׳ שמואל הלוי ע״ה

שמואל בן יחיאל קוהל ע״ה

Dedication

This book is dedicated to my dear wife of more than fifty years, Perle Cohen, nee Sternberg, who, like Ruth of the *Tanach*, left her birthplace, peaceful Switzerland, as well as her family — parents, brothers, sisters, nieces and nephews — and went with me, a lone survivor of the Holocaust, just a month and a half after our wedding, with just $80 between the two of us, to a strange land — Canada. We had neither relatives nor friends there, except for my friend Shlomo Yunger, with whom I have a special relationship, as we suffered together for three years at a sanitorium for tuberculosis in Davos, Switzerland. Since he had just immigrated to Canada, he sent us papers to enable us to come to this country.

Life was not easy, but Hashem helped us in every step with His *hashgachah pratis*. Perle is the mother of my five children *be"H*, whom we raised together *b'ruach haTorah v'yiras Shamayim* and *middos tovos*: my daughter Chana Leah Norman, our son Avrohom Mordechai, our daughter Gita Shafran, our daughter Chaya Tamar West, and our son Pinchas Elazar Tzvi (Eli). My wife has constantly been a source of courage and support in all aspects of my life, including every detail of my health and diet (due to my chronic digestive disorders). It is with her encouragement that I decided to put my wartime memoirs to print.

לז"נ

אבי מורי פנחס אלעזר בן צבי הכהן

אמי מורתי חנה לאה בת יצחק מנחם

אחותי גיטל

אחותי אלטה מירל

סבי צבי בן פנחס אלעזר הכהן

וסבתי פרומעט

שנספו בשואה הי"ד

Table of Contents

Foreword

The idea of writing about the suffering I witnessed and experienced in the ghetto and concentration camps occurred to me even during those times of oppression. Often while we were at work we would discuss whether people would be able to believe the heinousness of the daily affliction we had to endure, whether it was possible for the human mind to even fathom the misery, the selections, the beatings, the hunger, the humiliation, the degradation and the suffering of everyday life.

The ill-fated ones who were gassed, shot, burned, hanged or drowned died a relatively fast death. But the ones who were continually exposed to the frightful present, perpetually awaiting death – going out with their work details and not knowing if they would come back alive, confronting the strain and exhaustion of being overworked, and enduring starvation as well – were forced to face daily a special anguish: slow and agonizing uncertainty. I recall many who, when they were dying, begged others to let the world know of the atrocities that had been committed, and to take revenge on their murderers.

When I speak about my wartime experiences to groups of children or adults, I feel that I am fulfilling the last wishes of those who did not survive the Holocaust and were lost without a trace. I feel the same way about writing this book. Even though it is my personal story, it represents the story of the thousands of Sruliks and Cohens who suffered a similar fate. Let it be a testimony for generations to come, let them know what happened to their Jewish brethren. Even though I know that it is impossible for anyone who was not there to truly conceive what it was really like, I hope that readers will be able to connect with me, at least in some way, walking through the Valley of Death. Every morning, when I was driven to the *appelplatz,* with shouts, abusive language and beatings, to be counted and sent to work, I thought: Hell is not some place made of fire and brimstone. The *appelplatz* was the real hell, with horrifying scenes that the average person would not believe. We say in the *Haggadah* of Passover that every Jew should picture in his imagination that he himself was liberated from Egypt. Every Jew would do well to imagine himself in the contemporary Egypt in which I was enslaved.

My second reason for writing this story is to emphasize the *hashgachah pratis* that I was constantly witness to in my life. Whenever I speak to an audience, people ask me the same question that is on everyone's mind, including my own.

"Why did this happen?"

My answer is: I don't know, and no one else knows, not the most intelligent person, not the greatest *tzaddik* (righteous person). Anyone who attempts to rationalize the events in order to have peace of mind, or to satisfy himself, is deluding himself in his belief that he can understand the ways of Hashem, that His *hashgachah* can be fathomed by a tiny mortal brain. A Jew must not be afraid to say, "I do not know." We can only know that everything went according to a plan, a plan beyond our ken.

It is the same with the questions, "How was I able to survive, and how did all the others survive, when the Nazis' diabolical scheme worked so well to exterminate six million of our Jewish brethren? Were we righteous, and the others wicked? Why did Hashem not save all the great *tzaddikim*?"

If you say that it was random luck, then you deny the *hashgachah* of those numerous moments when I was at the threshold of death, and was saved, many times at the last minute. Could I possibly claim that I was lucky? Not at all. That I was smart? Not at all. I could feel the hand of G-d and His care for me, in not letting me die, in allowing me to survive for some reason that I do not understand.

I hope that my writing will inspire and remind others that we are constantly in the hands of the A-mighty, and that He guides us and provides us with the capacity to be good. Even now, I can still feel myself being guided and redeemed. Following this line of thinking, you will be better able to cope with life and all its vicissitudes, and be strengthened by your faith.

I thank the A-mighty for giving me life and health and the strength to put my memories into words.

I wish to thank my daughter, Gita Shafran, and her husband, Rabbi Avi Shafran, for their devotion and expertise in editing this book.

I also thank my children and my friends, and even the e-mail strangers who, having read bits of what follows here, encouraged me to write and publish the entirety. May those who read my stories benefit from them, and find the message that lies in each chapter.

An Appreciation

Not very long ago, at one of those all-too-rare-in-these-far-flung-times family gatherings where my beloved in-laws were surrounded by their children and grandchildren, my father-in-law, the author of this book, said something I will never forget.

The words were not his own; they were borrowed from the *navi Yeshayahu*, and the sentiments they embody are engraved on the souls of many a survivor, including my own dear father and teacher and my father-in-law, may they and their wives be well.

"Mr. Cohen" — as my father-in-law diminutively refers to himself, though he possesses the experience, knowledge and wisdom of an entire convention of rabbis — looked around at his daughters and sons and their spouses, against the lush and lively background of, *bli ayin hara*, grandchildren of a wide assortment of ages, all following in the proud Jewish footsteps he and his wife laid down over the years and continue to lay down, and, *be"H*, will continue to lay down for many years to come.

And then he said, quietly but with deep feeling: *"Mi yalad li es eileh?* Who bore me these? *V'eileh mi gidel?* And these, who raised them? *Hein ani nisharti levadi, eileh eifoh heim?* Behold, I languished alone, where did these come from?"

"I can't believe my fortune," he explained to those of us within earshot, who may have looked puzzled. "I can't believe that from lying in a pile of corpses in a burning concentration camp, starved and sick, I have been *zocheh* to all that I have today."

His words well reflect what you will perceive in this book: a deeply Jewish humility and honest appreciation of what *HaKadosh Baruch Hu* has bestowed — a most eloquent and moving embodiment of the sentiment Leah expressed at Yehudah's birth: "I have received more than my share."

What I know will impress and teach those who read my father-in-law's story — as it has me — is that his gratitude is no recent acquisition. It, and a deep trust in the Creator, imbued his heart and life even throughout the seven circles of hell that engulfed him over a half-century ago.

I owe him and my mother-in-law a deep gratitude of my own, not only for their cherished gift to me of my dear wife and the wonderful blessings that have followed our marriage, but also for the invaluable, powerful lesson that inheres in this book.

Rabbi Avi Shafran

Introduction

Israel Cohen, the author of *Destined to Survive,* is a Polish Jew, an Auschwitz survivor now living in Canada. I made his acquaintance in the small Hassidic synagogue in Palm Springs, where he comes in wintertime to enjoy the warm desert sunshine. A small, spare, quiet man, he volunteered to read the Torah on Shabat when he first visited, and has been doing so with flawless accuracy for years. It is a sad day for our little Chabad congregation when Israel Cohen goes back to Toronto around Purim time.

His cantillation skill was all I knew about him at first. If I gave an occasional *dvar Torah,* comment on the weekly portion, before services, he would sit quietly and listen. Now and then he might call my attention to one or another authority, or whisper a sharp point on the text. Soon I discerned that here was a man as learned as he was humble, a self-effacing *Talmid Hakham* who knew far, far more than I did. As our acquaintance developed, he disclosed that he was writing a book about his survival in the concentration camps.

Through the years I have had many encounters with survivors, especially during and after the writing of my novels *The Winds of War* and *War And Remembrance*. In the course of writing those works, I delved deeply into the published literature on the camps, and the multitudinous survivor documents in the archives of London, Paris, and Jerusalem. I did not imagine that there could be much new in Israel Cohen's book, nor was I sanguine that he would actually finish it and find a publisher. Nevertheless, I asked him to send me a sample chapter. I had come to feel a real debt to Mr. Cohen; not only because of his Torah readings, but because of the learning he shared whenever we talked. The chapter he duly sent me was intriguing, and I told him that if he succeeded in interesting a publisher, I would write an introduction to his book.

Years passed. He did finish his book, and found a fine publisher in ArtScroll. I have read his manuscript with care. In its bare bones as a survivor document, Israel Cohen's book goes over heavily ploughed ground, but his unpretentious account is outstanding for vividness – and most strangely – optimism. He was a lad of eighteen, a pious Gerrer Hassid, when he was swept into the maelstrom. He came out of it scarred in body and soul, yet still a pious Jew with undimmed faith in his Maker.

Without trying to fathom the religious challenges that the Holocaust poses, Israel Cohen simply tells how he survived. He has something like the novelist's eye for detail, and he has a unifying, uplifting theme; a perfect belief that the Lord guides every individual's destiny, though His ways are beyond our understanding. A skeptic might comment that Israel

Cohen, having survived while millions died, is entitled to his personal faith, but so what? This account is the riposte. The author paints a telling picture of the way a religious structure gives form and strength to life, and could do so even in Auschwitz.

The Jewish calendar becomes in his story a very narrow bridge of hope through the inferno. Cohen and his group from Lodz live from Shabat to Shabat, from holy day to holy day, always inching along the bridge. His tale of Hanukkah in Auschwitz – the lighting of a few drops of margarine in a spoon, with a wick unraveled from a ragged camp uniform, with Jews clustered around chanting the blessings and singing the songs – is memorable. The story of how he acquired that spoon, and how he sharpened one end of it to make a knife, risking an immediate bullet through his head if discovered, is one of a hundred life-giving touches in his story. The narrative of his experiences after his deliverance gives a fresh dimension to the book, especially the insights into postwar Poland.

Perhaps because he is so steeped in haggadic literature, Israel Cohen is a Maggid, a storyteller. *Destined to Survive* held my interest throughout. I recommend the book as a declaration of faith that has been tested in hellfire, and as an adventurous personal history wholly Jewish and wholly Godly. My latest book, *The Will to Live On,* is about the remarkable survival of God's people against almost impossible historic odds. In his personality, in his life, and in his book, Israel Cohen embodies that will to live on.

Herman Wouk

Palm Springs
Tammuz 5761
July 2001

Chapter 1

Jewish Life in Poland Before World War One

When I was about 6 years old, my grandfather brought my two older sisters and me to stay with him in his home in Brezezin, a small town about twenty-five kilometers from Lodz, where we lived. My father had left the country for Belgium, where he would remain for a few years. My mother did not have the financial means to take care of us. Thus began the special relationship I had with my grandfather, which only grew stronger with the difficult times which were to follow.

My grandfather was an active person, well liked by all, Jews and gentiles. His kindness and selflessness in caring for the poor, the sick and the lonely earned him the respect of people in all walks of life. A man of average means, he was always ready to help others and share his table with the needy. He was a Gerer chassid, strictly Orthodox, but he never demanded from the people he helped any attachment to religion. Wherever he went, in town or in the country, he would greet the people he met, and ask about their families, giving them his blessings.

A few months before my father left for Belgium, I was stricken with scarlet fever, which left me with an infected knee that became swollen and made it most difficult for me to walk. After consulting with one doctor after another and bringing me to therapeutic baths – all to no avail – my parents became desperate. The only solution any of the doctors could come up with was to put the whole leg in a cast so that the knee would become immobilized and nonfunctional. I would then have to walk with a limp. Finally my father, a Gerer chassid like his father, decided to go to the Rebbe for help.

Following the advice of the Gerer Rebbe *zt"l,* my parents brought me to the renowned Dr. Soloveichik in Warsaw, who, after examining me, sent me to an orthopedist who devised a special brace for my leg. Though heavy and cumbersome, after three years of being shackled to the contraption, my leg eventually returned to normalcy. Meanwhile, I had to travel every month to Warsaw to have my knee examined and my brace adjusted.

When I moved to Brezezin to live with my grandparents, I was still wearing the brace, and could not attend *cheder* (school), and so, my grandfather became my father, teacher and rebbi. I became very attached to him and grew to love him as I did my own parents. Even when my father returned from Belgium and my sisters and I returned to Lodz, I often longed for the wonderful times I had had when we lived with my grandparents.

Brezezin, where my grandparents lived, was a small town with a square, or marketplace, in the center, and four streets branching out in different directions. The Jews of the town made up about 50 percent of the population, and somehow, they lived in peace together with the Poles. But on Sundays and Christian holidays, when the Poles, who were devout Catholics, came out of their houses of worship, it was dangerous for any Jew to be out in the streets in the vicinity of the churches. The priests, most of whom did not have much sympathy for the Jews, rarely missed an opportunity to remind their congregants that the Jews had crucified their beloved savior, and therefore all Jews in all generations were guilty of deicide. Thus the people who attended the mass, mostly illiterate and ignorant farmers and laborers, were encouraged to harass the Jews, and unfortunate was the Jew who happened to pass by when the Poles were freshly inspired to avenge their savior. The hapless Jew soon became a target for verbal and physical abuse from the mob.

Every Thursday there was a farmers' market in the town square. All the farmers from the surrounding countryside drove in with their produce loaded onto their wagons, pulled by one or two horses. They parked their wagons in the marketplace and displayed their merchandise. In the summer they had fresh fruit, vegetables, chickens, eggs and butter, etc. The Jewish women came to buy food for Shabbos – chickens, potatoes for the *cholent*, and carrots for the *tsimmes*.

I remember visiting the marketplace with my grandmother on a Thursday morning. The farmers' wives were sitting on small low stools next to their bushels of cherries and onions. Some of the women had scales hanging from poles and others had measuring cups to measure their blueberries and beans. There were chickens in cages on top of the wagons, and the customers would feel them all over, and blow the feathers on their backs in order to ascertain their bulk. Butchers frequented the marketplace in order to pick out cows and calves for the slaughterhouses. Everyone was forever haggling over prices. Only a fool would pay the asking price of anything.

At the end of the day, townspeople returned to their apartments and farmers to their farms. Storekeepers brought their purchases to their stores to stock their shelves with fresh merchandise. Poor people could not buy in the marketplace, as they had no cash. Instead, they paid higher prices at the stores where they could buy on credit. Every grocer had a book in which he recorded all the money his customers owed him.

Many of the townspeople were tailors who worked at home for the wholesalers and storekeepers in Lodz. Some worked for individuals, making custom-made suits for them. Some had stores selling to townspeople or to farmers who came into town. Life went on at a slow pace.

There was one big synagogue, the official house of prayer, where most of the people prayed. It was a beautiful edifice, built expressly as a Jewish place of worship, housing an official rabbi who presided over services every Saturday, and on special occasions. There were also several *shtieblach* – small synagogues in private apartments – frequented by people with different customs, followers of different chassidic rabbis whom they greatly revered. My grandfather *davened* (prayed) at the Gerer *shtiebel,* where other chassidim – followers of the great Rabbi of Gura Kalvaria, a town near Warsaw called in Yiddish "Ger" – prayed together.

Friday was my favorite day, as on that day my grandmother baked *challos* (special loaves of white bread) and sometimes cakes and cookies, and sometimes even the blueberry buns that I loved. She also cooked for Shabbos, filling the house with delicious smells. We children would help prepare the food, and of course help ourselves to some bits and pieces.

About two hours before candlelighting time, my grandfather would prepare himself for the holy day. He put on clean clothing, and prepared two boxes to take with him to the *shtiebel*. One was a box of candies to give as Shabbos treats to the children who came with their fathers to the evening prayers, and the second was a snuff box – which contained a mixture of different brands of tobacco, with a few drops of perfume added, a treat for the men who gravitated to his corner of the *shtiebel* to partake of a bit of the snuff. The barrage of sneezes that ensued were evidence of the pleasure my grandfather gave to these people.

On his way to the *shtiebel* every Friday afternoon, he would gently urge the Jewish storekeepers to close their shops and go home to prepare for Shabbos. After the services, he would be the last to leave the *shtiebel*, but not because he was infirm or ailing. He was keeping an eye out for the transients – poor people who wandered from town to town on foot or hitched rides with passing wagons – who happened to pass the town on a Friday. As they had neither money to buy food nor a place to sleep (they often ended up sleeping on a straw sack in a room adjacent to the *shtiebel*), they would come to a house of prayer where people would invite them for the Shabbos meal. My grandfather, being the last one to leave the *shtiebel*, would take home with him anyone who did not get invited, sometimes even two or three people. My grandmother would be embarrassed, as she did not prepare for so many guests, but my grandfather would tell her not to worry, and he would share his portion with the others, giving the excuse that he could not eat then, or that he had a stomachache, so as not to embarrass the company.

On Saturday morning, before going to the *shtiebel* for morning prayers, people came to his apartment for tea. There was a big samovar, or teakettle, standing on a naphtha heater, with a spigot that dispensed the hot water. Not everyone could afford such a luxury. On a cold winter day when it was freezing outside, many a frozen visitor would thaw out with a cup of hot tea from my grandparents' samovar.

There was one event that sticks out in my mind. My grandfather won some money in the lottery, and he decided to dedicate a Torah scroll to the *shtiebel*. He paid a scribe to write out the Torah on parchment. It took more than a year to write it out by hand; the scribe used a goose-feather quill and special ink. When the written work was done, the scribe brought the skins to our house. On the final day before the dedication of the *Sefer Torah,* people volunteered to assist in sewing the skins together with special thread made from the veins of kosher animals, and our kitchen was full of women helping to bake cakes and roast the goose for the special meal honoring the completion of the *Sefer Torah*. The scribe would leave a few lines at the end of the Torah unfinished, and different people were given the honor of inscribing a letter onto the parchment.

About a week before this joyous occasion, two dozen Gerer chassidim, members of the Gerer *shtiebel,* rented a bus and traveled to Ger for the weekend. My grandfather went along with them, taking with him the last parchment of the *Sefer Torah,* before it was sewn on to the rest of it, so that the Rebbe could have the highest honor of writing the last letter of the Torah. To my great excitement and pleasure, my grandfather took me along with the group. We left on Thursday evening, and the trip lasted all night. As the roads were not yet paved with asphalt, but with stones, the bus, without adequate shocks, had us jumping up and down all night. At the sides of the road there were open ditches which served as a runoff for rainwater. The bus somehow landed in one of these ditches and almost overturned. We had to find a farmer with a couple of horses to pull the bus back onto the road. It was a great adventure that I, a high-spirited young boy, thoroughly enjoyed.

It was a very proud 6-year-old who went in with his grandfather to see the great Gerer Rebbe on that Shabbos night, with the parchment on which the Rebbe was to inscribe the last letter of the Torah. I gave him my hand, which he pressed, and I looked into his eyes that radiated warmth and kindness. After asking me a question that I almost did not hear, so great was my excitement, he placed a few cookies in my hand. My grandfather and I then made our way out of the room, walking backwards, still looking into his eyes.

Outside, we danced in a circle for a few moments, and then boarded the bus for the return trip home. I must have slept the whole night, for I do not remember anything about the trip. When we got off the bus in the middle of the marketplace, which was deserted because it was still dark, we once again danced a few rounds in the middle of the square, and then returned to our homes.

On the day of the joyous event of the dedication of the *Sefer Torah*, when all the parchment pieces had been sewn together, there was a big crowd waiting at the door of my grandfather's house. In the street there were some chassidim dressed as Russian Cossacks, riding on horses. (Our district had belonged to Russia until 1918.) The order of the procession was as follows: first the horsemen; then my grandfather, holding the Torah, encircled by a dancing crowd; then the orchestra members sitting in a large wagon drawn by two horses; and following everyone, a large host of people singing and dancing along the way, through the marketplace to the spacious house of one of my grandfather's friends.

It was apparent that the chief of police had been given a gift of some value, for he let all the townspeople know in advance that no anti-Semitic acts would be tolerated. There were policemen on guard at every turn, and no one dared disturb the procession.

Inside the house of my grandfather's friend, the celebration continued. People were called upon to come up and be given the honor of writing a letter in the *Sefer Torah*. Each time someone was called, the orchestra would start to play a well-loved tune, and everyone sang, drank and ate some of the delicious cakes that had been baked for the occasion. This continued until after dark.

When the *Sefer Torah* was finally completed, the procession resumed, this time heading for the city's big official synagogue. The scroll was carried under a canopy, like that used at a wedding, with men carrying torches and singing as they accompanied the "bride." Inside the synagogue, the rabbi made a speech, as did some government dignitaries who had been invited for the event. The cantor sang songs and chanted a blessing for the government.

So ended a great day for me. Everyone went back to the big house of my grandfather's friend where they celebrated with a huge banquet well into the night. I was not allowed to participate in the last stage of festivities, as it was past my bedtime and I had to go to sleep.

The next day, my grandfather and his friends went to the big shul to take the *Sefer Torah* from there to the Gerer *shtiebel*. At the *shtiebel* there were men who had taken out all the Torah scrolls there and, carrying them, went to meet the procession coming from the big shul with the new *Sefer Torah*. Again there were songs and dancing in the streets until a very late hour. The gentiles looked on with awe, not daring to disturb. The ones who hated the Jews, and these were not a few in number, were afraid of the police, who at this particular time guarded the peace very convincingly.

In this way, the Jews were able to live in the small towns in relative peace with their non-Jewish neighbors.

Chapter 2

My Early Youth

The late 1920's were turbulent times, and my father had to leave Poland and escape to Belgium. In the early 19th century, Poland had lost its independence and was carved up into three parts and divided among Russia, Germany and Austria. In 1918, at the end of the First World War, the Allies gave Poland back its independence. The Poles repossessed Upper Silesia from Germany, reclaimed Galicia from Austria, and took back Eastern Poland, including Warsaw and Lodz, from Russia. The Germans and Austrians had been badly beaten and left with no armies, and had no hope of regaining their territory, whereas the revolutionary Red Army was still very active, still involved in civil wars. The Russians tried several times to reconquer parts of Poland which until 1918 had belonged to them. The Polish generals and "pulkovniks" (colonels) led their armies in fighting long and hard against the Russians for many years. At one time the Russians even advanced to the gates of the capital city of Warsaw. In the end, the Poles beat the Russians back, even conquering parts of Western Russia and Western Ukraine, which was part of Russia.

These wars took a great toll on human life, and there was constantly the need for more manpower in the armed forces. The Polish military drafted scores of young men, single and married, with no regard for their wives and children.

Now, in general, the Polish commanders were very haughty and anti-Semitic. For example, in 1920, there was a general named Haler whose army, dubbed "the Halershiks," went on a rampage against Jews, especially religious Jews. Wherever they went, if they saw a Jew with a long beard, they would cut it off with scissors, and beat him up. It was dangerous for a religious Jew to venture out of his house and travel by train, or even just to show himself in the street. Jewish soldiers were excessively abused by the Polish recruits, and were always in jeopardy. They were forced to work on the Sabbath and Jewish holidays and were fed nonkosher food.

It was no wonder, then, that religious Jews tried any means to evade the draft. People would cut off their fingers or handicap themselves in other ways in order to make themselves unfit for the army. My father never told us exactly what he did, but he was court-martialed as a deserter, and condemned to be shot, despite the fact that he was married and the father of three small children, I being the youngest.

Somehow he escaped the death penalty. My mother told me that she went to army headquarters and pleaded for mercy. His case was adjourned, but, believing that it would be safer for him to leave the country, he fled to Belgium, where he lived for many years. Meanwhile, my mother and some friends worked on his case. Most likely they cleared him by bribing the right people, a standard procedure in Poland where the authorities practically solicited bribes. It was several years, though, until he was able to return.

My father was a well-educated and learned man, a thinker and a great scholar, not only in religious studies but in secular knowledge as well. He was fluent in many languages – Russian, Polish, Yiddish, Hebrew, German, French and Flemish. I remember leafing through his many books, trying to decipher the Russian alphabet, the German gothic script and the French words that were all Greek to me.

Unlike my grandfather, he was very strict with me, and insisted that I should learn to recite by heart everything I studied in school. He did introduce me, though, to the poems of the great Jewish poets of the Middle Ages and the Golden Age in Spain, and to the eminent Jewish thinkers and commentators of the *Tanach* like the Malbim, Radak and Ralbag. He was highly intelligent, and people came to him for advice in legal matters, and for help in writing letters and filling out forms for the government offices and the courts. He was a staunch Gerer chassid, and for him learning was the greatest pleasure. He was more of an intellectual than a businessman, and had a hard time feeding his family, having tried many businesses and trades but barely managing to make a living.

My mother was a very bright, warm and lovely woman, who tried to compensate for my father's strictness with a superabundance of love and devotion. She worked at home, designing and embroidering ladies' lingerie and tablecloths for the manufacturers of these products. Besides doing all the cooking and cleaning and domestic chores, she worked on the embroidery machine most of the day.

I can't forget the Friday nights when my father would test me on my learning by heart, which was usually torture for me, as my father liked me to know it perfectly, whereas, more often than not, I didn't, and punishment came swiftly and firm-

My mother (standing, left) at the matzeivah of her mother in Poland. Standing at the right is my mother's brother Aharon Dovid Wirstel. Sitting are my mother's sisters, Regina Rickel and Gitel.

ly. During the Sabbath-morning meals my father would study poetry and commentaries with me, and later in the afternoon, my mother would sing for my sisters and me old songs about Israel and the coming of Mashiach.

In the last year before the war, I was totally immersed in my studies in the Gerer *shtiebel*, from 5 o'clock in the morning until 10:30 at night, with a couple of breaks for breakfast and lunch. There were about thirty or forty of us young men learning there, the older ones teaching the younger ones.

During those prewar years, I traveled many times to Ger to see the Rebbe, staying for a few weeks and learning there with my friends. The traveling was rough, for with the little money that we had, we were only able to pay a truck driver a few zlotys to allow us to ride in his truck for a night's journey from

Lodz to Warsaw. Sometimes we rode in an open truck and the driver would cover us with a tarpaulin, and sometimes we would make the trip in a closed lorry in which we would be locked up for the night. In Warsaw we would stop at a synagogue for our morning prayers, and afterwards proceed to the little train, known as the "kolayko," that would take us to Gura Kalvaria. Very often we would get beaten up by Polish youth before we boarded the train. We did not worry much about food. If there was a boy among us who brought some food with him, he shared it with the rest of us. If not, we went about on empty stomachs.   But who cared about that? As long as we were able to go to see the Rebbe, we remained hungry but happy.

These good times ended abruptly for us on August 31, 1939.

Chapter 3

The Skies Darken

L ong before the outbreak of World War Two, the Jews in Poland were in an uneasy situation. Once the Nazis took over the government in Germany, anti-Jewish laws were enacted, and the propaganda war against the Jews began, spreading like wildfire in Germany and outside its borders as well. The anti-Semitism in neighboring Poland became unbearable. Jews were physically attacked in the streets. Pogroms broke out in many communities. There was a movement in the "Seim," the Polish Parliament, to ban *shechitah*, the slaughter of animals in accordance with the laws of the Torah. I remember every morning seeing new graffiti on the walls, hate-filled slogans like "The Jew is your enemy – Don't buy from a Jewish store!"; "Jews, go to Palestine!" and "Kill the Jews!" etc. Indeed, there were sworn anti-Semites and madmen who obeyed the signs. In many places Jews were killed right and left, even in big cities like Lodz.

When Hitler marched into Czechoslovakia, Poland became a partner to Germany and annexed a part of the Czech Republic. The Jews feared that Poland would not escape the impact of the German boot. It was just a matter of time.

I remember that when fellow Jews met each other in the street, they would ask each other, "Will there be a war?"

My father would speak to different kinds of people – rabbis, doctors, teachers and professors. No one could give him a suitable answer. It is stated in the Talmud that when G-d wants to punish His people, He makes their leaders and their guides blind (*Bava Kamma* 52).

The Polish leaders were also blind to the danger they posed to their own country by following the Germans. They were always eager to claim a portion of the spoils, and to remain on good terms with their neighbors the Germans.

"You took Czechoslovakia; we also want a part. You are staking a claim in Lithuania; we also want a share."

The Germans acquiesced to Poland's requests in order to maintain their support.

One Friday night when we were returning home from shul, we came upon a sizable demonstration of Poles lobbying for war against Lithuania. The crowd began to sing a Polish nationalistic hymn. As we were continuing on our way home, one big, fat Pole struck my father in the face, screaming, "You! Jew! Take off your hat!" (Apparently we had offended his sensibilities by not removing our hats for the song.)

Shortly afterwards, Hitler began with his demands from Poland – the cession of the port city of Danzig and the relinquishing of certain important rights in the Polish Corridor. It was then that the Poles turned away from the Germans, refusing their demands. But the Jews were still hated in Poland more than the Germans.

My last journey to Ger was for the holiday of Shavuos 1939. Thousands of chassidim came, every one apprehensive about the prevailing situation. Weeks before, during the holiday of Pesach, the Gerer Rebbe had shown some chassidim who were close to him a *kvittel*, a message, that an old chassid – who had been a follower of the Kotzker Rebbe, and then of the Chidushei Harim, and later of the Sfas Emes – had given him at the beginning of his leadership, in 1905. The *kvittel* mentioned, in the words of his great-grandfather, the Chidushei Harim, that there would come a time when things would be bad for the Jews, when the skies would blacken more and more, and a period of darkness – both physical and spiritual – would envelop the Jews of Europe. Only those who were deeply attached to the Torah would be able to still believe in it, and hold on to their religion. Now we knew that there definitely was something threatening in the air, something frightening and menacing. We felt trapped and helpless.

Even though the Gerer Rebbe encouraged his followers, especially those who had the means, to immigrate to Palestine (Israel), not many heeded the advice. (One needed to show that one had 1,000 English pounds in order to immigrate to Palestine.) Even the fiery Zionists, who strongly advocated moving to Palestine, themselves stayed in Poland to protect their fortunes.

On our way back from Ger, we were again attacked by Polish thugs who made fun of us and punched us as we boarded the streetcar in Warsaw.

On August 31, 1939, I came home from my studies. It was a hot evening, and I stood near an open window, listening to some martial music playing on the radio at a neighbor's house. Suddenly, the music stopped and there was an announcement that German airplanes were flying over Polish territory and bombing military sites. We were all to darken our windows, as the war was on.

The next day, on Friday morning, September 1, I went for the last time to the Gerer *shtiebel* at the usual time. Everyone was sad and worried, but still, we learned very forcefully, trying to forget the present. It was very hard to continue.

At noontime, we began to dance in a circle, with our eyes closed, holding hands, singing a chassidish tune. We all had the premonition that this would be the last time we were together as a group, and that we might not see each other again.

Every day, new things came up, such as having to run around, trying to get food. On Wednesday, September 6, the Polish army retreated in disarray through the streets of Lodz. Many Jews started running for their lives in the direction of Warsaw. Many were killed by the German planes that were roaming the skies undisturbed, machine-gunning soldiers and civilians alike. All the Polish planes had been bombed on the airfields before they could even take off.

On Friday, September 8, the German army entered Lodz, and hell began to rain down on us Jews.

Chapter 4

Ghetto Litmanstadt (Lodz)

W hen, on September 8, 1939, a mere week after World War Two erupted, the German army marched into Lodz, terror and catastrophe ensued, especially for the Jews. German soldiers shot Jews and beat them mercilessly; they arrested and assigned them to the toughest labor imaginable; they broke into Jewish homes and beat up the residents, plundering all their jewelry and valuables. Suddenly we were overcome with fear by day and by night – whether we remained in our houses or walked out in the streets.

I remember the day the German soldiers burst into our apartment, kicking in the door with their boots, carrying their rifles threateningly, and pulling out drawers, spilling out all the contents in their search for valuables. My father, who spoke German fluently and still remembered the German soldiers of the First World War, started to talk to the leader in German.

"But my friend ..."

Badge worn by the Jews

Before he could continue, the German punched him hard in the face and screamed, "Since when is a Nationalist Socialist a friend of a Jew?"

In February 1940, the Germans herded all the Jews of the city into a ghetto, situated in the "Balut" neighborhood, the poorest Jewish section of Lodz. We were ordered to leave our most valued possessions in our houses, while being allowed to take along with us only articles of minimal value, such as clothes, pots and other kitchen utensils.

On the first day of May 1940, the ghetto was sealed. From that moment on, we felt like hostages, but we were destined to experience far more suffering and hardship than we imagined. Incredible hunger and deadly epidemics soon spread; people were dying at home and in the streets, and the dead bodies multiplied like flies until the cemetery was filled to well beyond its capacity.

The starvation was so acute and widespread that some people ate their bread rations — which were supposed to last for eight days — in two days, because they were so famished. On the other six days they had only garbage and grass to eat, which caused them to become swollen and susceptible to all sorts of deadly epidemics, especially tuberculosis. The sick and the weak lay at home, waiting for the end. As there was no fuel for heating or cooking, people simply froze to death in their apartments, lacking resistance to cold and to disease.

Anyone who survived the ghetto years can tell you that the four years were satiated with misery, pain, suffering and fear. It was a miracle if a person could withstand the ghetto regime for the whole duration from the beginning to the end. From the approximately 200,000 people who were locked up into the ghetto in the beginning of 1940, only less than 10,000 remained to be sent off to Auschwitz.

There was always traffic flowing in and out. First there were deportations from the ghetto, and then the importing of Jews from all over Europe. Then there were again deportations, and then the bringing in of Jews from the ghettos in the small towns surrounding Lodz.

Those who were "fortunate" enough to escape the deportations were decimated by the hunger, the freezing temperatures and the various constant epidemics. When we got to Auschwitz, the "natives"– the veteran Auschwitz prisoners – told us of the lack of food and how the soup "stank." For us Lodz Jews, the soup was delicious. In the ghetto we would never be able to enjoy such a soup, with our inadequate rations.

The only advantage we had in living in the ghetto was that we were individuals living with our families in a Jewish enclosure. After work, we could still come together with other people, pray with a *minyan* (quorum), and make believe that although life was tough it was almost "normal." In Auschwitz, we were no longer considered human beings, only numbers, and we were treated like vermin.

In the ghetto, when we would occasionally receive a ration of kohlrabi, my mother would mince it, add some salt and saccharin, and then boil it. We would pretend that it tasted like minced fish or meat. If one took some of the burned grain called "ersatz," which was used as a coffee substitute, combined it with some ground kohlrabi, a little flour and a little sweetener, and fried it in a pan, with an extra dash of imagi-

Mordechai Chaim Rumkowski,
"King" of the Lodz ghetto

nation, the resulting dish could pass for a *kugel* or pancake.

We had underground religious schools, and other kinds of organizations. There were theatrical performances that big shots in the ghetto attended. Even Mordechai Chaim Rumkowski, the head of the Judenrat in the ghetto, would appear from time to time at such events.

After a long day of hard work, people would try to forget that their lives were constantly in danger. Every day we heard reports of Jews being shot if they happened to pass near the barbed wire surrounding the ghetto. There were some extremely vicious guards who shot at passersby just for the fun of it. Sometimes a guard would call out to a child or an adult that he should approach the wire fence. The person walking by, thinking the guard wanted to tell him something, would comply, only to be shot at point blank when he came into range of the guard's rifle.

I remember one event that could have been fatal for our whole family. When the ghetto was set up, there were some Polish districts that were included in the enclosed area. The Polish people who lived there were told to leave and settle in other districts around Lodz. As no order had yet been set up in the ghetto, people just grabbed whichever room they could find, trying for an apartment in the middle of the ghetto rather than at the edge. (There were only apartment houses in the ghetto, and each family was allowed only one room.) We were not the grabbing or the fighting type, so we ended up with a room in one of the Polish apartments at the very edge of the ghetto, on the second floor, with one window overlooking the barbed-wire fence. These apartments happened to be cleaner and nicer than the coveted more centrally located ones, but we had to always be careful not to stare out the window for fear of getting a bullet in the head. From the side, though, I liked to look out at the green grass and the freedom on the other side of the fence.

Every evening there was a curfew at 8 o'clock, when everyone had to be inside the building, with all the lights out, the rooms fully darkened. We would eat our "meals" beforehand, except on Friday nights in the summer, when we ate in the dark after the evening prayers. Next door to us lived a family who would not forgo the pleasure of eating the Sabbath meal in a lighted environment. The man put a blanket up on the window, making sure that no light would seep through to the outside, and so the electric light was on all night and all day, as they could not turn off the light on the Sabbath.

Unfortunately, one Friday night while we were all sleeping, the blanket fell off the window, which alerted the German guards to the fact that there was a light on in an apartment house. We awoke to some shouting in German, then heavy steps on the stairs, and soon a pounding on the door. Since our door was just opposite the stairs, they came to our door first. My mother covered me up, and opened the door. There stood some German guards with their rifles drawn.

"Why did you have your light on?" This was more of a shout than a question.

My mother answered that we did not have the light on, and we had been asleep.

One of the guards asked,

"Are there any men in the room?"

My mother and my sisters sitting up in bed said that there were none.

They left without harming anyone. This was a great miracle, as they shot people without even an excuse, and here there had been a great "transgression" against the German authorities.

Not much afterwards, the Germans took a part of the ghetto adjacent to where we lived and surrounded it with a double barbed-wire fence and a trench filled with water. In here they incarcerated a few hundred so-called "gypsies." They must have been very important political prisoners, as they were tortured mercilessly, and sometimes killed. Every night we could hear their agonizing cries, which frightened us and prevented us from sleeping. In the morning the Jewish burial commando was summoned and ordered to take the dead for burial in the Jewish cemetery that was in the ghetto. During the day, an orchestra played very loud classical music so as to drown out the cries of the victims. Afterwards, we were ordered to evacuate our premises, and we were given another room in a deteriorated house in the old part of the ghetto. It was not long before an epidemic broke out in the gypsy camp, and some Germans died from the disease. Then they shot everybody and liquidated the whole camp.

One day the Germans announced that every Jew must come to the ghetto market square. A rumor was spread that about ten Jews had been selected to be hanged, and the Germans wanted everyone in the ghetto to witness the hanging. Since we were behind in production, and there was not enough space for all the ghetto workers to watch the cruel spectacle, the employees in my factory were spared from having to view the actual ceremony. However, we were forced to come out on the next day to observe the hanging bodies. I will never forget the picture of those ten Jewish men, their bodies swaying in the wind, suspended by their necks. We were told to look, but I could not keep my eyes on this image. I walked with the crowd, with my eyes shut and a pain in my heart, all shaken up by the horrendous display. Their sin? They had tried to escape from the ghetto by passing as Poles on the Aryan side.

And so the days passed in misery and despair. Every day we heard rumors, probably the result of people wanting to believe that soon there would be a change for the good. We might be getting bigger rations, as the Germans needed our work for their war machine. When we heard that the Germans had conquered another country and acquired new territory in Europe or Africa, the optimist would say, "You see, the Allies want them to spread their supply lines, and so they handed them another country far from Germany, so as to thin their ranks."

Another of the optimists' themes was that we would be exchanged for German prisoners of war. The only problem was that the good news did not materialize. The bad news, however, turned out to be worse than we could imagine.

Meanwhile, even the healthy and strong succumbed to the hunger and nutritional deficiency we were subjected to from a lack of essential vitamins and minerals. At one point, after a terribly difficult winter, people suddenly could not walk; their joints would not function. And, since they had to go to work every day in order to get their soup, they walked with great pain.

One day, suddenly, the plague hit me. My joints ached so much that I could barely walk. It took me hours to go to work and to come home. My mother could not bear to see me in such pain and asked her neighbors and co-workers if they knew of any remedy. She found out that one could get from the black market a tiny bottle of vitamins called "vigantol." This was a wonder medicine, she was told. By just taking a few drops a day, one could start walking again. I told her that she should not believe in such nonsense. It was just a trick that the black marketers thought up to extort rations from some poor fools, as the price for the bottle of vitamins was a whole bread, worth about 4 or 500 marks on the black market.

Nevertheless, my mother started to save her own bread, until one day she brought home for me a small bottle containing that marvelous liquid. I was very upset, as I was convinced that she had simply been cheated out of her bread. But she begged me to take it, and she put a few drops into my mouth every day. Wonder of wonders, after only three days, I started to walk without pain, and by the time I finished the bottle, I could walk normally, as I had done before.

This was not the last of my afflictions. I developed swollen glands in my neck, and under my armpits. My grandfather's doctor treated me with needles of calcium, which helped a little, but not entirely. I had my glands pierced and the pus extracted, but after a while, the swelling would come back. I cannot understand how I could have passed by the infamous Dr. Mengele when we arrived in Auschwitz, to be sent to the right side, which meant life. I can only return to my theory that the A-mighty intended that I should live, that I was destined to survive by Divine Providence. By the time I arrived in Death Camp Number Four, Camp Kaufering near Dachau, the swelling had completely disappeared. There was no logic to this happening, but for the will of G-d.

❦

Despite all the suffering in the ghetto, we had the advantage of being "home." Somehow, we managed to celebrate all the Jewish holidays, including Passover. The "king" of the ghetto, Mordechai Chaim Rumkowski, agreed to supply matzos for the religious community. We could choose to receive two pounds of matzah for eight days instead of four pounds of bread. It was worth it for us to forfeit two pounds of bread in order to fulfill the mitzvah of matzah. Somehow we organized a *seder,* naturally without wine. The matzos served as a reminder of G-d having taken our forefathers out of Egypt. We didn't need any bitter herbs to remind us of the bitter life they had had in Egypt. Our own lives were bitter enough. During the day we were forced to go to work, even on the Sabbath, but then we tried hard to do the minimum amount of work possible, at least less than we would do on a weekday. At night we would reminisce about the times before the war when everything was normal, and we could go where we wanted to go, and do what we wanted to do, and dream about the future. We always finished with the words: *"Leshanah habaah biYerushalayim!* – Next year in Jerusalem!"

Chapter 5

Deportations From Lodz

From January to April of 1942, the Germans deported approximately 50,000 Jews from the Lodz ghetto. At first, since they wanted the Jews to come voluntarily, for appearances' sake, they concocted a story that they needed workers in Germany, adding that the living conditions were a lot better there than in the ghetto. As a further enticement they promised that families could remain together and that food would be plentiful at the new locations.

Some Jews volunteered, falling for the alluring deceptions of the Germans. That winter of 1941-42 was extremely severe – unnaturally cold, with tremendous amounts of snow. We had nothing with which to heat our flats, and we had long ago used the last pieces of furniture as fuel with which to cook the meager rations we received. The potatoes that the ghetto administration had stored for the winter had frozen, causing even greater starvation than we had thought possible. I remember that each night before I went to sleep I would have to eat a small piece of bread, about the size of a nut, which I had hidden. Otherwise, I wouldn't be able to fall asleep because of the great hunger pangs that gnawed at my insides.

At night I would put a bowl of water next to my bed with which to wash *neigel vasser* (hand-washing before getting out of bed) in the morning, but overnight it would turn to ice.

Many people decided to believe the Germans who were calling for people to volunteer for resettlement to another ghetto or camp, where life would be much better than in the Lodz ghetto. Because it was such a hard winter and there was a great famine in the ghetto, parents could not bear to see their children suffering from the cold and hunger, while the children found it hard to comprehend why their parents did not give them food, and allowed them to freeze from a lack of clothes and fuel. A lot of Jews calculated that wherever the Germans intended to take them, it couldn't be worse than in the ghetto, and so they appeared with their families at the deportation sites and left the ghetto, never to return.

Deportation from Lodz ghetto

The vast majority, however, did not trust the Germans. So a new tactic had to be employed. Rumkowski, the leader of the Judenrat in the ghetto, began by ordering his

Jewish policemen to take people by force. At first they took the Jews who had been caught in some "criminal" act such as stealing a piece of wood for fuel, or a potato, or dealing in saccharin in the streets.

Later on, letters were sent informing people that they were to appear for transport. Other letters ordered people who had received welfare from the ghetto administration but had not yet been given work — to present themselves for deportation. Once one family member was chosen to be deported, the rest of the family followed suit.

After that, the Germans seized anyone they could find who was hiding and did not want to volunteer for transport.

For some reason, our family got a letter from the ghetto administrator telling us that we should appear in a couple of days at the assembly point for resettlement. My mother said that under no circumstance should we go to be sent out of the ghetto. Instead, we should leave our apartment and hide, in order that we should not be picked up by the ghetto police. We tried also to get help from a distant relative who was a secretary to Rumkowski, the Jewish ghetto head, but who never seemed to be available to see us. She probably had many others who were turning to her for "protekzia." Finally, I decided to speak to the commissar of the tailor shop where I had just been appointed mechanic and foreman of buttonhole-machine operators. As there was a great shortage of buttonhole-machine mechanics, and since the buttonhole group was a vital section of the factory that manufactured German uniforms, the commissar, for his own sake, went to all the right places, and succeeded in taking us off the list of prospective deportees; I had told him that if any member of our family would be sent away, we would all go together.

Nevertheless, we had some very anxious moments, as very often the police had to fill their daily quota, without consideration of any exemptions. Each night we would spend in a different location. We were afraid to go out and redeem our food coupons as we might be picked up right then and there. People who had been sent their exit papers were immediately crossed off the rations' list, so that if one of these people came to try to redeem his rations, the police would instantly take him to the deportation center. Fortunately for us, the resettlement quota was soon filled, so a week or so later we could breathe a sigh of relief.

All the people who were transported out of the ghetto at that time were sent to Chelmno, not far from Lodz. There, in the hands of the *einsatzgruppen* (Death Squad), they were gassed in the trucks that had transported them, or they were simply shot in the forests and their bodies were burned.

This was another instance demonstrating that Divine Providence protected me and the people around me.

Chapter 6

Instructor: Part One

I n the Lodz ghetto, named Litmanstadt by the Germans, we were isolated from the rest of the world. Having lost our jobs and businesses, we no longer had the means of earning cash, which we needed in order to buy food rations. At first we managed by selling whatever valuables we owned and had brought with us into the ghetto. We tried to make this money last as long as we could, but eventually it ran out and we had to go hungry. My parents and two sisters could not find any work, and I, a chassidic yeshivah boy who learned all day in a Gerer *shtiebel,* lacked any work skills. Even if one worked, he could make only enough to feed himself. Mordechai Chaim Rumkowski, whom the Germans had appointed as the *altester der Juden,* or Jewish head of the Lodz ghetto, had plans of turning the ghetto into a large work center, in order to provide everyone with the money to buy food rations and all other necessities, and to give the Germans a reason to allow us to stay where we were.

I was always made aware of the presence of *hashgachah pratis*, or Divine Providence, in my life, especially during the war years. The smallest, seemingly insignificant event could, through the A-mighty's will, save those who were supposed to survive.

One of our neighbors in the ghetto, a certain Mr. Citrinowicz, was saying *Kaddish* for his deceased mother. On the Sabbath he had a *minyan,* of men praying in his apartment, and, since he needed someone to read from the Torah, I volunteered for the job. For this he was very grateful to me, and we became quite friendly.

Mr. Citrinowicz had owned a factory which manufactured clothing before the war. As he knew his trade well and had the good fortune to be friendly with Mr. Rumkowski, he was made an executive in the ghetto's central office over all the tailor shops, whose task it was to manufacture uniforms for the German army.

A tailor shop was composed of about twenty to thirty groups of tailors, depending on the building. In each group there were fifteen to twenty workers.

There were special machines for making buttonholes. These machines were supplied by a group of people who had owned the buttonhole machines before the war and had serviced the tailoring industry; now all machinery had been confiscated and had become ghetto property. However, since the operation of these machines was a complicated affair, the previous owners were retained to run and service them, and to oversee a staff of women and girls who worked as finishers, cutting loose threads and sewing ends together.

The competition in the buttonhole business had been fierce before the war. The owners of the complex buttonhole

Money used in the Lodz ghetto, called "Rurucks,"
signed by Mordechai Chaim Rumkowski

machines, now mechanics and instructors, were very posses-sive and reluctant to let anyone touch their machines, which they expected would be returned to them after the war. Nor did they want to teach others their trade, so as to avoid further competition after the war.

In the meanwhile, though, more tailor shops were opened. Rumkowski needed to feed the ghetto residents, but this was only possible through work and the cash it generated. Each instructor was put in a different shop and worked day and night. Earning two ghetto pfennigs for each buttonhole, he could make about 500 ghetto marks per week – more than any executive earned, but hardly enough to buy a loaf of bread on the black market.

As the factories expanded and the number of workers increased, production grew immensely, but there was a delay in the buttonhole department. It was not physically possible for the one or two buttonhole people per shop to make suffi-cient buttonholes for the completed uniforms. The Germans began to grumble and indicated that they would consider any delay as sabotage, with grave consequences for everyone.

Rumkowski, after meeting unsuccessfully with the buttonhole operators, who still refused to teach anyone else how to work their machines, decided to punish them severely. He assigned them to a work force whose task it was to scoop excrement and sewage from the latrines into special containers and, acting as human horses, pull the wagons holding the containers to their designated destinations. The stench, as well as the humiliation, were almost unendurable. After a few days they broke down and agreed to teach some new people how to work the buttonhole machines.

Mr. Citrinowicz immediately informed me of a job opportunity, as there were now openings for a hundred young people to learn how to operate the machines. Happy to be able to earn some money to buy my rations, I started to work at a tailor shop near the edge of the ghetto.

A team of twenty apprentices was assigned to learn and work the ten buttonhole machines in this group. There were two shifts, one from 7 a.m. to 1 p.m., and the second from 1 p.m. to 7 p.m. A pair of apprentices worked on each machine. My partner was Motek Gewertzman, a man much older than I, and, unlike my timid self, very outspoken, aggressive and bold. We became good friends, and we ignored the shifts, taking shorter turns operating the machine. We soon became proficient at our jobs and worked quickly and efficiently. Our instructor no longer had to work as an operator; he needed only to adjust and repair the machine whenever it broke down, which happened quite frequently. While we were paid 10 ghetto marks per week, hardly enough to pay for our food rations, the instructor still received his two pfennig per buttonhole payment, and, due to our ever-increasing efficiency, made quite a big salary. We dared not protest about our meager wages of only 10 marks, for we feared that the instructor would fire us or deliberately stall the adjustment of our machine. So we simply swallowed the injustice and continued our work.

After a few months, my partner took me aside.

"Look, Srulek," he said, using my nickname, "we are the fastest and most efficient workers in the whole group. Why are we allowing one man, who is the instructor, to work us like slaves, take for himself all the money that we are earning, and pay us a measly 10 marks a week?"

I answered, "We need him to keep the machines in good working order. Without him, we wouldn't even get the 10 marks."

"I think you could repair the machine as well as he does," Motek retorted. "I've watched you make minor adjustments and I can tell that you are mechanically minded."

He was all for breaking away and working on our own, but I, lacking in self-confidence, was afraid to take responsibility for both of us.

I said, "No, I will not rock the boat and make trouble for us both."

Motek, however, decided to ask the instructor for a raise, since we were the most productive of all the workers, always exceeding our quota for the day. The instructor refused to even discuss the matter. So Motek, now very upset, went straight to the commissar of the shop to complain that the instructor refused to give us even a small raise. He asked if we could work independently on one of the machines, in order to increase production.

After consulting with his superiors, the commissar agreed to allow us to work independently and get paid according to our output. The ghetto leaders were anxious to break the monopoly of the original group of buttonhole machinists. They had the power to halt the production of all the tailor shops, since they alone knew how to run the machines.

When Motek brought me the "good" news that we would be allowed to work on our own at one of the machines, I was frightened at the prospect of not having the instructor to service and repair the machine when necessary. When I protested, he told me that it was an irreversible order from the commissar. Reluctantly I agreed to work with him, but I was still worried. Since Motek worked rather forcefully and recklessly on the machine, I knew a breakdown was inevitable.

The first week we made more than 100 marks. Though happy with the money, we were still worried about a possible breakdown. The second week we did even better and made about 150 marks. But on the third Monday, as Motek was relentlessly racing the machine, we heard a loud bang and the machine stopped in the middle of a buttonhole. I was scared. The instructor eyed us with a gleeful smirk, as if to say, "Now they will come back to me on their knees, begging me to repair the machine and happy to get their weekly 10 marks." Motek looked at me with guilty eyes, and meekly begged me to save the situation. With my back effectively against the wall, I started to dismantle the machine, trying to figure out what went wrong. Some parts were broken and others were dislodged and out of place. I worked straight for two full days and nights, stopping only for a few hours of sleep, acquiring some new parts and straightening out others that were badly bent. Finally, on the third night, with a click and a whir, the machine started to work again. When Motek arrived the next morning and saw the machine working again he hugged me joyfully and said, "I knew you could do it!"

I, in turn, thanked the A-mighty for having given me my mechanical inclination and the opportunity to study the parts and workings of the machine so that I could repair it. From then on I had no difficulty repairing and adjusting any of the machines.

A few months passed and then came the terrible winter of 1941-42, which brought huge snowstorms and severe frost. Fences and abandoned shacks disappeared during the night as people ventured out to snatch any piece of wood they could find to heat their rooms and cook their rations.

Hundreds of kilograms of potatoes froze in the warehouses, causing a decrease in food rations. Then, within a period of three months, 50,000 Jews were deported from the ghetto. The Germans, deceptive as usual, and unwilling to risk an uprising, promised the people that they would be sent to Germany, to factories where they would have plenty of food and be together with their families. In fact, they were all sent to Chelmno, where they were gassed or shot in the woods.

Many people, distrusting the Germans, tried to hide, but most ended up being taken by force. Some, though, desperate because of the hunger and cold, thinking that nothing could be worse than the Lodz ghetto, went voluntarily to the assembly place where they would be taken to the trains. Among these was our instructor, who could not withstand the hunger and could not bear to see his family suffering. No one wanted to believe that the Germans would put such a multitude of men, women and children to death.

After the deportation, we arrived at work to find that there was no mechanic to repair or adjust the machines. The commissar came in and asked: "Is there anyone here who knows how to repair these machines?"

There was silence.

Again he asked, "Is there anyone among you who is able to look after your machines?"

Then Motek stood up and said, loudly, "Cohen knows how to repair the buttonhole machines."

The commissar turned to me and asked: "Is this true?" As a 16-year-old yeshivah boy with no mechanical training, I lacked self-confidence and was afraid to take responsibility for heading the whole group of about fifty operators and finishers that would come with the job of taking care of the machines. I said, "No, I can't."

But Motek again stood up and insisted, "Of course he can. He keeps our machine in perfect condition."

The commissar turned back to me and said, "From now on you will be the instructor, and I will not tolerate any excuses."

From that moment on, I became the youngest instructor in the ghetto.

Chapter 7

Instructor: Part Two

Thrust into my new position as instructor/mechanic in charge of a whole group of people, I began to feel panicky. I was not cut out to be a bully, or the kind of aggressive and power-hungry person who was usually appointed by the Germans to a position of power, cruel to the weak and hungry workers and forever yelling at and even beating up the poor souls who couldn't work at the pace that he, as foreman, demanded. "Power corrupts," they say, but I was young and I came from a Gerer chassidic background, which instilled in me the characteristics of being idealistic and humble and respectful of the dignity of other human beings. I did not want to be separated from my co-workers who had become my friends, nor did I want to be one of those foremen hated by most of the workers. I had no desire or temptation to become an exploiter of other people. Instead, I tried to use my new position to protect the workers in my group from the administration. When the commissar asked me to establish the minimum quota that each operator should achieve, I gave him a very low number – 600 buttonholes per shift. (I myself could do three or four times that number.) But there were some sick people who couldn't even do that many. When one worker came to report to me at the end of his shift, I asked him if he had finished his daily quota. He told me he had only done half of the required 600 buttonholes. When he showed me his swollen hands and feet, I told him to go home, and I finished his quota in less than an hour.

I had yet another dilemma. I had been one of those who resented our former instructor for the large amount of money he made from our hard labor. Now here I was in the same position, taking the pay away from the hard-working people in my group. Again, I was helped out of this predicament by *hashgachah pratis*. Just around this time, the administration of the tailor shops decided to have all the instructors become employees of the ghetto self-government and thus earn a fixed salary independent of production. We were given yellow armbands to wear, identifying us as ghetto employees. The other workers would from now on get two pfennigs for each buttonhole, eliminating the problem of jealousy. As additional compensation, the instructor would receive an extra food ration. Even if the ration was minimal, it was still better than money, for in the black market food and medicine were exorbitant.

During the infamous "Sperre curfew," which took place in August and September of 1942, when the Germans hauled away all the children to be killed, some parents somehow managed to hide their children. After the Germans stopped searching for more children, the ghetto authorities placed the ones who remained, ranging from 10 to 16 years of age, in different shops to work as messengers and couriers. Among the children who were allocated to our group were some religious boys who attended underground religious schools. I assigned these boys to the afternoon shift, while registering them in the morning shift, gave them tickets for their daily soup, and sent them away to learn. Although this was a risky business, I felt it was something I had to do and besides, being somewhat of a rebel, I had the satisfaction of knowing that I was defying the German authority by disobeying orders.

During my first year of being in charge of a group, an incident occurred that showed that even for an instructor and someone indispensable in the line of production, it was extremely risky to be different from the others.

The building in which our shop was located housed twenty tailor groups, each with its own foreman and each served by our buttonhole-processing group. The administration consisted of the technical supervisor, two foremen and the commissar, who had supreme arbitrary power. The commissar, an assimilated Jew and a former sergeant in the Polish army, was an arrogant young man in his late 20's or early 30's, rather contemptuous of his subordinates and workers. If an elderly worker ever left his place and tried to go home two minutes earlier than he was supposed to, the commissar would take off his belt and hit him over the head. His language was nasty and vulgar and he was constantly cursing and behaving like a tyrant, so that no one dared to defy him in any way.

One of the foremen in the tailors' group tried to befriend the commissar by flattering him and trying to impress him with his workers' rate of production, which he achieved by pressure and coercion. Now, whenever the uniforms were ready, they were sent down to my group for buttonholes to be made. We had a policy of "first come, first served," trying to be fair to everyone. The foreman, however, tried to get us to work on his uniforms right away, out of line, so that he could show that his group's production exceeded that of the other groups, but to his chagrin, he did not get any preferential treatment from me. I repeatedly explained to him that it wouldn't be right for the groups who brought their uniforms earlier to have to wait longer, while his got finished right away. As I was his equal in rank, he had no authority over me, so he tried to get his friend the commissar to use his power to force me to concede to his demands.

Now, in our workplace we had ten machines set up in two rows of five machines each, facing one another. Between the two rows there was a long shaft driven by a single motor, with several pulleys connected to the machines so that each operator could run his machine by pressing on a special pedal with his foot. These old buttonhole machines were very hard to operate, as the completed uniforms were cumbersome and needed to be moved around as the buttonhole was being made. The motor was needed in order to facilitate the foot operation, allowing a small amount of pressure to do the same work as moving a foot pedal back and forth.

One day the commissar visited our group and ordered me to take one of the machines and set it up on the third floor for the exclusive use of his friend the foreman. I explained to him that in order to work our machines we needed a motor because it was very hard to work with hands and feet at the same time. He went into his office and called the central office of the tailor shops to inquire about a motor, but there was none available. About an hour later he returned and said to me, "No matter what, you must supply a machine and operators to be put in this special group as soon as possible."

Ordinarily, a foreman or group leader would have the power to enforce any order given by the commissar. Anyone told to do a certain kind of work had to comply, or risk being put into jail and then deported at the first opportunity. But I knew I would have no volunteers in my group, and I didn't have the heart to coerce anyone to forgo the use of the motor. People were weak from the famine in the ghetto. (My own father had died in 1942 of starvation.) Similarly, when I had needed to move a female finisher from one job to the other, she refused, and I tried to be strict and explained that I had to enforce discipline as I was responsible for the work. But when I saw tears in her eyes, I gave up and tried to find someone else for the job. I was neither tough nor domineering, as were most of the other foremen. Whereas I had gained my position through my ability to service and repair the machines, the others had aggressively sought their positions of power so they could act as dictators, which I could not do. At any rate, I told the commissar that I would need to adjust one of the machines to be run by foot without a motor, which could take some time, and I would let him know when it would be ready.

This gave me a few days' time to discuss with my group what to decide on the matter. It also gave me the satisfaction of standing up to the dreaded commissar and his friend, making it difficult for him to enforce his order, something he was unaccustomed to with his other subordinates.

During the next two weeks I "worked" on the machine. I took it apart and put it together again numerous times, purposefully breaking some parts and making new ones, so that it would take more time to comply with the demand, in the hope that the foreman would change his mind and rescind his order for a special machine to serve his group.

One day, the commissar burst into our group's area and shouted at the top of his voice, "Why is the machine not yet ready to be set up for the special group?"

I had been ready to give him my excuse that it was extremely difficult to adjust the machine, but feeling affronted and resentful at his screaming at me in front of my whole group, I instead calmly said, "I am not deaf, and you can talk to me as to a human being, not a slave."

The commissar, not used to having one of his subjects answering him back, especially not a 17-year-old, could only utter one word, an obscenity.

I have no idea from where I got the courage to reply, "And your mouth is like a toilet. All that comes out of it is filth and scum. Why don't you learn to talk like a human being?"

By now all the people in my group were holding their breath in fear of what would happen next. The commissar, his face filled with rage, lunged at me with his hand raised to strike me. In my hand I held a heavy file, which I had been using to file metal. I was so tense and overwrought with emotion that I was ready to land a blow on his head with my file if he were to strike me, regardless of the consequences. He must have sensed the danger to himself, for he lowered his hand to his pocket and, to save face, took out a small notebook and scribbled something in it, and, without a word, ran out of the room. Time stood still for a couple of minutes, until the people in our group began to resume their normal activity. No one uttered a word about the incident, but all eyes clearly showed the sympathy and pity everyone felt knowing that my fate was sealed. I myself was in a daze, for the emotional drama had sapped my energy.

After work that day, I started to walk, for I needed to sort out my thoughts and calm my nerves. It was the middle of the summer and it would be a while before darkness would envelope the ghetto. I had no direction or purpose in my walk, but my feet carried me to Marishin, a suburban part of the ghetto, with small houses and greenery. Here were housed the new arrivals to the ghetto from Germany, Czechoslovakia and Austria. Most of these people were assimilated Jews who actually resented being housed in a ghetto with Eastern European Jews. But previously, I had seen one of the new arrivals, an elderly man wearing a yarmulke and studying a *sefer* (Hebrew book containing Torah thoughts) so I had approached him and had engaged him in a discussion of religious matters. He was a German doctor who had been rounded up with other Jews and told by the Germans that they would be taken to a safe place in Austria where they would be lodged and fed. Instead they were taken to the Lodz ghetto where they knew only extreme hunger and cold. After I had met him the first time, I visited him often and we became friends.

On that day as I walked aimlessly through the neighborhood, I noticed my friend through a window. Like lightning, a thought struck me and I entered his room, saying, "Doctor, please help me. I have a terrible pain in my stomach."

"I'm sorry, I can't examine you," he apologized. "They took away all my medical tools."

Then he put his ear to my chest and to my abdomen and said, "I can't be sure of what the problem is, and I can't prescribe any medicine for you because it is not available in the ghetto."

"Then please give me a note saying that I am sick and must be exempted from work for two weeks."

This he did, and I went home to my family and told them all that had happened that day. My mother and sisters were very worried but I said to them, "You can't change what happened already. You can just hope for the best. At least I won't have to face the commissar for another two weeks."

The next day I sent my sister to get my two soups. I was entitled to the extra soup since I was an instructor. The enraged commissar refused to give her more than one soup. I was satisfied with being able to stay at home. While I was "sick," I couldn't be seen outside. Things remained quiet for the next ten days.

On a Saturday morning, while I was saying the morning prayers at home, I noticed through the window someone approaching our flat. It was the technical adviser of our shop, Mr. Benkel, a middle-aged man, who came from the same city as my grandfather, and knew him well. He had become supervise both through his professional knowledge and by knowing the right person in the right place. As soon as I saw him I quickly undressed, got into my pajamas and climbed into bed. When he entered the room (there was only one room per family) he said "Good Shabbos" and I motioned him to sit down in a chair near me. I waited for him to speak and tell me what brought him here.

"You must come back to the shop and begin to work right away," he began. "We need you."

"You see that I am sick in bed," I protested. "How can you ask me to go to work?"

He smiled and winked at me, as if to say, "You can't fool me." Out loud he said, "I think we understand each other and I can see the nature of your 'sickness.' "

I said nothing, waiting for him to continue.

"You know," he said, "almost all the buttonhole machines are at a standstill. Nothing is being delivered from our shop to the Germans. The commissar was called to Gestapo headquarters and threatened with being shot because they suspect sabotage."

"That's his own doing," I said. "He doesn't care about anybody else. Why should I care about him?"

The supervisor said grimly,

"Don't you know the Gestapo? They can pick out five or ten people to be shot. My own life is in danger as well. Do you want to have all these people on your conscience?"

"Definitely not," I said. "Not even one person should be killed because of me."

"Then get dressed and come with me."

"Look," I said. "Today is Shabbos. Even if I have to sometimes work on this holy day, I will not start working today. But tomorrow I will come and have all the machines working again."

"All right," he said, and then he told me all that had happened while I was absent from work. The commissar had wanted to replace me with another mechanic, but there were no spare mechanics. So he begged another commissar to "lend" him a mechanic for a day. The second commissar obliged, and sent him a mechanic who could not fix even one machine. The workers in my group, wanting to help me, made sure that every day another machine was inoperable. The commissar then tried to send the unfinished uniforms to other shops to be processed, but each shop had its own priorities. The uniforms were piled up to the ceiling in many rooms, and the commissar was close to having a nervous breakdown because he knew that if the Germans were to come in, he would be the first casualty. So, swallowing his pride, he sent the technical adviser to try to talk me into resuming my work as soon as possible.

On Sunday morning I came into the shop. There was barely any place to move as the room was overflowing with uniforms. I sat down and began to work on the machines. At about 4 o'clock in the afternoon all the machines were operable. Now we had the problem of trying to finish the backlog of uniforms while new ones were constantly coming in to be buttonholed. I called in the technical supervisor and explained to him my plan, with conditions. I would arrange a night shift of workers, besides the regular shifts, but since it was very difficult to work on a night shift in addition to a day shift, each person who was working the night shift would have to receive an extra portion of bread and soup. The commissar was now ready to give in to any of my demands. I made a list of the people I needed and gave each one a turn on the night shift. Because of the extra food, everyone was very anxious to get a turn. We would start at 7 o'clock in the evening and work hard until about 11:30 p.m. or midnight. Then I would tell everyone to bed down on the uniforms and go to sleep. We did not want to catch up on our backlog too quickly because that would mean an end to our extra food. Then, at 4:30 a.m., I woke everyone up. We didn't want to be caught sleeping and not working.

It took us about two weeks to finish the backlog of uniforms. We were all grateful that this episode had a happy ending. Even the commissar began to show me more respect and when he would come to our group and talk to me he would address me as "Panie" ("Mr." in Polish) Cohen instead of "Hey, Cohen!" that he had previously used.

After the war, in February 1946, I came back to Lodz to look for my sister Mirel, who had returned to Lodz after her liberation in March 1945. (I found out that in July 1945, she had been killed by some anti-Semitic Poles.) There I met one of my former workers in the ghetto. After embracing each other and rejoicing over our having survived the camps, we reminisced about our former life in the ghetto. He mentioned to me that our former commissar was back in Lodz. I said that we should denounce him to the police as a collaborator with the Germans. He smiled and said, "You'd better watch out for him. You might end up somewhere in Siberia. He now works for the KGB."

This is the way of the unscrupulous person, who will work for any tyrant and will step on human corpses in order to serve his own purposes. It was the same story with the kapos in the concentration camps.

It is worthwhile to mention that very few of the religious, G–d-fearing Jews collaborated with the Germans to help them oppress their fellow Jews. Like the Jewish foremen in Egypt (shotrim), who took upon themselves punishment from the Egyptian supervisors instead of pressing harder on their Jewish brothers and sisters, religious Jews preferred to suffer than to be privileged as a result of hurting their fellow Jew.

Chapter 8

My Grandfather Comes to the Ghetto

fter the deportation of Jews from Lodz began in January 1942, with about 50,000 Jews being transported over a period of four months, ostensibly to an assortment of work camps, but in actual fact taken to be gassed or shot, the Germans began to transport into the Lodz ghetto Jews from Germany, Czechoslovakia, Austria and other places. These new arrivals languished among us for some time. Then, after a while, they too were deported.

A bit later on, there was another influx of Jews into the Lodz ghetto. The Germans rounded up the Jews from all the small towns in the vicinity of Lodz and crammed them in as well. These poor Jews had already been dislodged from their homes and squeezed into local ghettos, but in the summer of

1942, these smaller ghettos were liquidated. All Jews were driven out to the city square or marketplace. There the Germans made a *selektzia*, or selection. Older people, mothers with babies, and children under the age of about 15 were placed on one side of the square, while those apparently able to do hard work were pushed to the other side. The elderly and the mothers with their young were sent off to be killed. (They were told that they were being sent to a family camp where they would stay until the end of the war.) Only those judged suitable for labor were spared – at least for the meanwhile. Miserable and starving, these "fortunate" ones were now pitilessly forced to march to Lodz.

I remember well the day we heard that the Jews from the Brezeziner ghetto were to arrive in Lodz on the following day. Even amid the gloom that pervaded the ghetto atmosphere, my sisters and I could hardly contain our excitement and anticipation at the thought of seeing our grandfather again. We had no idea that the Germans were bringing only the young and labor worthy into the ghetto, so we fully expected to see him, and, fortunately, our hopes were not dashed.

We were waiting at the gates of the ghetto long before the sojourners were due to arrive. When they did, we eagerly watched everyone who passed through the gates, but at first we saw only young Jews – no children and no elderly people. Disappointed, we were about to leave when we noticed a few older people and young ones straggling in, and then – we saw our grandfather.

No sooner had we greeted him right there, at the gates of the ghetto, than the authorities began to separate the old and very young from their families. Within minutes, the Jewish police force, the arm of the Judenrat, hustled them, along with my grandfather, to an empty apartment house that happened to be very close to where we lived.

We found out about the *selektzia* the accursed Germans had made from some other Brezeziner Jews who remained. The very weak and young and old were sent to their destruction, while the ones who were still able to work were spared and sent to the Lodz ghetto.

My grandfather had been spared as well, through the good efforts of people who had hidden him and smuggled him into the Lodz ghetto, in gratitude for his constant efforts to help the sick people in Brezezin's hospital. They told us he would sneak out of the ghetto to barter with the gentile farmers for meat and butter and other fatty foods that could provide some sustenance for the sick in the hospital. Since he had risked his life for others, the doctors and other deportees from Brezezin had now smuggled my grandfather to relative safety in the Lodz ghetto among the others who had survived the *selektzia*.

My sister Mirel and I followed my grandfather and watched him being escorted into the assigned apartment building. After waiting outside for an opportune moment when we could smuggle him into our own house, our patience and persistence were finally rewarded, and we were able to bring him home.

After resting briefly from his painful journey, my grandfather told us how they had taken my grandmother — and the children — and the weak — from the ghetto. In truth the Germans always lied, saying that the children were being taken to a special ghetto, and the older people would be looked after separately, while in reality they were all taken to the gas chambers, or into big, enclosed trucks with the exhaust pipes vented inside so that the people were asphyxiated in an agonizingly slow death. Because of the inevitability of the situation, people simply went along with the Germans' promises, hoping — or pretending — that they were the truth.

After a while my grandfather announced that he needed to return to his assigned apartment to retrieve his suitcase. We tried to convince him that it was too dangerous to go back and get it, that he might be detained there by the police and not be allowed to leave. But he insisted on going, for his *tallis*, *tefillin* and other vital items were in his bag.

I decided to accompany my grandfather back to the apartment to secure his belongings. Since I was an employee of the ghetto authority, I wore an official-looking yellow band on my sleeve. At 17 years of age, I was serving as a mechanic for the buttonhole machines and as supervisor of about fifty people in a German army-uniform factory. I figured that the band on my arm might serve as our passport to come and go as we chose.

But as soon as we entered the apartment building, it was surrounded by ghetto police who barred anyone from entering or leaving. I, however, as a ghetto official, was permitted to leave and was told to do so at once. I walked home dejectedly, grieving over the fact that almost as soon as we had found my grandfather we had lost him again.

My sisters and I, rather than just sit at home and wait, decided to sneak back to the apartment building, which was not far from our house, and hide behind some bushes across the street. We had a good view of the building, so we waited to see what might transpire. Soon it grew dark, but we continued to lie there, just so that we might be able to see our grandfather one last time.

For several hours we lay waiting on the hard ground; each time a policeman approached our spot, we trembled from fear of being discovered. Meanwhile, my grandfather's prison grew dark and quiet. We assumed that everyone inside must have gone to sleep. Suddenly, at around midnight, the heavy steps of soldiers marching in our direction assaulted our ears. Soon we heard SS guards shouting in German that they were evacuating the building.

All at once, lights went on in the building, as the word was given that everyone was to leave their apartment and be waiting outside within fifteen minutes. Soon afterwards the frightened Jews were told that they would be taken to "another ghetto." By then people started to suspect that they were being taken to their deaths.

We could hear some people crying, others awakening their children to get them dressed and ready for the march to the ghetto gates.

In the warm summer night, through an open window, I heard a small boy crying and telling his mother plaintively, "What do they want from us? I'm so tired and hungry. I didn't eat anything all day. I can't get up now. Why don't they just let me sleep?"

Our hearts filled with sorrow and our eyes with tears. We wept along with him, knowing that there was nothing we could do to help him. (To this day, I can still hear the child's cries ringing in my ears, as if I had just heard them yesterday.) Before long, the SS soldiers were screaming, *"Los! Los! Forward! Forward!"* and then, "Everyone stand in line!" In the dark and confusion we tried to spot our grandfather. We listened as the people marched out, guarded by the SS soldiers and the Jewish ghetto police. We listened hard and carefully, but to no avail, until suddenly we heard my grandfather's voice say, "Moshe, do you have the bottle of water handy so that I can wash my hands?"

Before we could stop her, Mirel, the younger of my two sisters, jumped up from our hiding place, ran in the direction of my grandfather's voice and disappeared among the crowd of marching people. Gone!

Our hearts became cold as stone, fearing for the lives of my grandfather and now also my sister. As the last few people were removed from the building, everything became quiet.

We returned home with heavy hearts. My mother wept bitterly for my sister Mirel, 18 years old and now surely lost. "Why did she go away?" she asked repeatedly. None of us were able to fall asleep.

Chapter 8: My Grandfather Comes to the Ghetto □ 75

At about 2:30 a.m. there was a knock on the door. Fearing the worst, we ran to open it. Standing in the doorway were my sister and grandfather, feet caked with mud, and clothes full of tar and dirt.

We fell all over them, kissing and hugging them. We had thought that we would never see them again, but here they were with us once again and our joy knew no bounds. After we all returned to a calmer state of mind, and the rescuer and rescued one had washed and changed their clothes, my sister told us what had happened earlier that night.

When she heard our grandfather's voice, she felt an irresistible compulsion to join the line of people and find our grandfather. She did, and they marched side by side. When they came to a streetcorner where everyone else was turning left, she pulled our grandfather away and proceeded straight ahead instead. In the dark, no one had noticed their disappearance. Avoiding the main street, they scrambled through the bushes until they arrived at our house.

We all sang praises to the *Ribbono Shel Olam*. We marveled at Mirel's selfless courage. Soon afterwards, in the darkness of the night, I went back to the apartment building to fetch my grandfather's suitcase before it would be removed by the ghetto police.

My grandfather remained with us in the ghetto for almost another year and a half.

Chapter 9

The Curfew

The summer of 1942 passed. Things became a little quieter and we began to receive slightly larger portions of food. We began to think that perhaps the Jews would indeed continue to work for the Germans – either for the military or for privately owned German firms – and that the Germans were pleased with our labor. Perhaps now we would be given a bit of repose from the bitterness we had known until now.

But even the slight increase in food rations did not help my father, for he was slowly dying of starvation. His body became swollen, and the doctor said that he was suffering from severe malnutrition. In the end, he became pitifully thin, and we saw that there was no hope for him. He passed away on the fourth day of the month of Av. He was buried in the cemetery in Lodz, where there were so many dead bodies that there was no room to bury them in coffins, even if there were coffins to be had. We did not, however, observe the custom of sitting "*shivah*," as we were forced to go to work, no matter what.

The Lodz ghetto was different from the Warsaw ghetto, where people left the enclosed area to go to work and were able to smuggle things in and out, and were able to maintain some contact with the outside world – with the Polish people who lived on the outskirts of the ghetto. Thus the Warsaw Jews were more familiar with current events and with what the Germans were doing to the Jews elsewhere, and with what the Germans were proposing to do.

In contrast, the Lodz ghetto was hermetically sealed. Outside the ghetto there were only Germans, as Lodz had become incorporated into the German Reich. Hence, we were oblivious to what was going on outside the ghetto. Our first knowledge of the reality of concentration camps and gas chambers came to us only upon our arrival at Auschwitz.

We had grown more optimistic when we had started to get a bit more food, and the deportations had been brought to a halt. In this improved situation we had thought that we would stay here until the end of the war, come what may, and until then things would remain at the status quo. Then suddenly, at the end of August, the German police sealed off the ghetto streets near the hospitals. Entering and exiting were strictly forbidden. With the premonition that something terrible was about to happen, we grew tense and frightened.

The following morning when we entered our workplaces, people were whispering to each other about the events of the previous day. The Germans had come with trucks and had escorted all the invalids and the sick out of the hospitals, bringing them to some unknown destination outside the ghetto. Several Jews who had attempted to flee had been shot on the spot. With their newly found optimism now blown sky-high, people grew apprehensive and restive. Yet most people still thought that those working for the Germans would not be disturbed. Several days later notices appeared on the walls in the ghetto announcing that there would be a strict curfew lasting several days and that provisions should be prepared for the shut-ins. Anyone seen out in the streets would be shot instantly. We began to speculate that the Germans were planning a new round of deportations. We heard that they wanted another 25,000 Jews.

Once again we were reminded that the ghetto would become a labor camp. Those who could not work, such as children under the age of 12 or the elderly over the age of 65, would be shipped to a special camp for those incapable of working.

Hysteria mounted, as those with young children or older parents grew desperate with the notion that their families were about to be split, perhaps forever. But we were all helpless.

It wasn't long before we learned that the Germans no longer trusted the Jewish police to carry out their orders properly. One day they came in with their trucks and a number of horse-drawn carriages and, with the assistance of the Jewish police, surrounded several buildings. Then the Germans ordered all residents to come out of their flats. In a flash the Jewish police accompanied by German soldiers hurried into the apartments and began to rush everyone out. They then conducted a thorough search of each flat, breaking into closets, chests of drawers, even tearing down walls, investigating any place where they suspected someone might be hiding. If anyone was found hiding, he was escorted out to the courtyard, where he was shot in the presence of all the other tenants of the building.

In the courtyard, people were lined up in rows, as the Germans began to hold one of their notorious *selektzias*, wherein a portion of Jews would be directed to go to the left side, from which they would be transported in wagons to a spot outside the ghetto. Anyone who dared to run away was immediately shot. Children were torn away from their mothers and thrown into the wagons. After the ordeal was over, those who remained trudged back into their apartments.

The shrieks and the agonized moans of mothers from all around the area tore at the hearts of all those who heard them. Before long the line of German vehicles came to our building, in which over twenty families were living.

My mother told us to hide at all costs. At once we moved into action. My sisters hid in the beds, and my mother stuffed me into a laundry hamper, which was extremely narrow, and covered me with heaps of dirty laundry. Being rather small boned, I folded myself in three and squeezed my scrawny body into this obscure spot where I would hopefully not be easily found. Hearts thudding with terror, we waited for the moment when the Germans would enter.

Silently, I kept repeating to myself Chapter 118 of *Tehillim,* in particular the *pasuk, "Min hameitzar* ... From the straits did I call G-d." Certainly this was a *meitzar* – a desperate situation. Then I heard the police enter, and I shivered as I heard the German officer screaming that they should break open all the armoires and closets and then leave. Thank G-d, they did not find any of us.

At the time, my grandfather lived in the same building, but in another apartment. We had pleaded with him to hide as well, or the German murderers would surely transport him, but he remained in his bed for he was now weak and frail.

When we went back up to my grandfather's flat after the selection had taken place, he was no longer there. We assumed the Germans had taken him away. The next day we were tremendously relieved to find that my grandfather had made his way back to the flat. He told us that he and a group of others had been taken to an assembly point, where they were guarded by the Jewish police. By offering a policeman a little bag of sugar that he had collected from his rations in exchange for an agreement to look the other way, grandfather managed to sneak out to safety. In this way, my grandfather saved himself from certain death. By the grace of G-d, he managed to live for almost a year and a half in the Lodz ghetto, and merited a Jewish burial, something countless others did not receive during the war.

In November 1943 my grandfather became very ill, which was no wonder with all the epidemics that continuously plagued the ghetto. Although he had access to more than his share of food rations – through all his acquaintances from Brezezin, and also from a relative with connections in the upper administration of the ghetto – he became very weak and had to remain confined to his bed. During the time that he was bedridden, my grandfather received constant medical care from doctors who had known and respected him in Brezezin. They visited him daily and provided him with medications that were both rare and expensive. Also, some young men and women from his town, in recognition of all he had done for them, regularly came to clean his room and give him the care he needed.

I clearly remember the afternoon that my grandfather adamantly insisted that he would not be able to eat the food that I was about to prepare for him, despite my protests and entreaties for him to eat. No, he said, he is already a *gosses* (dying person), and this would be his last day in the world.

Then my grandfather proceeded to instruct me regarding his last wishes, assigning me the role of executor of his last will and testament. In his suitcase he had a package that contained some gold coins and several hundred American dollars. These he directed me to keep as a fund for my sisters' dowries. He showed me his *tachrichim* (shrouds) and told me that he wanted to be buried in his Yom Tov *tallis,* which he had worn when reciting many a tearful prayer, but the silver *atarah* (ornamentation) I was to take for myself. There were a few more instructions, and then he fell asleep, while I napped in a chair nearby. So the night passed.

In the morning, my grandfather asked me to wash his hands, and then light some candles at his bedside. He closed his eyes again, and I sat there, sad and perturbed. After a while, he opened his eyes and asked me if I had already said my morning prayers. As I hadn't done so yet, he said, "Put on your *tefillin* and start *davening*."

About a half hour later, he asked me if I had davened *Shemoneh Esrei* (the Eighteen Benedictions) yet. I had just finished. He said, "Take off your *tefillin* right now."

I did so, all the while watching him as he moved his lips in silent prayer. Then he said out loud, "*Shema Yisrael Hashem Elokeinu Hashem Echod* – Hear, O Israel, Hashem is our G-d, Hashem is the One and Only."

Then he uttered three times, "*Baruch Shem Kevod Malchuso leolam vaed* – Blessed is the Name of His glorious kingdom for all eternity." After that, he said seven times, "*Hashem Hu HaElokim* – Hashem, He alone is G-d."

These were the same prayers that we say in *Ne'ilah*, the final prayer of our Yom Kippur services. Witnessing all that he was doing, I was stricken with both grief and awe at the same time.

My grandfather coughed and breathed loudly and then there was a sound like a balloon bursting. I began to call him, but his head was limp and lifeless.

I ran outside and called out to passersby to come up, as my grandfather was dying, but no one heard or cared. They all continued on their way as if nothing unusual was happening. In the ghetto, a death was a normal occurrence.

Returning to August 1942, those who had not managed to escape the curfew were led by the Germans to Chelmno, where they were either locked into special sealed trucks in which they were asphyxiated by the carbon monoxide fumes emitted by the motors, or else they were taken into the nearby forest and shot. Having been spared from the last selection, we thought we were out of danger, but remained terrified. Neighbors seemed to resent the fact that we had not come down when ordered to and thus remained intact as a family, whereas they all were missing children, parents or other family members.

One such jealous person suggested that when the Germans returned they should report the fact that we had been hiding. In their bitterness people speculated that had there been more at the selection their own family members would have had a greater chance of surviving. This was sheer nonsense.

Before long we heard that other selections were being conducted in other areas of the ghetto. These reports were confirmed as true, and once again terror entered our hearts.

Rosh Hashanah came, and although we were not allowed to be out in the streets, we organized a *minyan* in our apartment building. The outpouring of tears during the *tefillos* was heartrending. Those who had lost children or other family members expressed their great anguish to the *Ribbono Shel Olam*. Those who had survived the selection trembled and begged the Creator, "*Kera ro'a gezar dineinu,*" abolish the evil decree.

While we were blowing the shofar, several people appeared with panic written all over their faces. German vehicles had entered our street.

People began to run in confusion and terror. In the pandemonium, everyone searched for his own family members and then, as quickly as possible, made his way into his apartment.

Through the window I could see a coach filled with German soldiers parked at the end of our street.

Then I saw a German officer on a motorcycle approach the large group of soldiers and speak with them. In another moment the Germans turned around, and for some reason, went back to where they had come from. While we breathed a bit more easily, our nerves were frayed to the breaking point. Barely a half hour later the Jewish police arrived with the news that the curfew had ended and that on the following day everyone should go back to work.

We thanked the A-mighty that our worst experience had been fear, and that our lives would continue on the next day in the factories. There were some children between the ages of 10 and 13 who had survived by hiding, or by falsifying their documents to show that they were older than 16. They now worked in the factories as messengers, thus able to remain among the living in the Lodz ghetto.

The guardian angels of the Divine Providence were still protecting us.

Chapter 10

The End of the Lodz Ghetto

In early 1944 a large number of SS personnel along with groups of German industrialists arrived in the Lodz ghetto. Hans Bibov, the commandant of the ghetto, accompanied them on a tour of the factories, offices, kitchens and storage houses throughout the ghetto. They also visited the distribution centers where we received our daily rations, according to our ration cards.

When these officials came by, I, as an instructor, mechanic and supervisor, was obligated to straighten myself upright, as if I were a soldier of the Reich, and scream "*Achtung! Attention!*" My heart always beat violently during such moments, for fear of not meeting their approval, if the expression on my face or the tone of my voice might betray my feelings. Anyone was eligible for the severest beating at the slightest suspicion of lack of subordination.

While these visits were taking place, the remaining Jews in Lodz had the feeling that something was about to happen. Sure enough, in the month of March an order was issued announcing that the ghetto must provide a certain number of people for transport out of the ghetto and for work in other locations.

At that point in the ghetto's brief history, everyone who was there was already working. There were hardly any people to spare. Rumkowski, the head of the Judenrat, ordered all foremen to provide lists of workers in the factories who might be considered expendable, that is, without whom the factories could manage. The foremen thus had to give much thought to determine who was not a vital contributor to production.

Shortly after these lists were submitted to the Judenrat, those Jews whose names appeared on them were sent notices informing them that they were to report for deportation. In order to minimize the sense of alarm, the notices also stated that each person was allowed to bring along twenty kilograms of baggage, and would receive a special bread ration upon departure.

People began to hide. Others avoided sleeping at home. In response to this, the Jewish authorities put the names of these fugitives on a blacklist, which meant that these people and their families would be deprived of their rations.

Most Jews, however, preferred to remain hungry rather than place their trust in the Germans and their "offers." In a backlash to this lack of cooperation, the police began to grab people off the streets, holding them in prisons until their transport would be arranged. Not surprisingly, the German authorities kept increasing the numbers of people they intended to transport.

When my sister Gittel received a notice ordering her to present herself for deportation, our entire family went into hiding. Fortunately, through the intervention of the commissar, the administrator or "czar" of the factory in which I worked, I was able to arrange for my sister's name to be removed from the list. This was because I was one of those mechanics without whom our factory could not function. So our lives continued in the ghetto for many weeks.

Not long afterwards, we started to hear every night, off in the distance, Russian guns being fired and cannon explosions. Occasionally we would see long convoys of German military vehicles in retreat, carrying aboard them their wounded. The filthy, ragged uniforms of these soldiers returning to Germany provided a sharp contrast to the polished elegance and impeccable attire of the SS guards.

As we watched the convoys rolling by, there sparked in our hearts the faint but real hope that soon the Russians would arrive and liberate us from the German murderers. However, I always kept in mind what my grandfather had once told me, when I had wanted to cheer him up with the news that the Germans were suffering severe blows and military setbacks and that the war would probably end soon: "*Oy*, my child, when you see the German guards dressed so elegantly, clad in their shiny black boots, know that they have not yet been defeated."

Soon rumors once again surfaced to the effect that the Germans were now preparing to send out a new mass of people from the ghetto. Then came the rumors that the entire ghetto was about to be liquidated. We could not help but wonder: "What are the Russians waiting for? Why are they not coming to free us?"

So the days and the weeks passed by, with our doubts and despair mounting steadily. Once again we began to fear the worst. We also began to work more nimbly and efficiently in our factories, in a vain attempt to convince the Germans that they needed us to work for them.

In the end, our hopes were completely dashed. It started one day when large posters were nailed to the walls of the ghetto streets, announcing that all residents of the ghetto must gather in a large central square where Bibov, the ghetto commandant, would personally address the Jews of the Lodz ghetto. I was afraid to go, so I stayed at home. Afterwards, I learned from others who had attended the assembly that Bibov had sworn, by the life of the Fuhrer himself, that the ghetto was simply going to be relocated in the Saxony province of Germany, and that everything would be restructured as it had been prior to the relocation. He gave his "word of honor" that we would all continue to work at the same jobs we had here in the ghetto, and that all the ghetto's residents would continue to live with their families as before.

"Do you not hear the Russian cannons?" he asked all the Jews assembled before him. "We will put up a strong resistance in Lodz, and many houses and factories will be destroyed. If the Russians conquer Lodz, they will most certainly send you all to Siberia. But since you have all so loyally served the Reich, we wish to repay you by sending you all to safety.

"In gratitude for your efforts," he continued, "we are granting you a certain amount of freedom, so that every factory will travel as a group, machinery and all, in order that as soon as you arrive in Saxony, the authorities there will be able to restructure all the factories quickly. We greatly appreciate your work for us, and therefore we want to help you. Everything that you will need you will find there – bedding, clothing – except for cookware. This you must take with you, as all metal has been used for the armament."

Ninety percent of the residents of the ghetto did not believe a word he said. They thought that they would be able to work in the factories a little longer, while waiting for the Russians to arrive, and avoid the terrible fate that awaited them if they would listen to Bibov.

However, almost immediately the Germans brought the operations of the factories to a total halt. They removed all the materials and the machines, claiming that the workers who had worked with them would continue to do so inside Germany.

As noted, the vast majority of the Jews did not believe the Germans; this disbelief was soon borne out as, a few days later, our freedom was in fact curtailed.

The Germans reentered the ghetto. One section at a time, they surrounded several housing blocks and dragged out everyone whom they found, escorting them to the ghetto prison on Czerneckago Street. The following morning they were led to the train station to meet the train that would take them away.

Where to? No one yet knew.

The immediate response of the ghetto Jews was the formation of an underground, which supplied information as to where the German troops and SS were headed next. This gave the Jews in that area advance warning during which time they could go into hiding. Our family hid for about two weeks in this way. At one time we found refuge in a cemetery; at another we hid in a bombed-out building in a street that had already been liquidated and evacuated and was therefore considered safe.

Once we ran into a house that had been emptied out, when suddenly a group of SS troops arrived and began to search the apartment. We managed to quickly dash into the cellar, careful to replace the floorboards on top of us after we had all descended. From down below we heard the heavy footsteps of the German soldiers overhead, and our fear was unbearable. Some of us were unable to suppress our natural tendency to relieve ourselves. In the end the Germans left the house without noticing the cellar, most fortunately for us. The penalty for going into hiding was death.

We had no more food. Rations were now a thing of the past. We tried to nourish ourselves from the raw beets which people had planted in their courtyards, or any other possible location, and which they had had no time to harvest. At times there were other ways to find food, as, for example, when residents were snatched by the Germans and shipped out without notice, perhaps leaving behind them a small cache of food.

Another time I was alone in the house in which we lived when suddenly a search party appeared. I had only enough time to dive into a storage room where some mattresses had been stacked up. I quickly squeezed under them and waited, holding my breath. As the German soldiers entered the room, they made their way to the closet, stepping right on top of the mattresses. I thought that my end had come, but, miraculously, they did not discover me.

Thus our family managed to stay together for a while longer. Two weeks passed. Usually it took the Germans about two weeks, with the assistance of the Jewish ghetto police, to clean up an area, removing all the residents who had been hiding and then transporting them. We remained as long as we could in one spot. If we heard that the Germans would be searching another neighborhood in the ghetto, we stayed put in our spot.

Finally, one day, our time came. We happened to be looking out the window, as we had heard some shouting coming from outside, when suddenly we saw a group of German soldiers entering the yard of our apartment building to conduct a search.

We quickly went up to the attic where there was a water tank. Using a portable ladder, we climbed through the ceiling through a trapdoor.

As soon as we were all in, we lifted the ladder through the

opening, closed the trapdoor, and hoped and prayed for the best. But before long we heard the Germans shouting, "*Alle herunter*! Everyone down!" (Later we learned that we had been denounced by a Jewish policeman who thought that by informing on us he could save his father, who lived in that building.)

We did not respond, but soon we heard someone bring up a ladder. Then the trapdoor opened and we helplessly faced the German soldiers who had uncovered our hideout. One of them began to beat us all on our heads with a large rubber baton. Then he placed himself by the door through which we were ordered to get down, delivering blow after blow upon our heads as we each took our turn down the ladder. We could not tolerate much more after this lashing. When my turn came, I received such a violent blow to my skull that I jumped down from the ladder rather than climb the rest of the way down and prolong the ordeal. The swelling from the single blow I received did not subside for several weeks.

After we assembled in the courtyard below, we were marched off to the central jail on Czerneckago St. As the prison was already overcrowded, we had to wait in the yard that was surrounded by brick walls. My mother and my two sisters began to speculate about what would happen next. We had not eaten all day. We were totally surrounded by a high brick wall, with German soldiers guarding the entire perimeter of the compound so that no one could escape. My mother said to us, "Children, save yourselves. Run away if you can. I will stay here, but you are still young and should try to escape."

We did not want to leave our mother by herself, so we said, "We must stay together." She insisted that we must try to run away. Then my older sister said to my younger sister and myself, "You two run away. I will stay with Mammashee."

Half dazed, and with heavy hearts, we moved toward a corner of the brick wall where no one would see us, and we climbed to the top of the wall. Below us we saw a German soldier pacing back and forth, his machine-gun under his arm. We froze, not daring to move until we saw him entering a doorway in the corner, after which we quickly jumped down and ran between some houses, unnoticed.

Under cover of the dark night we meandered our way through the alleys until we found ourselves back in our own flat. The moment we entered we were horror struck by the devastation all around us. The doors were broken; the beds were overturned; any remaining possessions had been scattered on the ground. We sat on the floor in the midst of the tornado's aftermath, and began to discuss plans of where we could hide. We could not, however, avoid the painful question tugging at our hearts: How could we abandon our mother, leaving her alone with our sister?

This brought our discussion back to the option of returning to the prison compound where our mother and sister were held. Rationalizing that this might be the best course of action to take, we figured that perhaps we would still be sent to a concentration camp in Germany — and perhaps we could still remain together as a family and help one another.

We debated back and forth nearly the entire night, until we reached our decision. We would return to the prison and reunite with Mammashee.

Getting back into the prison grounds was easy. We merely told the guards that we were voluntarily presenting ourselves for deportation, and we once again joined our mother and older sister.

We were just in time. An hour later there arrived a special detail of SS guards with black uniforms, and markings of skulls and crossbones on their hats and armbands. This was the dreaded *Einsaztgruppen* – Death Commando, the worst of all the SS guards – who instilled in us a fright that we had never yet experienced. Yet we knew all too well that we were totally defenseless, with no alternative whatsoever.

We marched until we came to the train station from which the Jews were being shipped out of Lodz, through which others from the towns around Lodz had been transported in the earlier stages of the ghetto. We were ordered by the Jewish police to form rows, as we were herded to the wagons, which were already waiting for their next cargo.

These were closed cattle cars, which had two tiny windows on each side to let in air, covered with iron grates to prevent anyone from jumping out. We climbed aboard the cars by crossing over a wooden ramp leading to the doorway of the car. We were each handed an entire loaf of bread by the SS guards. This relieved us somewhat, for we assumed that if we were about to be killed, the Germans wouldn't be wasting these precious loaves of bread, valuable commodities as they had been in the ghetto.

The cars filled up very quickly to beyond capacity, so that we all had to stand squeezed tightly against one another, with no room to sit. We placed our large knapsacks, which we had taken along with us when we were told we could bring baggage weighing twenty kilograms, on the floor of the wagon, and we tried to sit on top of them, but there was no room for our feet.

As soon as we heard the doors being slammed shut and then locked with chains, we were all filled with a sense of panic. It occurred to us that we were now like cows being carried to the slaughterhouse.

As the train pulled out of the station we heard a flurry of command calls being shouted by SS guards. We were soon riding in a direction of which I had no idea and towards a future which was dubious, to say the least. Before long, night began to fall, and we tried to arrange a *minyan* for *Minchah* and

Maariv. At this many of the passengers began to laugh at us, taunting us with their remarks. "Chassidim! Fools! Here too you won't give up your religious beliefs?"

We replied that the *Ribbono Shel Olam* is everywhere, and we believed that He was with us right there in the cattle car. We added that we were beseeching Him for His help. Consequently the passengers of our car became involved in a lengthy discussion that lasted well into the night.

Afterwards we attempted to snatch a few moments of sleep, which was not easy at all. I felt like partaking of some of the bread we had been apportioned, but my neighbor advised me against it. "Don't start eating your bread yet. Back in the ghetto I heard that this trip to Germany might last an entire week. Keep the bread for tomorrow, and the day after tomorrow — and the day after that. If you start eating your bread now, you will die later of hunger."

Hunger was gnawing at my insides and I could certainly have eaten the entire loaf at once, but I listened to the sound advice of my neighbor, and left the bread whole and untouched.

For weeks afterward I was tormented by the fact that I could have eaten the entire bread and stayed my hunger, at least for a while. Instead I ended up losing the entire loaf, for on the following day, upon our arrival in Auschwitz, the precious bread was confiscated from me.

Day broke once again. Nature made its regular demands of us, but we didn't know where to do what we needed to do. After we selected a corner for a makeshift latrine, everyone suddenly began to push toward that corner. In a few minutes, the stench in the wagon was unbearable. I forced my way to the window to see where we were. To my surprise, I saw Polish gentile peasants with their wives and children standing near the railway tracks and laughing at us. Some made horrible gestures, often obscene. Some motioned with their fingers to their throats suggesting that they very much enjoyed the notion that we would soon be slaughtered.

In my mind there sprang a verse from *Tehillim* (79:10): "*Lamah yomru hagoyim, ayeh Elokeihem?* Why should the nations say, 'Where is the Almighty?' " Then I remembered a *pasuk* from *Eichah* 1:7: " ... *ra'uhah tzarim* ... her oppressors have seen her (Yerushalayim) and they have laughed over her downfall."

Soon the train began to slow down to a crawl. I looked out between the bars of a window and saw a strange sight. People dressed as what must be described as clowns, who were nothing but skin and bones, roamed about, while others were chasing them to and fro. The latter had abnormal-looking faces with huge jowls, showing them to be extremely well fed and physically nurtured, so that they hardly looked human to us ghetto Jews.

Then I looked a little further on, and I saw off in the distance blocks of low buildings surrounded by barbed-wire fences and cement poles, several rows wide. Every few meters there were elevated guard posts suspended above the wires. I had never seen anything like this before and I and others who were with me were overtaken by a terrible and almost unnatural fright.

A moment later the train pulled through a gate with the inscription "Arbeit Macht Frei" across the top. With all of the agonies and tribulations which we had already experienced, we nevertheless had no inkling that we had now arrived in the most notorious concentration camp within the Reich – a place which rendered the suffering which we had endured until this point mere "child's play" in comparison with what awaited us here.

Chapter 11

First Day in Auschwitz

We arrived in Auschwitz on Friday morning, *erev* Rosh Chodesh Elul, 5704 (1944). We were confused, overcome with fear, and in a state of shock. In the Lodz ghetto, we would rarely have anything to do with the German soldiers, as all matters were directly handled by the Jewish authorities of the Judenrat, headed by Chaim Mordechai Rumkowski. Only when we would look at the barbed-wire enclosure would we see SS guards there, every few yards, pacing slowly, machine-guns nestled casually on their shoulders. Now, in this new place where terror lurked in every corner, there was a sudden swarm of SS troops running to and fro, barking orders at us, shoving us in all directions, beating us indiscriminately. It was frightening beyond words.

"Leave everything! Leave everything behind! Out of the wagons! *Schnell!*"

From the ghetto we had brought with us backpacks into which we had hurriedly stuffed clothes and other belongings. Now, as we disembarked from the railcars, we were ordered to leave these behind, and to run.

We had arrived in the valley of sorrow — in the valley of death.

I grabbed my most precious possession, my *tefillin,* and began to run in the direction I was ordered to. At once, I felt a stinging blow to my back and my head. Turning to face my assailant, I realized he was a kapo, one of the many overseers appointed by the SS to help torment us, who began shrieking in a frenzy, "Do you want to get killed right here on the spot?"

Grabbing the *tefillin* from my embrace, he tossed them, like a baseball, right onto a pile of personal effects that was off to the side. Then, without warning, he shoved me into the mass of people that continued to move from the direction of the train in an endless human flow.

The scene is permanently etched into my memory – SS guards and kapos of different nationalities, running around like vicious sheepdogs, yelling, "Forward! Run! *Schnell!*" raining a steady stream of blows on us with their sticks.

Shortly after, the next phase of our affliction took place, as the segregation commenced. First, the men and the women were separated, husbands from wives, brothers from sisters. Families were ripped apart mercilessly, with no chance for parting words or a hug from a loved one. Children were torn away from their mothers amid panic-filled shrieks of agony. People were pelted right and left to prevent them from running back into the embrace of a parent or child beckoning to them helplessly.

Somehow my mother managed to throw her arms around my neck for a fleeting moment and to utter her final blessing with tears in her eyes. "May Hashem grant you the same grace that Yosef was favored with in Egypt."

Then we too were forcibly separated, with no time for a good-bye.

Numb and distraught, I felt myself being pushed along with a mass of men until we came face to face with an SS officer, standing on a podium, shiny black shoes on his feet and a whip in his right hand. Almost capriciously, he motioned to each of us in turn, "Right!" or "Left!" As the infamous *selektzia* took place on this hellish spot, one line grew on either side of the clearing, maintained with the assistance of the SS guards. I proceeded forward, dumbfounded and totally bewildered, not even noticing where I was headed, unaware that a simple word, either "right" or "left," would be the determinant of my life or death.

"Line up in fives!" the SS guards now yelled at us. They told us to march like soldiers. "*Links, zvei, drei, vier!* Left, two, three, four!" and to march in rhythm, like the well-fed soldiers of the Third Reich. If one of us did not catch on to the beat and the pace, an SS guard would help him to catch on, with the use of a whip or a stick. How I managed to march, I can't recall; my mind was blurred. I simply remember being motioned off to the right and continuing to drag my feet amid the constant screaming and cursing.

Suddenly, from a distance, I heard someone calling excitedly, "Srulek! Srulek!" Surely there were others with the same name, but the voice was unmistakably that of my sister Mirel. I looked around and saw her being led along with a large group of women in the opposite direction.

She was sobbing as she called out to me, "They have taken Mammashee to the left." At the time I did not realize the significance of that statement. I simply assumed that it meant that my mother and my sisters had been separated.

Within the next few minutes, we were herded into an enormous barracks, where we were ordered to stand off to one side. At the front of this low structure there stood a couple of large barrels and a blanket. While absorbing our new surroundings, we saw several SS guards enter the building, followed by a large group of kapos, who immediately began to walk around us, trying to instill order. "Silence!" they shouted, and used the backs of their hands to enforce their demands. Few of us were spared the force of their hands, as their purpose was to intimidate us, which they were quite successful in doing.

When a total hush was effected, one of the SS officers positioned himself at the front of the barracks and announced, "You will remove any and all valuables from your pockets and deposit them into these barrels. These include gold, silver, watches, pens or anything else. In a short while, you will each be inspected. Anyone who will be found in possession of any of the aforementioned items will be shot on the spot."

The kapos weaved in and out of the mass of people, shouting and cursing as they conducted a person-by-person inspection. Within moments, as if from nowhere, mounds of valuables began to form at the front of the building, on top of the blanket. A pile of watches here, a heap of gold coins there — pens, golden chains and American dollars.

I had in my pockets my own little cache of personal effects. One item was a precious golden pocket watch on a golden chain, which I had inherited from my beloved grandfather. I also had a few small pieces of gold and some U.S. dollars that my mother had sewn into the lining of my garments.

With a trace of defiance growing inside me, I decided not to allow the cherished pocket watch to fall into the hands of any accursed German. I would rather simply break it. I looked about me to make sure I wasn't seen, and dropped the watch on the floor, then placed my foot over it in order to crush it.

Suddenly a kapo appeared out of nowhere and treated me

to a stiff punch in the ribs, and then said, "Pick up that watch and throw it into the barrel." More quietly, he added, "You're lucky that I'm the one who saw you. Had it been another kapo, you would have been on this day hanged from one of the poles outside."

Had I succeeded in carrying out my little venture, the SS would have considered it sabotage. Naturally I wasted no time in picking up the watch and throwing it into the barrel.

As I returned to lose myself in the crowd of inmates, I saw my good friend Yosef Carmel, with whom I had learned together in the Gerer *shtiebel* in Lodz, so I moved toward him. We were both elated to have discovered each other in such an unlikely spot so we resolved to stick together and never to separate. Then he turned to me and said, "Yisroel Yitzchok, what do you see when you look down at the ground beneath us?"

Looking down, I replied, "Nothing in particular," and wondered what he was getting at.

"If you look underneath the surface," he said, "you will see a type of white sand that is limestone." Before I could ask him what the significance of limestone was, he continued. "In the Lodz ghetto, I heard that the Germans murder Jews in certain places, bury them there and then spray limestone powder over the bodies to cause them to disintegrate."

I looked at him incredulously, and he continued. "I think that this will be our final resting place. Here we will meet our end."

While his shocking words shook me to the core, I tried to compose myself, and commented, "Do you remember the *gemara* in *Berachos*, where Chizkiyahu said to Yeshayahu Hanavi (Isaiah the Prophet), 'I have a tradition from my ancestors that even if a sharpened sword is placed on your neck, you should not despair of Hashem's mercy'? Hashem can still help us."

In that manner we stood there for a number of hours, as if

suspended between the realm of the living and the realm of the dead. Finally, we were once again ordered out of the barracks and told to line up, in a strange military style, in rows of five. Then we were marched some distance away to a red brick building, while the cool of night began to descend upon the end of a chaotic day. An entire day had passed, leaving us with only fear and dread of what was yet to come.

Suddenly, we were being shoved into a blockhouse. In Auschwitz, we learned, inmates would be jammed together into one half of the block, while the other half remained empty. Then the kapos shouted out their instructions at us (kapos were forever shouting out instructions in Auschwitz) that we remove our clothes as we were going to the showers to bathe. Anyone who was even slightly reluctant to remove his clothes, or who was slow in doing so, promptly received a different kind of shower – blows from the stick-wielding kapos.

The forbidden question entered my mind, "*Ribbono Shel Olam*, what are You doing with us?," but I could not continue my train of thought, as I noticed a kapo rushing in my direction. Aware of the sticks always poised to beat us, I swiftly removed my clothes and placed them in a neat pile to the side, so I would be able to recognize them later on. When we had still been in the Lodz ghetto, a couple of days earlier, in preparing ourselves for the transport, many of us had donned several shirts, two pairs of pants, sweaters and other garments, figuring that we would need them in the days ahead. Also, my mother had sewn some small pieces of gold coins and a few American dollars into the lining of my jacket. But I didn't have too long to worry about the fate of my clothes, for sure enough, all our clothing was immediately carried off by the kapos and thrown into large piles. For any of us who dared voice any disapproval, a rain of blows on the head would be the response, along with the explanation, "Fools that you are, you will not be needing your clothes any more, anyway."

The panic, the shock, the shouting, the beatings and the fear of the beatings removed from us any trace of levelheadedness, and we were unable to think clearly. Even our ability to worry was impaired. But, once again, any opportunity to think was curtailed by the next phase of our initiation. Event after event occurred so quickly that we didn't have the time or the ability to digest the happenings.

We were suddenly rushed to another large chamber of the building, where a crew of kapos met us with scissors and hair-cropping machines in hand. Within minutes we were further "refined," as our heads and our entire bodies were completely shaved.

The procedure was torturous as well as humiliating. Using razors and machines that were dull, the kapos, victims in their own right, were under pressure to process a few hundred inmates within a short time. With their blunt instruments, they hurriedly tore out our hair as much as they shaved it off. We emerged from that department of horrors bleeding painfully. To further dehumanize us, they dealt each of us a sudden violent blow on the back so that we doubled over in pain, at which they took the opportunity to check inside our bodies for any items that might have been concealed there.

Very frequently and regularly during the ordeal we would be given a whack with a stick, in order to ensure quick compliance with their orders. The method worked well, for the fear of further pain induced in us instantaneous obedience and submissiveness, stripping us of any urge for self-control and independence.

We were made to file into an enormous room that had dozens of showerheads jutting out from the ceiling overhead. We were all packed into the shower hall, too small to contain the mass of people.

Horror dawning on his face, my friend Yosef turned to me and said, "I heard in the ghetto about a room with showers, but instead of water coming out, people are showered with gas and end up dying from suffocation. It looks like those rumors were true."

I did not know what to answer him. It was too incredible to believe. In the ghetto we had been forced to work for five years to aid the German war effort, and now they were about to kill us, in cold blood. It made no sense at all.

But even the logic of my reasoning did not fully convince me, as we waited for several endless minutes, the smell of sulfur going to our heads and further amplifying our fears. Then, all at once, water came down. At first we were still afraid that perhaps some sort of poison was being rained down on us. But after a few moments of panic, we relaxed somewhat as we realized that the liquid was water indeed. Then, spurred on by a new drive for survival, we began to vie for a better position, to obtain more of the water.

But just as quickly as it had started, the water was shut off.

The initiation process went by rather quickly. We suffered the worst while we stood in line waiting our turns. But there was more to come.

For our next trial we were moved into another room in the same building, an ominously dark room, with a recessed floor filled with blackish liquid. It was an enormous pool of water heavily treated with what smelled like sulfur and disinfectant, into which we were ordered to enter and dip in over our heads, while SS guards watched us from above to make sure that our heads went underwater. The strong chemicals in the water caused the fresh wounds we had acquired from our shearing experience just minutes before to sting excruciatingly.

When we stepped out of the pool we were driven out of the other side of the red brick building, and pushed outside, as we were, naked.

By now it was the dead of night. For a brief moment I stood there, among others like myself, who were perhaps also reflecting on the events of the day, as I was, wondering how to account for the passage of time of the past twelve hours in particular, so terrible and harrowing had been the events that had occurred. The black sky and the chill of the Polish early autumn night brought a shiver to my bones. Suddenly the darkness around us was obliterated by the blaze of powerful floodlights.

The hunger that we all felt gnawing at us was not yet uppermost in our minds, as we experienced the next segment of our transformation into proper citizens of Auschwitz. Off to one side, there were immense piles of various articles of clothing, with a kapo standing next to each pile. We were made to file by, one by one, and receive one item from each pile. First I was given a pair of briefs, then a shirt. From a third pile I was handed a pair of trousers and from a fourth a jacket. The last item I received was something that looked like a rag, and I hadn't the slightest idea of what to do with it. First I thought it might be a sock, but then I saw other people putting theirs on their heads, like hats.

Looking all around me, I realized that everyone was in disguise. We all resembled a bunch of clowns. Here was a tall man in a jacket several sizes too small, and there was a short man with sleeves amply covering his entire hands, and on all of our heads, rags. Were it not for the tragedy of our situation, we could all have enjoyed a bout of hearty laughter while viewing the Purim characters we had become.

We had barely finished getting dressed outside of the bathhouse, when the kapos recommenced their vicious behavior, shouting curses at us, and peppering their words liberally with hefty blows from the whips and sticks that they held. After being beaten once again into total subservience, we were marched to yet another block, where we were supposed to sleep.

Once again, we were squashed into one side of the block. The building was divided along its center by a low red brick wall, a couple of feet in height. On one side of the wall, approximately 500 of us were packed in like sardines, while about half a dozen or so kapos ran around the other side of the room, empty, save for them.

As we scrutinized our surroundings, trying to figure out what would happen next, a long whistle blast pierced the din. One of the kapos approached the low wall, climbed on top of it and called out, "Silence!" As if on cue, the other kapos followed suit, shouting at us to be quiet, and threatening us with blows to the stomach for any word spoken out of turn.

There was instant silence in the room, as we all held our breath, waiting to hear what the kapo had to say. To our amazement, he began to speak in Yiddish.

"Friends. *Yidden*. We are also prisoners, like you. We went through everything you have gone through today. We beg you for your cooperation. In a moment the SS will be walking in here and each of you will be frisked, and thoroughly inspected. If anyone is discovered having any gold, silver, currency or valuables, he will either be shot on the spot, or hanged on this pole." He paused, to show us a pole standing in the middle of the barracks. I had noticed it earlier, but never guessed its purpose. "Dear Jews, be aware that yesterday there also arrived a large transport from Lodz, and the SS ended up hanging fifteen Jews right here in this room. If anyone has any contraband with him, and will admit it right now, of his own free will, we will convince the SS not to punish him."

The silence on our side of the barracks was deafening, no one daring to utter a single word. Neither did anyone speak up in order to admit to having smuggled anything in. A few quiet moments passed dramatically, when all of a sudden the kapo turned to us in a rage.

"Animals! Swine! Do you think we don't know that you have smuggled gold pieces and money into this building? When the SS come in, there will be innocent people shot. Why should any of you suffer because of some other swine? If anyone here knows of anyone who has smuggled valuables in with him, please come forward and tell us. You will be rewarded with food and drink."

Again, silence. Our nerves were frayed to near breaking point. Our bodies were about to collapse, after we had been standing on our feet for two days and a night. In the railcars we had had barely enough room to crouch in, let alone sit. Only now, after having undergone shock after shock, terror after terror, I could ponder the fact that I had not eaten or drunk for two days. And yet here we all were, still standing – in sheer fright of the kapos who stood over us and of the SS guards whose appearance was now apparently imminent.

Then the kapos proceeded to do what they had threatened us would be done by the SS guards. They made their way to our side of the barracks and began to frisk and inspect us, making sure to remove our shoes, which were the only things we had been allowed to keep. There ensued shouts and snarled orders by the kapos interspersed with cries of pain, but no pandemonium broke loose, and we maintained our equilibrium as well as possible.

Suddenly, the lights were extinguished, and an insidious darkness enveloped us. We could still hear moans from people being beaten amid the continuous screaming of the kapos. Then, we heard the head kapo's voice call out above the din, "We have already caught several people who had valuables with them and did not admit to it."

Was this a warning, or a mere observation? We could not determine the answer. We could only listen, as we heard what sounded like a few people being forcibly taken to the other side of the barracks. Then, loud, heavy footsteps pounded in the darkness as new shouting, now in German, could be heard.

"Five people will be hanged at once, and everyone in this

block will be severely punished!"

More heavy footsteps and loud breathing were all we could hear in the devastating silence. Then, all at once, a heart-rending cry shattered the stillness. *"Shema Yisrael!"*

There are no words that exist to describe the dread and shock we all felt at that moment. Immobile, we continued to stand in the dark, pressed one against the other. Then, as time passed, with no further disturbance, our numbness gave way to fatigue. We all began to kneel down, keeping our legs spread apart for fear of losing some of the meager space apportioned to each of us. Somehow we all made our way down to the floor, crouching rather than sitting, a fitful slumber overtaking our anxieties. We remained in that position, crammed into each other, half awake, poised to hear the slightest sound that could possibly be a harbinger of newer atrocities to befall us.

We were awakened at about 4 o'clock in the morning. In the dim, predawn light we could see no sign of anyone having been hanged. Suddenly we understood that the entire scene played out the night before had been nothing more than a charade. Dreadful theatrics had been enacted by the kapos, Jews themselves who had sunk so low as to prey on our paranoia in order to extract a few precious valuables from a distraught mass of victims, who had already endured so much suffering and anguish. To add to their despicable, mean-spirited behavior, they had abused the holy words of *"Shema."* We could ascertain from this that a person without the fear of G-d in his heart will not respect his fellow human beings, but will step on people's heads in order to become rich or just for the pleasure.

That night's ordeal indelibly scarred our hearts. The fear which was instilled in us that night, the absolute terror, so degraded and demoralized us, that no one who was there could ever be totally cured of the injury sustained from the experience.

Nevertheless, life in Auschwitz went on. We did not have the luxury of pensive idling and pondering over events as they occurred. Each day brought new dangers, new tribulations, and new threats to our lives. Our Sages taught us that new afflictions cause one to forget the old.

Chapter 12

Life and Anguish in Auschwitz

At 4 o'clock that morning we were harshly awakened from a fitful sleep to the realization that the nightmare we had lived through on our first night in Auschwitz was indeed a reality. After the overwhelming experiences of the preceding days, the journey in the stifling, sealed railcars, the *selektzia,* the tearing apart of families, the baths and the marathon standing sessions – all to the steady accompaniment of a stream of bloodcurdling screams and a relentless hail of blows rattling our weary bones, courtesy of the SS guards and the kapos, many of them Jews – we had yet to endure a frighteningly cruel drama orchestrated to frighten us into yielding any valuables that the kapos suspected we still had concealed somewhere. That night's torturous experience left an indelible mark on us. In addition to the sheer terror we experienced, we had to endure the inhumane crowding of hundreds of us into half the block area, denying to many the faint hope of possibly being able to sleep for a few hours. No words can accurately describe our feelings during that night's ordeal.

At 4 o'clock that morning, the kapos ordered us to go outside, where we were made to line up, as usual, five to a row, between the barracks buildings, in the pitch black of night. Battered and bruised, having eaten nothing for a couple of days, our endurance having been tested to the very limits, we stood and shivered in the chill of the predawn air. The kapos did not seem to be bothered by the cold, well fed and warmly dressed as they were.

They ordered us to stand motionless in formation. However, when it appeared that they would be gone for a while, we all drew together, one against the other, back to back, to try to keep warm. But it was not long before they returned, and, when they noticed how we were huddled together, they proceeded to pry us apart with their batons, beating many of us freely and to the point of bleeding.

Curiously enough, as soon as the kapos left again, the masses of Jews standing there instinctively drew together again, like magnets. The freezing air was so biting that we once again gravitated to each other in our efforts to keep warm.

For about three hours we stood there in our miserable formation. At about 7 o'clock, SS guards arrived to count us. As strict and severe as the kapos had been about the way we stood, the Germans were far worse. Woe unto the person who was spotted slouching even the tiniest bit, or standing in less than a perfect manner. Right away, that poor person would be ordered to leave the line and assume his place in front of the whole group. As the rest of us looked on, the miserable victim would be ordered to bend, to dance, to run or to do an assortment of other gymnastics, as the SS guard's whip kept pelting him mercilessly, on his face, on his back, until the poor man's blood soaked the ground beneath him.

As soon as the SS had concluded their exercise and left the scene, the kapos would continue the task with renewed vigor. If anyone were foolish enough to express the slightest protest or disapproval, he would be treated to an even stronger dose of punishment, being beaten until his body would lie still, in a lifeless heap in front of the rest of us.

That morning, as on every morning following, when the ordeal of the *appel* (roll call) was over, we were ordered to file back into the block. As we reentered, the line moved more slowly, as the block "elder" (one of the kapos) stood and handed each person a cup of hot black liquid that they referred to as coffee.

In a matter of moments we had ingested our "coffee" in its entirety, the first "food" that we had received after days of starvation. Almost at once we were again overcome by the pangs of hunger that we had been suffering.

After a while, we were ordered to leave the block again. This time we were left to roam around and do pretty much as we pleased, until the afternoon hours. On that first day we wandered from block to block in search of others we might know – a relative, a friend, or just a familiar face.

Not far from our block was a series of barracks which housed Jews from Hungary. The four months that they had already lived in Auschwitz had taken their toll, for they looked worn-out and spent. These were the fortunate ones among the Hungarian Jews who had come to Auschwitz, for most of them had been taken immediately to the gas chambers upon their arrival, and murdered.

As we began to mingle with them, they told us about Auschwitz and what we could expect here in the weeks and months ahead. In the Lodz ghetto we had known of atrocities, but had never been prepared for what we had so far experienced in Auschwitz and what we were told by these "old-timers." They educated us with the gory details of the selections that were carried out almost daily in the camp, and with what happened to those who were selected for death. They told us about how masses of Jews would be crowded together in the gas chamber, a building in which people were gassed by poisonous fumes, and how the piles of bodies would then be carted away to the adjacent crematorium to be burnt.

They directed us to look out into the horizon and view a number of tall brick smokestacks that steadily belched forth pillars of ominous black smoke, intermingled with columns of flames that would shoot out periodically.

Our instincts would not allow us to believe what we were told. We did not want to accept the fact that living, vibrant human beings – parents, children – were being murdered en masse. Yet the way these hard and long-suffering Hungarian Jews were looking at us, compassionately, yet mocking our naiveté in our unwillingness to come to terms with the reality which faced us, caused us to suspect that maybe they were in fact telling us the truth.

Slowly, though, we became resigned to this new order, that human life had little or no value, and we realized that no one could possibly know when it might be his turn to lose his own precious life. For now we were alive, but what the next hour or minute would bring, no one knew.

During those first days, I spent some time in the company of the Hungarian Jews. I noticed that they seemed to have slightly better living conditions, and they were astounded to learn that we slept directly on the floor, while they had been given boards on which to sleep on top of the ground. Whereas we were clothed in rags, they had been given striped uniforms and berets of sorts. Their clothes looked like pajamas, but were better than what we had.

One day, I was amazed to see one of these Jews take out a pair of *tefillin*. In my spiritual starvation, I begged him to allow me to put them on. I couldn't wear them for very long. It seemed that as soon as I had put them on, I already had to remove them. We were all too frightened at the possibility of a kapo or an SS guard suddenly entering, for if one of them saw that pair of *tefillin*, the situation would be bitter indeed.

After removing the *tefillin*, I returned to my block, where I proceeded to wander about aimlessly, wondering at how my real world had dissipated into a satanic world of make-believe. As difficult as it was to digest all that had occurred in the past few days, we did not have an abundance of time to think and to analyze, as we needed the proverbial thousand pairs of eyes to keep a sharp watch on everything, simply in order to be aware of the many dangers that lurked everywhere.

At one point, I saw a kapo walking towards me. The short, heavy-set man stopped an inmate and asked him a question. Too far away to hear the exchange, I had little doubt that the inmate's answer did not meet with the kapo's approval, for, without warning, the kapo raised his hand and brought down the stick he was holding full force on the poor man's head. Within seconds, the inmate fell, blood gushing from his fractured skull.

I learned the lesson that in Auschwitz, one must not open one's mouth. In Auschwitz we received a new type of education that taught us that we were nothings, mere worms. We discovered here that our survival could depend on the caprice or whim of anyone in a position of some authority.

I returned to my block just as the bell rang to signify that the daily ration of soup was about to be handed out. Within seconds, hundreds of inmates were lined up in front of a huge cauldron, waiting for their turn to receive their portion of the vile gruel that the block elder began to ladle out. Actually, every two people would receive one portion of soup, which they would have to share, giving us all a lesson in forced camaraderie. We were not even given spoons to eat with, which only added to the difficulty. (On the first day, we all looked around for anything, even a simple flat piece of wood to use as a spoon. Anything we could find that could be used for that purpose we guarded as if it were the most precious commodity.) On top of that, we had to get down on the floor to eat our watery ration, in a most degrading fashion.

I watched the block elder distributing the soup and noticed how he looked into the faces of those who stood before him in line. If anyone found favor in his eyes, he would dip the ladle deeper into the cauldron and dig up a bit more of the solid stock that would sink to the bottom. Once in a while, a lucky person would happily find a small piece of potato in his bowl.

On the other hand, if the kapo did not like the face of the person standing before him, the ladle would skim the top of the pot and the inmate would receive a very watery bit of broth.

As we ate, we all took great care that the person we were sharing our portion with should not get an extra mouthful or a few extra drops of the soup. We abided by the strictest rules – one helping for you, and one helping for me.

The anguish of our predicament reached its peak when we heard loud disputes breaking out among people who could not bring themselves to give back their bowls to their partners, or when a brawl would erupt over — a piece of potato. And we felt all the more agony over having to witness the debasement of our fellow Jews, as the scores of people who had not been able to find a piece of wood to use as a spoon were forced to attempt to eat the soup with their fingers.

In almost no time at all, the rations were consumed. Then, as soon as the block elder left the area for a minute, everyone suddenly began to run. We had no idea where they were running to, but we all just ran along, in order to find out what was happening, and why everyone was stampeding. A moment later, we discovered the reason for the commotion. Right where the cauldron stood, there were dozens of people pushing and shoving and vying for a better position from which to scrape the side of the cauldron in an attempt to salvage ever the tiniest bit of food that may have been left behind by the kapo. Some men tried scratching the inner walls of the pot in the hope of getting something – anything. After the commotion had died down, I was able to walk over to the pot and take a closer look. It had been thoroughly cleaned, and there was not the tiniest speck of anything left over.

This was lunchtime at Auschwitz. Ravenously, we devoured the paltry portion of soup we were given, and the hunger in our bellies lingered practically unchanged. But we had no opportunity to dwell on our hunger, for as soon as we had finished eating, kapos and block elders once again made themselves evident, shoving and ordering us about. Some of us were told to sweep, while others were instructed to tidy the entire barracks, and a few more were ordered to carry the heavy wooden soup cauldron back to the camp kitchen.

The kapos were not satisfied unless we were constantly busy with something, never able to sit and relax for a spell. So we tried to second-guess them, and dance to their wicked tune. We quickly learned that we were best off just to keep walking quickly, so as to appear busy with some imaginary task already assigned. While we were constantly consumed by fear of the kapos' batons and whips looming over our heads, and of the gallows post – a steady and grim reminder of camp justice – we also viewed life as a challenging contest, whereby we would try to see who could outsmart whom, inmate or kapo, like a game of cat and mouse.

After we were rushed around for a while, being assigned different tasks, a bell sounded again, and we were hurried over to one side of the block by the kapos.

During most of the day, we were not allowed in the block-house. Whether in pouring rain, in sweltering sun, or in the chilling cold, we were forced to remain outdoors, and we learned that we were never to sit, nor to appear idle.

We were told to line up in rows of five, to prepare for being counted. This formation of five to a row enabled the SS guards to count us more easily. But, as we stood there waiting, the kapos "educated" us further about camp life. Like in a macabre game of "Simon says," they barked orders at us arbitrarily.

"Hats off!"

In a flash, thousands of inmates standing near their blocks removed the raglike hats from their heads.

"Hats on!" they barked again, and instantly the rags were back on our shaven heads.

This same charade was repeated, not just once, or twice, but dozens of times. We were being molded into a veritable army, an army of miserable prisoners of the Third Reich.

Then came a different command.

"Down on your bellies!"

Within seconds we had to stretch out on the floor, prostrate. Then, "Up!" We were back on our weary feet standing once again in formation. Among us there were many older Jews for whom this training was a slow and frightening process. The sticks of the kapos were ready and waiting to be used liberally on the heads of those who took a split second longer in carrying out the meaningless and capricious commands of our tormentors.

The kapos had other assorted punishments for those whose obedience they felt was wanting. One of their favorites was to order the victim to stand in front of the columns of inmates, and then have him crouch without letting his knees touch the ground. Thereupon they would force him to raise both his arms and keep them suspended in front of him, and then put a brick in each hand, and he would have to stay in that position for what must have been a backbreaking eternity.

Anyone who grew weak, and either let his hands down or objected to his ordeal, would have only the A-mighty to look to for assistance, for such a wretched individual would end up having to be carried away with broken ribs and a smashed skull.

After an endless series of the "Simon says game," we heard the footsteps of the SS guards approaching for the count. On good days, if we had good fortune, they would make their rounds quickly, and then as soon as they were done, we would once again line up outside the block as the block elder, standing at the doorway, handed each of us his daily bread ration, after which we entered the barracks for our final "meal" of the day.

At this point, we were so starved that we would keep a hawkish eye on the sizes of our bread rations, as sometimes one person would be given a piece that was smaller than that of his friend. We were, however, not allowed to complain, nor to utter any sound at all.

Finally, we sat, eating and making slight conversation in our few moments of relaxation. After a few minutes passed, the block elder announced that there was to be absolute silence in the block, so the kapos could sleep.

Thus ended another day in the frightful, abysmal place called Auschwitz-Birkenau, as we slipped into a fitful sleep laced with angst and the foreboding of what the next day would bring.

Chapter 13

The Spoon

After a while, I saw that wandering about aimlessly for an entire day was terrible and useless, so I began to volunteer to do any sort of work in and around the camp. One day there might be a need to carry bricks or wood. Another day I could be useful digging trenches for the sanitary drains. But anything was better than roaming about the camp pointlessly, when at any time I could become the object of a kapo's cruelty.

One day, after our daily soup rations had been distributed, I did not wait until we were ordered to carry back the big soup cauldron. Rather, my friend Yossel and I picked up the big pot by its metal handles and lugged it back to the camp kitchen that was at the other end of the grounds. As we neared the kitchen, we saw all the other cauldrons that had been brought back from all the different blocks.

Even though we knew we were not allowed to enter the kitchen, we saw that the door was open, so we took the pot inside. The kitchen was empty. No one was around. I was really afraid that someone would come in and kill us. My friend, however, was braver. He walked up to the stove, grabbed a small pot that was sitting there, placed it under his jacket, and left. Somewhat encouraged, I looked around for some other article of food that I could grab, but there was nothing.

My skin was prickling with anxiety, for I knew that any second someone could come in. But after dashing outside, I saw on the ground at the side of the building a large pile of potatoes – and an SS guard pacing back and forth, carrying a machine-gun. Without thinking too long, I waited until the guard turned around and was walking in the other direction. Then, as I passed very close to the mound of potatoes, I bent down and snatched a few, stuffing them into my pockets. Immediately I walked on, without looking back to see if the German guard had seen me. I figured that if he had, he would already have shot me from behind.

I returned to the barracks with five potatoes in my pockets. For a while I wandered around, wondering what to do with the potatoes. Then I arrived at the block where the Hungarian Jews lived, and I realized that here might lie the solution to my potato dilemma. Having been in the camp for several months already, the Hungarian Jews were more aware of what was going on, especially with regard to the underground trade in soup rations, bread and other items.

As I neared the block, I saw a Hungarian boy walking around with a bowl, which I noticed had in it a soup of rice and milk. This boy was an assistant to the block leader, who was apparently trying to acquire something special by offering the soup for a possible trade.

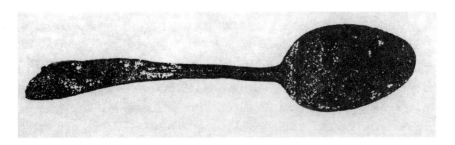

The "spoon"

I had no idea of what the trading value might be, but I offered him my five potatoes. When he immediately agreed, I thought that maybe I had offered him too much, so I told him that I also wanted the spoon that was in the bowl of soup. At first he hesitated, but in the end, he agreed. I gave him the potatoes, and as soon as I had the bowl of soup in my hands, I began to eat it. I could not remember the last time I had eaten such a soup of rice and milk, sweetened with sugar yet. Not only did I not have to share with any partner, but I also had a spoon to the bargain.

Now I began to wonder what I should do with the spoon. I would have an easier time eating my regular soup ration the next day. With the right partner, there would be one spoonful for him and one for me, but – I had to find an honest partner, one whom I could trust, who would not, Heaven forbid, take away my spoon.

The greatest advantage to my having the spoon was that after the soup was distributed and everyone had attacked the empty cauldron and scraped its walls with their fingers, after everyone was gone, I was able to get at some scraps of food with my spoon that the others could not get at with their bare hands. With my friend Yossel, I went from one cauldron to another in search of morsels to fill our perpetually empty stomachs.

Several days passed, more or less uneventfully. Then, one day, a loud bell rang throughout the camp, and everyone had to rush back into his block. This meant that there would be a *selektzia*. As the blocks were locked up our hearts filled with trepidation. We did not yet know exactly what a *selektzia* signified – how, as it says in *Unesaneh Tokef,* we would be made to pass by like sheep, and it would be determined who was to live and who was to die ... who would be taken for work, and who would be taken to the gas chamber.

We were locked into our block with no bread and no soup rations. There we spent the entire night. The following morning we were taken to another place that was far away from the barracks, where we were joined by others from other barracks. All together there were thousands of Jews from Lodz. After standing in one place for hours, we were led to another area, where there stood a table at which sat several SS officers, as well as civilian Germans. Around them stood numerous SS guards holding weapons and sticks.

After a while, we were ordered to strip off our clothes and leave them in one place, except for our shoes which we were allowed to take with us. We were made to walk in single file across the front of the table, after which we were told to go either to the right or to the left. Then we were ordered to run into another barracks where we were once again locked up.

Several hours later, the door was opened and once again we were led to a bath, a pool which smelled of sulfur, and which stung our flesh. Several SS officers stood over us to make sure that we all dipped in deeply enough so that the water covered our heads. After some time, we were led outdoors and given undergarments, new striped uniforms that were like pajamas, and berets. (I was lucky to get long warm underwear, while others got thin underwear. But later, in Kaufering, or Camp Number Four, the warm ones became breeding grounds for lice.) We felt that we now looked more human and presentable than before, when we were dressed in rags.

During the whole procedure, I never parted with my spoon, hiding it in my shoe, clutching it in my hand, or concealing it under my arm.

Once again we were led into a block and locked up. Somehow I still felt a little calmer knowing that I had my "wonder utensil" with me. This was already the second night that we spent without food or drink, and the pain of hunger pierced my stomach. I felt sapped of all my strength. We lay nearly lifeless on the ground, dozing off, exhausted from the day's harrowing experiences, and always — the fear. Thus we spent the night.

The next day, in the late morning, all at once, the doors opened, and the kapos began shouting, "Everyone out!" Starving and fatigued, we had to run. I realized that our bodies were functioning through nervous tension now, not physical energy, though I did not have much opportunity to ponder the fact, as we were now constantly being treated to blows and shouts by the kapos, which made thinking rather hard.

In a few minutes we found ourselves standing in an open area. We were made to stand in rows like soldiers, about 3,000 men. Again there was a table at which sat several SS officers and civilian Germans. As we came closer to it, we were lined up in single file, having to register at the table as we passed it. Now my thoughts began to focus on my spoon, my entire fortune. Where could I now conceal this treasure? Since we had no pockets, I opened up a seam in my uniform, and stuck my spoon in it. No one would find it there, I assured myself.

It was a beautiful day, with a clear blue sky and a bright sun to warm us. Before long our row began to move and we approached the table, around which sat three men, three angels of death. Near them stood SS men with machine-guns and with sticks, and also kapos to help maintain order.

As we got a bit closer, I was suddenly struck with horror. Before each prisoner came near the table, the kapos frisked him to see if he had anything with him. Overseeing the procedure were SS guards, standing nearby. My precious spoon again popped into my head. I took it out of my hiding spot, about to throw it down on the ground next to my feet. I would lose my prize, but at least my life would not be endangered. Just then, a metallic sound was heard. Another man standing in line had thrown something down in order that it not be found on his person. Immediately, kapos and SS guards came running, shouting, "Who threw the money down?" No one admitted to having done it.

But there, in Auschwitz, justice was dealt collectively. Since the culprit did not identify himself, the people who were standing near the place where the coins had been dropped were all taken out of line. Once trial and sentencing were hastily completed, the hapless "criminals" were horribly beaten, on their faces, chests, not to mention their heads. After a few minutes of this gruesome punishment, the victims lay on the ground in pools of blood. These men, we knew, would not continue in the procession to the table. Their next stop would be the crematorium.

"Ribbono Shel Olam," I thought to myself in a panic, "what shall I do now with my spoon?" In that second, in that moment of private anguish, the A-mighty injected a thought into my head. Usually a person who is struck with fear is unable to think lucidly. Plainly, Divine Providence had flashed the brilliant idea into my head. I removed my beret, wrapped it around my spoon, and held the beret in my hand. All too soon, the SS and kapos were standing over me ready to frisk me.

"Put your hands up," one of them ordered. I was glad to comply, raising my hands high with the spoon inside the beret, still in one of my hands. I was tapped and frisked from all sides, but my secret was not revealed. All the while, my heart banged like a hammer with fright.

With the help of G-d, I was found clean. Soon I was standing at the table. Anxious to cooperate, I answered their questions quickly and clearly. They asked me for my name, age, place of birth, names of my parents, and everything was recorded.

From here we were led to another spot not far from where we had arrived a couple of days earlier. There train cars were waiting, I knew not why. Once again we were lined up in a row, this time to receive a soup ration. Now I remembered that the last time I had eaten was two days ago. The hunger was gnawing at my insides. There were Hungarian youths wandering around, distributing bowls of soup at the instructions of the kapos and block elders.

In heightened anticipation, I approached the large soup pot. In front of it stood a kapo ladling portions into bowls, while a second kapo handed each person an entire loaf of bread. We were told that we were being taken to Germany for work, and that we would have to travel by train for several days. I took my soup and bread and looked around for a corner where no one would watch me eat, or more specifically, where no one would see what I was eating my soup with. I was able to finish my soup ration in a few seconds, thanks to my spoon. I also ate almost the whole loaf of bread, not thinking about what I would do for the next few days, on our way to Germany.

Even after this meal, I was still famished from the past few days in Auschwitz, and even yet from my previous days in the ghetto. While roaming around, I saw the Hungarian boys collecting the empty bowls, which they began to distribute to those people waiting in line for their soup rations. On the spur of the moment, I suddenly began to shout like them, "*Miski! Miski!* Bowls! Bowls!" and I managed to gather about twenty empty bowls. At that point I began to distribute these to the men waiting in line. As I was about to hand out my last bowl, I held on to it and slid into line, joining the others waiting for their soup rations. I did not stop to consider what might happen if I were caught.

With the help of Divine Providence, I received a second bowl of soup, and half a loaf of bread. Because I had my spoon, I was able to finish my soup much more quickly than the others who had to use their hands or a small piece of wood and were still working on their first ration.

Because the soup was salty, we became very thirsty, and of course, there was no water to drink. By and by, the kapos and SS guards started to shove us into the railcars that had become stiflingly hot in the late summer sun. Before they slammed the iron doors of the cattle cars shut, the Germans placed a single bucket of black "coffee" into each cattle car, just as we began to move.

The heat and the overcrowding in the cars were unimaginable. People began to fight over a drop of coffee and in the midst of the scuffle, the entire pail was spilled on the wagon floor. Our thirst mounted dramatically. I tried to push my way as close as possible to the door, which was chained shut from the outside. Noticing that there was a small crack, I kept my mouth open over the crack, and, as the train moved on, a bit of fresh air entered my mouth and lungs, so that I could breathe.

It was not long before our bodies had to submit to their natural urges. In addition to the heat, the crowding and our terrible thirst, the stench only made matters worse — until someone thought of the idea of removing one of the floorboards of the wagon. This became our toilet. Through the hole, some air came through as well, and the tension was somewhat relieved.

Nevertheless, the night passed as a nightmare. I did not dare move from my special place near the door for fear that someone else might grab my spot. I tried to sleep standing up but it was very difficult. Others tried to sit and the crowding grew worse. People pushed at one another until they became too tired to do so. Slowly slumber descended upon us miserable slaves.

Day broke. I felt a bit refreshed from the cool night air. Still standing in the same spot, I looked around and saw that others were just as wiped out with fatigue, for many had not slept at all. As the train rhythmically chugged along the tracks, I watched enviously as people started to eat the bread that they had received in Auschwitz. Regretfully, having eaten my share, I had none left for now.

The day became brighter as the sun rose higher. As morning turned to noon, the iron roof of the railcar conducted the devilish rays inwards, turning the car into an inferno. Once again we were afflicted with an unbearable thirst. In this way we rode on, until the train came to a halt, in a small town in Czechoslovakia. We saw people outside walking about, and several SS soldiers wandering around. These were our guards, who were traveling aboard a special railcar.

When we saw them, we all spontaneously began to beg them for water. They ignored us. We began to shout, "Water! Water!"

We could hear some of them begin to cock their rifles. Appearing alongside the wagons, the guards aimed their rifles through the portholes, shouting, "If you don't be quiet, we will shoot!"

But our fear now was only secondary to our thirst, which made many totally delirious. We began to scream even louder, "Water, or shoot!" They knew that shooting us all there was not an option. We had been sold as slaves, and they needed us for their work. So they opened up the wagons and the SS soldiers told a few men to disembark. Before long, the group of people returned carrying pails of water.

By this time we had learned to be more organized. The night before we saw that when each person fended for himself alone, everyone lost. Therefore, the water was now distributed in an orderly way, with each person getting a cup that he was able to keep.

Although I was very thirsty, I held myself back from drinking up all the water at once. I sipped it slowly, and with each sip, I actually felt my strength returning. Everyone else drank up his water quickly, but I kept a little bit in my cup for later. In the Lodz ghetto I had learned to make a bread last for eight days. Despite fierce hunger, I learned not to eat tomorrow's portion today. But now a Jew came to me with a proposition. He still had half a bread left, but he could tolerate his hunger more than his thirst. "Let's trade my bread for your water," he offered. This was a difficult decision to make, perhaps a decision between life and death. I felt unbearable hunger, while my thirst seemed slightly more tolerable. Perhaps my having stayed near the door with my mouth open over the crack, allowing the wind to blow into my lungs, helped me to overcome my thirst. I decided to make the switch, to our mutual satisfaction.

Naturally, I immediately began to eat the bread, thus quieting my hunger somewhat. Once again, we began to travel, with the iron wheels grinding against the rails – "Ta Ta Ta Ta" – and night descended yet again. By this time, having become slightly used to our new surroundings, we managed to organize ourselves a bit. We sat crowded together, but we sat! And we were able to sleep. So ended another day.

A new day dawned. Our third day aboard the train was a bit easier to tolerate. The fiery ball in the sky was hiding behind the clouds overhead. Thus we were better able to deal with our hunger and thirst. As the train sped through the Central European terrain, we peered through cracks, seeing nothing but forests and fields. In a mood of relative calm, we began to engage in conversation, recounting animatedly to each other the extraordinary chain of events that had brought us here. We also speculated about what might be awaiting us when we reached our new destination. While most of us agreed that we could hardly expect things to be worse than they had been at Auschwitz-Birkenau, inevitably there were pessimists among us who brought out our worst fears. These were countered by the optimists' more favorable predictions. But no one really knew what to expect.

At dusk the train came to a stop. Again we looked out and listened as the guards ran this way and that, hollering orders. Then suddenly the iron door of our wagon was flung open, and we were ordered to jump off. It was shortly after sunset, but outside it was still much brighter than in the wagons. Once my eyes got accustomed to daylight, I could see that we had arrived at a small station, where there were no civilians in sight, only SS personnel, wherever we looked.

After being ordered to form rows of five people to a row, we were told to march. Although our ordeal aboard the train during the past three days had considerably weakened us, the coolness of the September evening air was somewhat rejuvenating. Luckily, it was raining as we marched, and I was not the only person to position my mouth and hands in such a way as to catch a few precious raindrops to quell the thirst raging in our parched throats.

It was not easy, though, to try to crane our necks upwards, as the SS guards were constantly hurrying us forward. "Quickly! Quickly!" they shouted over and over again. We marched thus for hours, through fields and through woods, with hardly the ability to notice where we were heading. Every so often, we would hear the crack of pistol fire, or the rat-tat-tat of a machine-gun. The man walking next to me, probably sensing my puzzlement over these sounds, explained to me that he had heard from others that if someone would fall or falter out of weakness, he would be shot instantly by the SS guards who were accompanying us.

Hour after hour we marched, yet I could see no indication of arriving at any camp or any point of civilization. Panic welled up inside of me, as I started to feel my strength dissipate. I was terrified that I would not be able to keep up with the rest, and I knew full well what was the fate of anyone who could not do so.

I muttered to my neighbor, "I can't go on. I can't keep up. My strength is going."

"I won't let you fall," he answered. "You must not sit down, not even for a second." He grabbed my arm, powerfully, and held on to me as we walked on. Still I could not muster the stamina to push my legs any further, and I entreated him to let go of my arm. "Let me go," I pleaded, "or you will fall together with me."

Suddenly, I felt him push into my hand a few bread crusts. My mouth fell open in amazement, as he said to me, "Listen, I don't have good teeth, and I can't eat these hard crusts anyway. You eat them, and you'll be able to gain some strength back."

I could not accept his magnificent gesture.

"How can you give away the bits of bread which you yourself need?" I asked him.

Still, he did not want to hear my argument, and shoved the crusts right back into my hand. Making peace with what had obviously been arranged for me by Hashem, I began to chew at the crusts. Almost immediately, some energy began to seep back into my body, and I felt strong enough, and determined enough, to continue the march.

Thinking back to this episode, I am struck by the fact that I never got a look at the man's face, as at that point, it was pitch dark. I don't think I even asked him his name. Sometimes, I imagine that this man may even have been an angel sent by the Creator with the express purpose of keeping me alive, perhaps the same angel who sustained me whenever death stared at me in the face. Could it have been otherwise? It must have been the will of Divine Providence that I push on, that I survive the horrors. I don't know in what merit I was privileged to receive this Heavenly intervention, but I have learned that the grace of the Creator does not necessarily follow a predictable pattern.

Hours passed, spelling out an eternity. Even the well-fed SS brutes were beginning to find the march too much to handle. Then, far off on the black horizon, we were suddenly able to make out lights, towers for the guards, with a number of wooden huts silhouetted against them, and an enclosure of barbed wire. In no time at all, we were passing through the entrance, being counted by the guards as we made our way inside. A few seconds later, or so it seemed, we found ourselves inside the barracks, where we all collapsed in a death-like fatigue upon the wooden floor planks — and we slept.

Chapter 14

Camp Number Eight

The next morning we were roused from our slumber, at about 8 or 8:30 a.m., judging by the position of the sun. (None of us had a watch.) After the shrill ringing of the camp bell stirred us into a state of awakening, the SS guards accosted us with a whole new slew of instructions. We were told to leave the blocks and line up at the assigned assembly spot outside, called the *appelplatz*.

It seemed that the SS guards who had accompanied us on our death march needed to catch up on their sleep a bit longer than usual for SS guards. We had time to look around and see that we were in a small camp, comprised of fifteen to twenty blocks. Each block had been constructed by first digging, along the entire length of the block site, a long trench, wide enough for a wooden plank to be placed along each side of the trench. These planks, when covered with straw, became our beds, and each block had the capacity for about thirty people (but we were actually forty) to lie side by side like sardines along the length of the hut. The roof consisted of boards arranged on either side of the trench, sloping upwards from the ground and meeting at midpoint. It was a low triangular structure, covered with dirt, with grass on top, to camouflage the location from enemy aircraft that might fly overhead.

There was a narrow brick building to the side which was the camp kitchen, encircled, like a fortress, with a barbed-wire fence. Outside the camp there stood a number of more traditional-looking barracks, which comfortably housed the SS soldiers. All around the outside of the camp there were guard towers for surveillance of the entire enclosure. And in the front of the entire area lay the *appelplatz*, an empty expanse in which we were presently standing and where we would be ordered to congregate every morning just prior to our being sent off to our work details.

This was Lager Number Eight, which was to be our "home" for the next three weeks.

Now, again, we were ordered to line up in rows of five. I was instantly struck by the difference in the atmosphere here from the one we had just left in Auschwitz. Here the SS guards appeared to be somewhat more human. They did not shout at us, and did not beat anyone. Nor did they rush us. Everything seemed to be moving slowly here.

After waiting for a while, we saw the man whom we presumed to be the camp commandant approach us and take his place in front of the formation. He was a middle-aged, somewhat corpulent SS officer, who did little more than survey us at length. We were now his charges, the newest inmates in his domain. After counting us, he simply dismissed us and told us that we could return to our huts.

This was not Auschwitz. Here we did not have to feel uncertain of surviving the day, or even the hour. Now we could perceive Auschwitz as having been a bad dream, but one that we could not eradicate from our minds, nonetheless.

We felt slightly more relaxed now, free to mingle with one another. We were about 500 inmates, all of us Jews from Lodz. As we wandered about, looking for familiar faces, we naturally struck up conversations with our fellow inmates. We speculated about whether we would be getting anything to eat or drink, and about what would be happening to us in general, what kind of life awaited us here.

About an hour later, we were ordered by some SS guards to assemble once again in the *appelplatz*. Then the commandant resumed his place in front of the lines of Jews, and he began to deliver a welcoming address. As strange as it was for us to picture a concentration camp without kapos or block elders, we were even more amazed to hear this camp commandant speaking to us in a normal tone of voice, not yelling at us, not barking his instructions as the dogs of Auschwitz had done, but actually addressing us quite humanely, as if we were human beings after all.

He explained to us that we were located in a small camp that was a satellite of the larger concentration camp, Dachau. We would be working in the construction of roads and industrial facilities to assist the German war effort.

"In the meanwhile," he said, "for the next three weeks, you will all be quarantined here in this camp to ensure that you have not brought with you any contagious diseases into the German fatherland." During this period of time, we would not be made to work, except in helping to finish the camp's construction together with the German workers, but we were to be ready and prepared at a moment's notice to carry out any orders that the SS would give us.

I could not help but wonder if the commandant had any special connections in Berlin that enabled him to be exempt from being sent to the front lines to fight the Allied armies who were approaching from all sides. He must have had some pull which helped him acquire this sinecure, managing a small camp where he could relax much of the time.

At the end of his discourse, he asked, "Who here could serve as camp leader?"

Naturally, we all desired this coveted position, and a forest of hands shot up in the air. He moved closer to our lines and began to walk among us. Then he stopped and pointed out a Jew to be the camp leader. I noticed that this man seemed to be rather healthy-looking, considering the circumstances. I doubted that he had grown accustomed to much fasting in the Lodz ghetto. He had probably been an employee of the ghetto administration or of a food-distribution center. The man followed the commandant to the front of the lines.

Now the commandant again posed a question to the ranks of inmates.

"Is anyone here capable of being a cook?"

Again hundreds of hands were raised up to the sky. With a smile on his face, the commandant again walked amid the rows of inmates, and picked out a young man who appealed to him, telling him that he would now serve as the camp cook.

He then turned to his two new assistants, and in a voice that could be heard by all, he told them,

"Now pick out a few helpers and go immediately to prepare food for all the inmates. Everything you will need is already in the kitchen."

After these somewhat encouraging events, the SS guards disappeared again into their blocks, leaving us free to wander around, conversing idly. The subject of our discussion was mostly speculation about what was going to happen next.

Impatiently, we anticipated the soup rations and the bread that we were about to receive. During this time, the assistants who had been appointed by the camp officer attempted to discipline us into some sort of order, but this was no simple task. No one recognized them as superiors, with positions of authority, for to us, they were just plain Chaim or Moshe, like any one of us. Things were starting to get a bit unruly, when the kitchen workers finally arrived, and proceeded to dole out our portions.

We were told to stand in a line that started at the door to the kitchen. Right away, the starving inmates began to push and to shove, screaming at one another while vying for the best position in line. It mattered very little at the moment that we were all going to receive a ration, sooner or later.

The line slowly moved forward. I observed that as each inmate came before the man who doled out the ladles filled with soup, he kept his eyes fixed on the man's hand to see how deeply he would dip the ladle into the cauldron. There were potatoes at the bottom of the pot, while the top consisted mostly of watery broth. Now and then a complaint would be lodged against the server. "I didn't get any potatoes," or "The ladle you served me with was not full."

The same thing happened when the bread portions were distributed. Everyone seemed to feel that everyone else had received a larger measure of bread than he himself had. But although no one was satisfied with his share, we all ate ravenously. In a matter of minutes, we had finished eating, and we all made our way slowly back to the barracks where we lay down to sleep.

Thus passed the first day and night. The next morning we awoke calmly, after the sun had risen. Expecting to find our traditional black beverage, our morning "coffee" waiting for us, we were disappointed that it was not there, where our food was usually distributed. Some of us headed for the kitchen and dared enter it to investigate the mystery of the missing "coffee." This would have been a risky move elsewhere, but here it seemed we could afford to be a bit bolder. Just as we entered, the kitchen workers were hauling out large pots filled with the hot black liquid we knew as "coffee," which was, in fact, brewed from burnt grain.

A little while later, we were summoned to the *appelplatz*, where we stood to be counted by the SS guards, who, once the counting was completed, again disappeared into their blocks, and left us to our own devices. More time to wander about aimlessly in Camp Number Eight seemed to be what was in store for us for the time being. Almost immediately, we began to organize *minyanim* for *Shacharis*, during which people recited what they had committed to memory in days gone by.

A few days after we arrived, a group of German officers came by asking for Jews to work on fixing the barracks in the camp. Since none of the inmates was anxious to volunteer his services, the Germans instructed the newly appointed camp leader, with his squad of helpers, to recruit a number of workers. The inmates, however, met this move with resistance. Their feeling was that just because the Germans said he was a block leader did not give him the right to tell them to go to work. In the end, though, with the help of the Germans, just a few inmates were selected, and the group of workers was provided.

Soon the Germans were asking for mechanics to help with specific tasks. Though I wasn't a general mechanic, I volunteered my services because, as I mentioned previously, I tried to offer my services for work details as often as was feasible. My reasoning was that anyone who was wandering around idly would be the first to be picked for a much more difficult task, so I opted to offer myself for a job that was, in my estimation, at least manageable.

So began my work as an assistant to a German master mechanic in electrical work outside the campgrounds. I was to perform smaller, menial tasks that were necessary, but not too difficult, entailing no hard work. Sometimes I even dared to ask him to bring me some bread, which he did.

One of my jobs was to file small metal implements with a special file. While doing this work, an idea occurred to me, a clever, but dangerous idea. I would take my precious spoon, which I had smuggled at great risk out of Auschwitz, and, using the tools to which I now had daily access, I would convert its handle into a knife. I did this by pounding one side of the handle with a hammer, and then filing it until it was sharp enough to cut with. I wasn't even sure what I needed the knife for, but I figured that it might just come in handy one day. I also imagined that I could use the knife to cut our daily bread ration into segments, so I could have a portion for the night as well as the day. So now I was equipped with a spoon and a knife – I was rich in cutlery. But looking back, I marvel at the great risk I took, first in making the blade, and then in keeping it. If any Jew were caught in possession of a knife, he would be shot instantly.

Every day, when I returned to the barracks from work, my companions would bring me up to date on the events that took place that day in camp. On the third day of our arrival at Camp Number Eight, I heard that a few Jews had gone to the SS commandant of the camp and informed him about certain goings-on and inequities among the inmates. We could only wonder about the nature of these denouncements. A few days later, we discovered that the *altester* (camp leader) was going to be replaced, for it had been leaked to the camp commandant that he had been seen sneaking a piece of bread, upon which he had had the nerve to spread marmalade, and then eating it in the privacy of the camp kitchen. Then we were told that the camp cook would lose his position as well, because it had been reported by the same people that he had the habit of dipping the ladle deeper into the cauldron when dishing out a portion of soup to one of his personal acquaintances, digging up more potatoes for his friends and giving mostly water to those whom he did not know. The commandant promised the Jewish informants that their grievances would be settled.

The next day, two new prisoners showed up in Camp Number Eight. They were Germans who looked well nourished, and who wore green triangles sewn onto their jackets, signifying that they were common criminals. On the day that they arrived, the commandant introduced them to us during the *appel.*

"This one," he said, pointing to the short and stout one, "will be our new camp leader. And this one," he pointed to the taller one, "will be the new cook."

As soon as these announcements were made, disappointment spread among the men who had been helping the previous cook in the kitchen. They had been deluding themselves with the belief that each of them would at some point have opportunity to become the main cook, but now their aspirations had been dashed.

The newly appointed camp leader, who had been an inmate of Dachau for several years, assumed his new duties with great zest, while discontent spread among all the camp inmates. At the first *appel,* he introduced us to the new order and rules of discipline that he had no doubt learned during his stay in the dreaded concentration camp.

We were all mostly Lodzer Jews who had been together with our families in the ghetto under an exclusively Jewish administration. Indeed, we had experienced the hellishness of Auschwitz, but only for ten days, not long enough to actually become accustomed to concentration-camp life. Our new camp leader, with baton in hand, soon showed us clearly the fate of the person who might stand somewhat crookedly during *appel,* or of someone who dared come even a few seconds late. As his shrill voice screamed out orders at us, the new camp leader regularly brought the stick crashing down on our heads. The orders alone were enough to drive us insane.

"Run! Stand! Run again! Stand again! Lie down! On your feet!"

Over and over again they were repeated, twenty or thirty times, with no point and no purpose, other than to dehumanize us further. And woe to the unfortunate one who could not fulfill the order to the second.

When the time came for the soup to be ready for distribution, the line would form in the customary fashion, while the cook stood over the cauldron ladling out to each inmate a bowl full of the gruel. But the difference now was that the new cook would cruelly pour the soup ration to the side of the bowl, making sure that a portion of the soup, which was so vital to us all, would spill to the ground and be wasted.

We quickly found out that any man who dared complain that he had not received a full portion of soup would immediately be rewarded with a whack of the heavy iron ladle full force on his head. In seconds the man would be lying on the ground, blood gushing from his skull. The first time we saw this happen, we stopped even entertaining the possibility of ever again protesting against anything.

These adverse developments only occurred because of complaints that Jewish informants lodged against fellow Jews. Thus, after the first three weeks at Camp Number Eight, our lifestyle was transformed from one of relative tranquility to one of unrest and tribulation. Again we would be awakened needlessly at 4 a.m., ordered to run out to the *appelplatz* in the early morning chill, where we would be counted, forced to run, stand, lie down, get up, and so on, seemingly ad infinitum. And to add insult to injury, every day we would be treated to a special address by the German camp leader, during which we learned that, as Jews, we were identical to gypsies, vermin, worms, garbage, pigs and dogs.

"You will all end your lives in the concentration camp. Before long you will be nothing but smoke and earth. Your days are numbered."

And, of course, we had to stay busy the entire day, and just keep on working for the sake of working, even if at nothing constructive, never relaxing, never sitting, never being allowed to enter the barracks at will, back to the same hellish routine we had had at Auschwitz. All this because of Jewish informants.

Chapter 15

From Camp Eight to Camp Four

One night, in Camp Number Eight, I awoke in the pre-dawn silence with a start, sensing that something was crawling about in my ear. I tried to extract the invader with my finger, but to no avail. With growing frustration, I turned onto my side, then over again to my other side, in the hope of getting rid of the pest, but I could find no rest.

With all my fidgeting, I inadvertently awakened those who were sleeping around me. They began to complain that my moving about was preventing them from sleeping. Certainly, anyone's movement had an impact on his neighbor, as we were forced to sleep in the most cramped conditions, on wooden boards, squeezed tightly against each other. It was comically absurd, that if any one of us needed to turn over, those who lay nearby had to turn over as well. Now my neighbors were on the verge of shouting at me, for I needed to move constantly due to my new agony.

I got up and went outside to the water tap, and for lack of a better solution, I tried to pour some cold water into my ear, in order to flush out whatever it was that was crawling around. This too proved futile. I went back into the block, but at this point I couldn't push my way back into what had been a few minutes earlier "my" place on the board. So I headed back to the door of the block and sat down on the stairs leading into the structure, where I waited until everyone else would wake up from their sleep.

It was not long before the bell rang and everyone got up and shuffled outside into the brisk early morning air. As they approached me, I noticed that my acquaintances expressed shock when they saw me. Apparently, one side of my head had become terribly swollen. What was causing me severe pain was in fact a badly infected ear, but I could not even try to have my problem treated just yet. First I had to endure the daily *appel* along with its accompanying gymnastics, all to the discordant tune of the camp leader's hoarse shouts and lectures.

Hours passed before I could go to the camp infirmary and visit with a young man who was referred to as "the doctor." He began to inspect my ear, and then started poking around with his hand, at which I yelped with pain. To my horror he informed me, "We have no medications in the camp. Make sure that you keep your ear warm and let no cold enter it."

Neither did he have any bandages with which I could carry out his prescription. Instead, he gave me several yards of paper to wrap around my head and encase the infected ear. Of course, to add to my frustration, the makeshift bandage fell off after just a few hours and I was left again with nothing.

There seemed no respite to the excruciating pain. I tried to keep my ear warm, as I had been advised, but I had to spend most of the time outdoors, trying to appear as busy as I could. I was determined to avoid the scrutiny of the malicious camp elder, an objective that was not so simple to achieve. I was worried that the Germans might determine that I was physically unable to tolerate conditions in Camp Number Eight, so I mustered up all my energies in order to appear hardy.

The pretending and dissembling made me feel as if I were part of a game of cat and mouse. But the human being is capable of becoming accustomed to an immeasurable amount of stress and pain. In this way I remained in my miserable predicament for about a week and a half.

At about this time, which turned out to be our final few days in Camp Number Eight, an incident occurred which provided us inmates with a good deal of satisfaction, if nothing else.

It had been raining all through the night, no simple rain, either, but a heavy downpour. As a result of the torrent, the campgrounds, which we had helped to construct, were almost completely covered with pools of mud, which our sadistic camp elder chose to use as a means to further demean us. After we were rounded up for the *appel*, he began to shout his orders at us. "Run!" and then, "Lie down!" he repeated endlessly, or so it seemed. Using his stick forcefully, he made us get down on our stomachs and sink our faces over and over again in the viscid, smelly mud. For hours he continued to torment us in this fashion, until he became hoarse from all his shouting.

When the ordeal seemed to be over, we were told to stand in the *appelplatz*, where the commandant and the SS guards counted us. Suddenly, the commandant, taking a closer look at the prisoners standing before him, became visibly perturbed, and, calling one of the inmates over to him, asked him, "Why is your jacket, which you just received brand new in Auschwitz, all smeared with mud?"

The inmate, trembling with fear, did not reply. His was the

classic inmate's dilemma, for he was bound to suffer reper-cussions from whichever one he displeased. He therefore chose the approach which, he figured, would be the safest – silence.

Undaunted, the commandant summoned several other inmates, whose clothes were also black with mud, and pro-ceeded to ask them the same question. One prisoner, obvi-ously of a bolder nature, stepped forward and, pointing a fin-ger at the camp elder, said, "He forced us to lie down in the mud."

At this the SS commandant called the camp elder over and said something to him, which we could not hear. Then, with-out warning, the commandant's fist rose and landed a resounding blow on the man's face. After two more whacks, much to our added entertainment, blood began to stream from his brow. But the camp elder, more familiar with camp proce-dure than we were, did not respond at all, although his defeat was apparent to us all.

Several minutes later, the commandant headed back to his lodgings, but our illustrious camp leader, having been rebuked and humiliated in front of us all, and probably having been given new orders, was a changed man. He no longer dared to resume his bravado and power-hungry practices. Never again would he torment or even raise his voice against us as he had before his downfall. Unfortunately, our respite was to last for only a couple of days.

Rosh Hashanah was approaching, and we again organized, secretly of course, a *minyan* in one of the blocks. Each of us who remembered any portion of the Rosh Hashanah prayers said it out loud while the rest of us chanted along. We felt more relaxed since we were no longer being terrorized by the fiendish *lager* head. However, on the second day of Rosh Hashanah, rumors began to circulate that in a short time we would be leaving the camp. Sure enough, in the middle of our prayers, we were summoned to the *appelplatz,* where we quickly had to line up five to a row. After we were counted, the SS guards marched us out through the gate and escorted us on a hike that lasted a few hours. Along the way, several inmates tried to tear up some grass from some nearby fields to eat, but the SS shot at anyone who left the formation. Finally, we reached a small train station, where there was a train already waiting for us.

We were herded into the cattle cars, sealed in, and the train began to hurl itself forward. We flew past fields of bountiful corn and wheat, and caught glimpses of cows and sheep grazing in pastures of never-ending green, while birds overhead soared across the bluest of skies. As we gazed at the picturesque countryside we could not help but envy the beasts their

Kaufering Camp Number Four. Note double barbed-wire fence at right.

freedom, and recall how once we had also lived in unfettered tranquility.

The contrast between the world outside the train – with the sun pouring out of the clear blue skies, the fresh green fields, and the fruit-laden trees – and our own stench-filled surroundings, replete with barbed-wire fences, machine-guns and a grey, stifling atmosphere, was stark and depressing. But we could not dwell for very long on our dismal thoughts, for soon the train stopped in the middle of a field.

"Everyone out!" the SS guards shouted as they opened the wagons. We all disembarked from the train, and lined up, once again, five to a row. Then we marched until we arrived at the gates of yet another concentration camp, our new "home," the infamous Lager Four, or Kaufering, later called "the Camp of Death."

Chapter 16

From Bitterness Came Sweetness

Each day that we endured in the ghetto or in the camps became a chapter in our lives full of suffering, adversity and perilous situations. Death and drama lurked in every corner, and fear was our constant companion. Every night we wondered how we had managed to survive yet another day, and every morning we awoke with the dread of what new misfortune would occur or whether the next catastrophe would mean the end of our miserable existence. I myself would speculate about whether I would live to record all these chapters in print, or if my dream of writing a book would evanesce with my own demise.

As we stood at the gates of Camp Number Four, waiting to be counted by several SS officers and a group of kapos, we contemplated our future here with more than a shudder. Once we were counted, we marched through the gates while SS guards all around us shouted, "Caps off!" Quickly we removed our berets, as kapos took control of our ranks. They escorted us to the *appelplatz* where we were made to stand and wait. We could see that we had arrived at a much larger camp than Camp Number Eight, much like a miniature Auschwitz, with more advanced facilities, but with no crematorium.

After we had waited for some time, several dozen kapos began to move this way and that, blasting out orders, shouting, beating and shoving. More shades of Auschwitz. Then two more kapos arrived to lecture to us about our expected conduct in this camp. We were here to work, and to heed the orders of the kapos and block elders. If there were no discipline, life would be bitter for us indeed.

We were sent to several different blocks, and were told that on the following day, we would not yet be dispatched to our work details, as we would have to be registered and issued new numbers, after which we would become full-fledged citizens of Camp Number Four.

To my good fortune, when we entered our blocks, I met my friend, Yossel Carmel, from whom I had become separated when we had left Auschwitz. Again we vowed not to separate, to stick together like magnets. We brought each other up-to-date on our respective histories since we had last seen each other. I learned from Yossel more about Camp Four, and was duly horrified to hear that the kapos were vicious murderers, and that the work was backbreaking.

In turn, I related to him my experiences in Camp Eight, which, it became evident, had been a paradise in comparison to Camp Four.

I decided to go out of the block to see if I might discover other acquaintances. Upon hearing two people speaking Hebrew to each other, I approached them and said "Shalom!"

As a reward for my trouble, however, I received a slap on the face that made me nearly fall off my feet.

I moved away from them faster than a bullet. Later, a veteran inmate of Camp Four told me, "Didn't you know that those two were Greek Jews who became kapos, and subhuman, wild animals at that?"

This was yet another lesson I learned about the barbaric existence in concentration camps.

I returned to my block. We had arrived at the end of another day, without having received any food, as we were new arrivals, and had not yet worked. With bodies aching from starvation and minds worrying about the next day's happenings, we fell into that unsettled sleep which we had become accustomed to in the camps.

We were awakened before dawn, at about 4 o'clock. While everyone got dressed, the block elder announced that all the new arrivals from Camp Number Eight need not go out to the *appelplatz*. The guards would be counting us later on, and would assign us numbers to be sewn on to our clothes.

It was just then that I felt a need to answer nature's call, so I went out of the barracks to the latrine, which was adjacent to the *appelplatz*. On my way back to the block, I suddenly received a blow to my head from a kapo.

"Why didn't you go to the *appelplatz*?" he screamed at me.

I replied that I was one of the new arrivals from Camp Number Eight, and that we had been told to remain in the camp in order to receive numbers. In response to this, he dealt me several additional blows to my head, shoulders and face. Then he shoved me out to the *appelplatz*, and stationed me with a group of men whom he was about to lead out to work.

I still had not absorbed the basic principle of the camps: Never argue with a kapo.

Meanwhile, I was extremely agitated because now I would have to go to work while my companions from Camp Eight

Our workplace

would be allowed to rest. I turned to a Jew who was standing near me and asked him, "What sort of work do you do here?"

He groaned and said, "We work for the Moll Company and have to haul fifty-kilo sacks of cement for them."

This unnerved me, so I surreptitiously edged closer to a different work commando. Again I asked a man what sort of work his group did. He replied, "We work at Held and Franke.

One of the jobs we have to do is to fix rails for the trains. It is extremely painful to haul the heavy iron rails and wooden rail ties. On top of that, we need to set up heavy stones and wooden beams as supports for the heavy rail ties."

Without hesitation, I slipped over to a third commando that stood nearer to the block, with the hope that I would be able to return to my block unnoticed. But here there were so many kapos that it was impossible to separate from the group.

When I asked someone in this group what sort of work they did, I was told that they labored on a construction site, where the work was life threatening, and where they were beaten mercilessly by the SS guards. So I quickly moved on to the last group, which was nearest to the block. This time I found out that there was no job assignment here, but that the people standing around were patients from the camp infirmary, waiting to be counted, after which they were to be taken back to the infirmary.

At this point, I figured that my best bet would be to stand there until all the other commandos would leave for their workplaces. Then I should be able to steal away to my block. No sooner had I made this decision, than a doctor – or maybe an infirmary kapo – appeared on the scene, approached me, looked at me straight in the face and said, "You are not from the infirmary. You are trying to sneak in." With that, he slapped me a few times, and then shoved me away from the group.

Since I was rebellious by nature, I instinctively tried to use all my resources to remain in the camp, taking great risks in maneuvering my way from one work detail to another. Kapos were everywhere, using their truncheons liberally in order to prod inmates to go to work. In this hellish atmosphere, I risked my life in order to stay with my original group from Camp Number Eight. At the same time, I grew fearful that I would be punished if I did not show up for registration and receive a number along with the rest.

After a while I found myself all the way at the other side of the camp, where one final group remained after all the other inmates had been taken to work. After joining the group and pretending to be part of it, I suddenly noticed, to my horror, the "doctor" of the infirmary approaching us. I had unwittingly resurfaced among the camp sick, oblivious to the fact that they had been marched from one end of the camp to the other.

Again I received a generous share of blows. However, this time I was not to escape with so minor a retribution. The man pulled me by my arm directly to the office of the camp commandant, an SS officer, and said, "This one has been evading his work detail."

The officer looked me over, but said nothing to me. To another officer present he announced that I would be sent back to Auschwitz.

I was immediately marched to a special cellblock, and pushed through the door, which was then locked from the outside. Inside the block, I discovered a number of other inmates all of whom had been similarly told that they would be sent back to Auschwitz. We sat there in the block, consumed by an agonizing sense of doom. My thoughts turned to my friends and what they would think when they noticed my absence. For about half an hour we sat there, when suddenly the door was unlocked, and in walked a kapo.

"What are you all doing here?" he demanded of us.

We replied that we had been locked up in this block, and were supposed to be shipped back to Auschwitz. The kapo then rushed us out of the block to join about another twenty prisoners who were already standing in formation. After we took our positions in line with the rest, two SS guards escorted us out through the camp gate to where a transport truck stood waiting. Then we climbed aboard the back of the truck and soon were rolling along the German countryside with two SS officers and a kapo who accompanied us. We figured that soon we would arrive at a train station from which we would be transported by rail to Auschwitz. Yet somehow, it did not seem logical to transport the few of us all the way back to Auschwitz. Perhaps to Dachau, of which Camp Number Four was a satellite camp. Overcome with both doubt and despair, I decided that whatever would happen had already been decreed in Heaven, and was supposed to happen.

The truck slowed down and came to a halt at a farm, where the SS guards began to speak to a farmer and his wife. A few minutes later, they told us to jump off the truck and led us to a field that had been plowed by a tractor, thereby extracting the potatoes that were growing there. There they gave each of us a large basket, and ordered us to gather the potatoes into these baskets, and deposit our harvest into a large wagon which, when full, would be taken to the farmhouse.

Then the SS guards went to town, leaving the kapo behind to oversee our work. This kapo, a young Dutchman, happened to be a humane sort, never shouting at us or beating us without cause. He only did what he absolutely needed to. When the farmer returned a second time, his wagon now empty, the kapo urged us to continue our work. We felt as if our backs were breaking from the strain of constantly bending over, while hunger incessantly gnawed away at our insides, for we had not eaten in two days.

After filling up our second wagonload of potatoes, we began to converse with the farmer, informing him that we were starving, and consequently could not work well under these circumstances. We asked him if he could bring us something to eat. The German farmer drove his wagon full of potatoes to the village, and then, after what seemed like only a few minutes, returned with a basket full of bread, rolls, marmalade and drinks.

We immediately sat ourselves down on the ground and greedily watched as the German farmer apportioned a hefty chunk of bread for each of us, larger than any we had ever received in camp. In addition, he handed each of us a roll smeared with marmalade. We attacked our meal with great relish.

After we had finished our feast, we returned to our work with revitalized energy. Not that the work was easy. It involved constantly bending over and hauling our full baskets to the wagon. But now we felt an obligation to show appreciation for the splendid breakfast the farmer had provided for us. After a while, with renewed courage, we begged the farmer to bring us something for lunch. He said he would ask his wife to cook something for us.

Our hearts rose in joyful anticipation. Just a short while ago we had been in a situation in which we were starving even after having finished our daily camp ration. Then just a couple of hours ago we were treated to an incredible breakfast, and now, we were waiting to receive lunch as well. Furthermore, the SS guards had disappeared, and the kapo in charge of us did not beat us. We almost felt as if we had been liberated from camp, whereas earlier we had thought we were going to be transported back to Auschwitz.

At about 1 o'clock in the afternoon, the farmer and his wife reappeared, carrying plates and pots brimming with food. They served us large chunks of bread along with steamy bowls of soup, thick with potatoes and meat, which they had just finished cooking. At the end of the meal, we were each handed a bottle of beer. We were overwhelmed and gratified, for such a meal we had never even dreamed of.

Echoes of hunger still lingered in our minds, so we brazenly asked the farmer and his wife if they could bring us more food that we could take back to camp with us, as there starvation was our constant companion. The farmer told us that at that moment there was a huge pot full of potatoes cooking, in order to feed his pigs, which he would be glad to give to us instead. With gladdened hearts and emotionally strengthened, we once again resumed our work.

We were supposed to work until 5 o'clock, but at around 4 o'clock, an hour before the actual ending time, our SS guards suddenly appeared, to bring us back to camp. Immediately we were assembled in the field, and then we rode back to the farmhouse. When we stopped there, the farmer's wife begged the SS guards to wait just a few minutes longer, until the potatoes would finish being boiled. But the SS guards would not listen and ordered the truck driver to quickly leave.

After enjoying our recent good fortune, we were naturally disappointed, but, in any case, helpless. Then, just as the truck started off, we saw the farmer's wife come running out of her house with a basket. She raced after the truck and heaved the basket, full of pears, onto the back, where we were sitting. We all grabbed what we could, and then sat watching the farmer and his wife standing near their house until they were out of sight.

We returned to camp just in time for the distribution of the daily soup rations, along with the bread portions.

All my acquaintances from Camp Number Eight clustered around me, asking me where I had been. So I related to them the saga of my day. I also shared with them the pears that I had brought along. After hearing my story, everyone was quite envious of the good fortune I had been blessed with that day.

(After coming back to camp from our work detail, I was sure that the commandant's order to send us back to Auschwitz was just to frighten us. But later on, I read in a

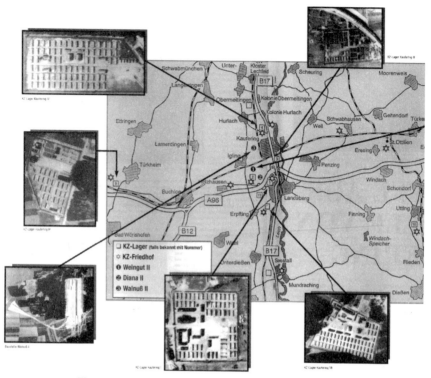

The camps around Landsberg, all satellites of Dachau

German publication, "Landsberg in the Twentieth Century," that several transports of ill-fated inmates were indeed sent to Auschwitz from Camp Number Four, directly to the dreaded gas chambers.)

I was given my new number, which was 97603, but I only had it on paper, not sewn onto my jacket, as everyone else did. Here was another way that Providence provided me with an opportunity to evade danger, as I could always intentionally make a mistake in the order of the numerals, when registering my number every morning at work, since it could not be verified. Later on, this circumstance would save my life.

Chapter 17

Yom Kippur, 5705

After my first day in camp, a day which ended up being a rather fortunate one for me, "normal" camp life began. At 4 o'clock the next morning we were roused from our sleep and ordered to rush outside to the *appelplatz*. There we stood in tortured expectation, thousands of slaves, waiting to be taken to their slave labor. We were going to work for the Moll Company, a construction firm which constructed enormous factories in the dense forests in the vicinities of Munich, Dachau and Landsberg.

It was amazing that amid the sprawling, dense Bavarian forests there were paved roads, crisscrossing the landscape in all directions. There were pipelines that had been laid, for gasoline as well as for diesel fuel, for miles, as far as the eye could see. In this way the Third Reich was able to conceal their magnificent munitions industry from the Allied planes that sortied overhead. From the vantage point of the skies above, the area was thick, innocent forest, while at ground level below there teemed a complex system of production feeding the German war effort.

Not all of us would be taken to serve the munitions plant. Some were going to work for the notorious Holtzman Construction Company, while others would be forced to perform the backbreaking task of laying new steel rails and wooden rail ties.

While we were waiting at the *appelplatz*, we were subjected to the vicious attempts made by various kapos to ensure that each of them had the correct number of workers in his commando. It happened frequently that a group would suddenly be short a few men. As a result, the kapos would shout at the inmates, rallying them forward with inhuman beatings to move out of one commando, into another, manipulating people as if they were pawns in a game of chess. Thus no one could be sure where he would end up, or with what sort of work.

I ended up being in the group working for the Moll Company. At approximately 6 a.m. we finally marched out through the gate of the camp, a couple of hundred prisoners, in the direction of the railway stop about half a mile away. As soon as we arrived, I saw a train that was already waiting to take us to the construction site.

The labor that we were forced to do was indescribably strenuous. We had to carry fifty-kilogram sacks of cement, or steel girders, or piles of lumber, on our already overstrained backs.

Upon arrival, each inmate was required to register his personal number before commencing his work detail. Everyone had this number sewn on the front of his uniform jacket, except for me, because of the previous day's events. I had to record my number, 97603, verbally.

It occurred to me that it might be a good idea to give an incorrect number, either by reversing the order of a couple of numbers, or by changing one or two numerals. In this way, if I ever stepped out of line, and would be required to receive some sort of punishment, I would not be able to be found. On the other hand, if I would be discovered, I could simply claim to have made an error in my number, an oversight easily understood, I believed. (I discovered, however, that mistakes were not tolerated, either. People were shot for lesser errors.)

That first day of work at the construction site seemed to last for an eternity. I was not in the least bit accustomed to working so laboriously for a full day. Consequently, I was very anxious to find out from the more experienced inmates how to possibly secure for oneself work tasks which might be some-what less taxing on one's physical strength.

When the end of the workday finally arrived, we were transported to the railway stop to be brought back to camp. During the train ride, we were subjected again to the cruel sport of the SS guards who sat in each railcar with us. When the train came to a stop, we were again rushed off, told to fall into line, and marched back into camp.

"Five to a row! Faster! Faster! Run!" the SS guards shouted at us, over and over again, as if they were in a tremendous hurry, for some reason.

As soon as we reentered the campground, the kapos greeted us with their own shouts.

"Caps off!" they ordered. We immediately removed our uniform hats from our heads, waiting once again to be counted.

Then we were marched to the place adjacent to the camp kitchen, where we were given our soup rations – gruel that was little more than a watery substance with what appeared to be a few blades of grass floating around in it. It was a rare occasion for celebration when some fortunate soul found a small piece of potato inside his soup ration.

After our "dinner" we were herded into our block, where the block elder and a kapo distributed our daily bread portion to each of us. We viewed our individual piece of bread as if it were a treasure, but worse, some of us beheld our neighbors' rations with blatant envy, for the other person's portion always seemed larger.

"Why do I always have to get the smallest piece?" people would commonly be heard to grumble.

I observed how people would eat their rations. Some gulped nearly their entire portions at once in the hope of quelling the intense hunger that pervaded their entire beings. But the diminutive portions were hardly big enough to appease our starvation. Still, many figured that the safest place for storing their bread rations was inside their stomachs, from which they could not possibly be stolen.

Others, however, were able to exercise more caution and foresight, saving a part of their bread ration for later on, or for the next morning. I was envious of those people who were able to control their hunger in this way, for I myself could not do this every time. They would have something, small though it would be, to chew on the next morning, while others would have nothing until the following evening, after another harrowing day of slavery.

And so the days passed, in this miserable fashion. Several times I tried to switch to another work commando, in the vain hope of somewhat alleviating my plight. But my fate seemed to have in store for me even more strenuous types of work, supervised by even more cruel kapos and SS guards.

On *erev* Yom Kippur morning, I found myself standing in the *appelplatz,* wondering what was in store for me that day. As I looked around, I noticed the Dutch kapo, the same one who had conducted our group to the German farm a few days earlier, organizing a group of a hundred men for a work commando. Without any hesitation, at the first opportune moment I headed straight for that group in the hope of being included in their work team. I risked my life in doing so, for had the kapo of the group in which I was originally standing noticed my move, he could have killed me on the spot.

I tried to find a place in the new group where I would be lost among the inmates. I spent those first few minutes in fear, until I saw my original work commando being marched out through the camp gates.

Even so, while I stood there with the Dutchman's group, I felt a moment of panic every time I saw another commando on its way out, for I could not help but fear that I would be noticed by someone and then plucked out of the new detachment. When I finally saw the last of the other commando groups being ushered out of the camp, leaving only our group standing there, I thanked the A-mighty for allowing me to stay with this group. Meanwhile, we started to wonder somewhat impatiently what was in store for us as the kapo and an SS guard became involved in a seemingly endless discussion.

Moments later, an enormous transport truck arrived, aboard which half the inmates were instructed to climb. A moment later, a second truck arrived, and the remaining inmates, myself included, were told to get on. A pair of SS soldiers climbed into the back of each of the trucks, while another, smaller vehicle pulled up alongside our truck, carrying about half a dozen more SS guards. Shortly afterwards, the convoy pulled out of the campground.

After a long drive, we arrived at a German airfield near Landsberg, which had been largely devastated by Allied bombing raids. We enjoyed viewing the charred remains of what had once been Luftwaffe airplanes, as well as the ruins of the hangars that had contained them, even before considering what we would have to do here.

To our surprise, the SS guards disappeared, leaving us in the hands of the Luftwaffe. The German airmen did not seem as cruel as the SS guards were. In fact, many of them seemed quite sympathetic toward us.

Before long, we were taken to a large warehouse where we were each told to take either a pickaxe or a shovel. From here we were taken to the airfield and told to work in pairs. One of us would soften the earth with his pickaxe, while the other would use the shovel to dig a trench. (In any other work detail, we would have had to each use both tools in rapid succession. Here one of us could rest while the other one worked.) The trenches were in fact part of a zigzag pattern of ditches being formed all across the field, designed to protect the Luftwaffe men from overhead fire.

Not only did we all get a chance to relax while our partners did their share of the job, but we were also fortunate in that our kapo was of a different breed. He didn't shout at us, nor did he strike us, as was the norm among all the other kapos. Even more noteworthy was the absence of the SS guards, who would never let us even stop to catch our breath, all the while casting constant terror into our hearts.

There were also Russian prisoners of war working in the airfield, who were treated a lot better than we were. They had freedom and mobility of a sort that for us would be the object of idle dreams. Although we were forbidden to communicate with these Russians, as is often the case in such situations, we were able to understand one another simply through the use of eye contact. As a result of this nonverbal interchange, they took the initiative in preparing for us a huge cauldron of cooked potatoes that they managed to position at the side of the field. One by one, we found an excuse to walk to that part of the field, and as we passed by the pot, we grabbed a few precious potatoes, stuffing our pockets and our mouths at the same time.

This went on for a large part of the day, until at one point we brazenly asked the Luftwaffe soldiers when we would be receiving our daily soup ration. They told us that before we could be given more food they would have to bring in a military kitchen installation from another location, as the Allies had all but destroyed everything that had been there on the site. Encouraged by our good fortune, we began to converse with the Luftwaffe servicemen, who talked with us freely, in sharp contrast with the SS soldiers who would never deign to chat with us.

Late in the afternoon, we were allowed to stop working. We sat idly waiting for the kitchen crew to arrive with our rations. Finally they appeared, and wasted no time in ladling out the soup, which was thick with flour and generous chunks of potatoes, quite unlike the watery gruel that was the measly fare of the other commando groups.

Shortly afterwards the trucks that had brought us to the airfield reappeared, and carried us back to the camp. We arrived quite a bit earlier than the other commandos, and now received the camp's daily soup ration, but this time there was no shoving and hollering accompanying the distribution, because we were the only ones who had returned from work. After we had eaten our soup, we made our way back to the block, where we sat around in a rare, leisurely manner, discussing the good fortune that had come our way. We had lighter workloads, more food, and we got to leave camp later than the others and return earlier. Our kapo had instructed us to assemble on the following day at a specific spot in the *appelplatz*, as he would be taking with him only those inmates who had worked under him on the first day.

Just as night fell, we were each given two candies in addition to the daily bread ration. This was highly irregular, to be sure. However, as the sweets were being handed out, a very disturbing episode occurred. Apparently the block elder, or the kapo, or both, had stolen a number of the candies and had stored them away for their personal use. Now, since there had been exactly enough sweets for the number of inmates in each block, there was a shortage of candies for all the inmates. Here the kapos invented a story, that several inmates had obviously taken double portions of candy, thus robbing the remaining inmates of what was rightfully theirs.

Many of the inmates were still greenhorns, unaware of the protocols of concentration-camp life. A number of them began to object loudly that there was no candy left for them. Infuriated at this spontaneous protest, the block elder swore that he would immediately teach the whole lot of us what the repercussions of such a demonstration in a concentration camp would be. He announced that we would immediately have to retire for the night and would not be allowed to walk around freely as we would ordinarily be permitted to do.

Mentally I cursed our hard luck. This was the night of Yom Kippur, which was possibly why we were treated to the candy in the first place, perhaps to tempt us with an irresistible treat on the night of the sacred fast day. I had been counting on being able to go from block to block to try to form a *minyan* in one of them. Instead, being forced to stay in my own block, I spent the time searching my memory for the text of the *tefillos* of the day, noticing at the same time that most of my blockmates were already falling asleep. My friend Yossel Carmel and I started reminiscing about how we used to spend Yom Kippurs past in a peaceful Lodz, during the prewartime years — and of our trips to Ger for the holiest of days.

Suddenly, the block door opened and in walked the notorious Max Libermann, a Polish Jew who had lived in Paris, France, prior to the war. An avid communist, he told us that he had stood on the same platform as Leon Bloom, first Jewish socialist prime minister of France. This man especially hated religious Jews with a passion, and beat his fellow inmates mercilessly. Now he shouted, "Everyone up!"

We jumped up out of our beds, and he began to lecture us.

"You are all low lives, all of you, stealing from one another and taking double portions!" (The scoundrel had stuffed himself with the candy that had been earmarked for other prisoners in our block.) "Now, as a punishment, you will all have to go outside and stand naked, throughout the night."

We began to file out of the block, passing under a barrage of blows from his stick. Once outside, we obediently fell into line in front of the block. In the frigid night we began to shiver with cold. To make matters worse, we were neither allowed to move, nor to utter a single word. In that way we stood for about an hour, freezing in the autumn frost, when another kapo came by and asked us why we were standing there.

"Max Libermann ordered us to stand out here," one of the inmates replied.

Immediately, the second kapo went into our block and called Libermann out.

"What do you want from these people?" the kapo demanded. "Don't you know that today is Yom Kippur?"

We could not hear the exact words of Libermann's reply, but the tone was brash and flippant. The other kapo, who must have been Max's superior, and stronger than him, was clearly not impressed, for he suddenly smacked Max's face with such a wallop that he nearly keeled over.

Our "redeemer" turned to us and said, "All of you go back inside and get to sleep. If Max ever so much as bothers you again, just come and tell me about it, and he won't be alive much longer."

Exhausted, but much relieved, we dragged ourselves back inside, lay down on our planks, and fell asleep, for once with a rare sense of satisfaction. Max Libermann had gotten his just deserts.

Early the next morning, when we were once again lined up at the *appelplatz,* my friend Yossel whispered to me that he was going to try to avoid going to work that day because it was Yom Kippur, though he knew he was taking a great risk.

I was involved in my own quandary, struggling with the decision of whether to go to work, and hope that somehow I could be spared doing any actual labor, or whether to try to avoid going out with the work detail altogether. I was afraid that if I missed a day of going to work I might lose my coveted position in the work unit which served the Luftwaffe, which was treated to a military soup and which was given much less strenuous work than the other details.

Finally I decided that I would try to stay back from going to work, for perhaps the A-mighty was testing me to see if I was willing to give up a good thing – moderate workload, more food and no beatings – for the sake of the holiest day. Maybe if I could manage to hide, I might even be able to assemble a group of people to pray. Weighing all these risks in my mind, I felt somehow that I would succeed. Having been in Camp Number Four already for a number of days, I was growing adept at finding ways of staying out of danger's path and avoiding the watchful eyes of the kapos as much as possible. Thus I ended up being one of about five men from our block who avoided the work units and chose not to go to work that day on account of its being Yom Kippur.

The work commandos had left, and with them, the kapos. Even the block elder seemed to have disappeared. We stood near one another, trying to piece together the Yom Kippur *davening,* reminding one another of the beloved passages.

Suddenly, at about midmorning, the door swung open, and we heard a bloodcurdling shout, "Everyone out!"

In a panic, I turned around and saw a few SS guards escorting a number of other inmates whom they had collected from other cellblocks. In an instant, we were all being marched out of the campgrounds.

We all trembled with trepidation, wondering if they would beat us, or torture us, or simply shoot us. A short distance away from camp, we stopped, were handed shovels and ordered to dig. I grumbled to myself that I had sacrificed a good spot in a decent work detail for this – for having to profane the holiest of days after all. However, I found some consolation in knowing that I had done what I could to try to prevent myself from desecrating Yom Kippur. Now I was being forced to work under the threat of the barrel of a machine-gun. Since I was not working voluntarily, I was not responsible for my actions, and was thus "exempt in the eyes of G-d."

With shovels in hand, we dug and dug. What we were digging for, we did not know. We were afraid that perhaps we were digging our own graves, as the Germans used to order Jews to dig their own graves before shooting them. Whenever the opportunity arose, such as when the SS guard supervising us turned around, or else wandered off for a few minutes, we would chant whatever highlights of the prayers came to our minds. "On Rosh Hashanah will be inscribed and on the fast day of Yom Kippur will be sealed ... who will live and who will die." We would stop praying whenever he would turn back to us, digging with greater vigor in order to avoid suspicion.

Then we would start again,

"And You are the living, eternal King!"

We continued in this way as the day passed on, digging under the watchful eyes of the SS guard, chanting the Yom Kippur prayers when we thought we could get away with it. Uncertain of our fate, we pondered over whether the Germans knew that today was Yom Kippur, the holiest day of the Jews, and merely wanted to make us work out of spite, or if they had already decided to shoot us and bury us in the ditches we were digging.

After a few hours, our SS guard received some message from a higher authority. We were then ordered to fill up the ditches and return to the camp. We breathed sighs of relief, and went back to our blocks.

Yet we still managed to observe Yom Kippur to some extent, at least. Later in the day, we were handed our daily ration of bread. The temptation to eat it was overwhelming, as the hunger gnawing at our insides was compounded by the great stress. But we overcame the trial, almost all of us stashing away our portions until dark.

The next morning, normal camp life resumed. We returned to the hell of the *appelplatz* where the kapos, vying to fill their personnel quotas, snatched their men, shouting and dealing heavy blows to emphasize their actions. I lay low as I scouted around, looking for my Dutch kapo, and raced over to his group as soon as I spotted it. I noticed that the commando had doubled in size. Apparently word of its favorable conditions had spread.

I took my place within the group and waited, when suddenly, someone turned to me and asked me if I had my "paper" with me. I didn't answer him, but overheard two other men discussing the fact that on the previous day, which was Yom Kippur, the kapo had distributed to his group special papers to identify them, so no newcomers would be able to join the work detail. My heart sank for I realized that I would be discovered with no identification, and be sent off once again to work for the Moll Corporation. I watched apprehensively as the kapo made his rounds, checking each worker to make sure that he had his paper in hand. Whoever did not have this vital document was taken out and violently handed over to the custody of another kapo.

I stayed in line, without any paper, and watched as the kapo approached me. He saw me, noticed that I was paperless, and continued on his rounds, allowing me to stay. He recognized me, it seemed, from the day before yesterday, at the airfield, or maybe from the first excursion to the German farm.

Perhaps he remembered me because I was still wearing the head bandages for my ear infection. In any event, he let me stay in his commando. I managed to stay in his work commando for approximately two weeks. This was the best period of time I spent in the accursed world of the concentration camps.

While looking back at this episode, and many other wartime experiences, I clearly see the hand of G-d testing us to see how much we would be willing to sacrifice for the sake of the Torah commandments, whether between man and G-d or between man and man. At times it is hard to comprehend how young people like ourselves were able to risk our lives for the sake of Heaven. But we knew that we had to make our decisions, and be ready to sacrifice, leaving all else up to Providence, or *hashgachah pratis.*

Chapter 18

A Rather Brutal Cure

On the day after we had arrived in Camp Number Four I had tried my luck at the camp infirmary where I had hoped to secure the assistance of a doctor.

Before long, a "doctor" approached me, took a look inside my ear, and then disappeared. A few moments later, he was back, holding a razor blade.

"We are going to have to operate and cut out the swelling inside your ear."

In a panic, I simply refused. I was certainly not ready to let myself be cut up right then and there. The doctor became furious and bellowed,

"Get out of here, and don't come back! We can't help you here."

Stubbornly, I begged him to at least give me some aspirin, but he resolutely chased me out of the infirmary.

Just before leaving Camp Number Eight, we had each been given a thin towel to take along with us. I had been using mine to bandage the side of my face and ear in order to keep my ear from getting cold. I walked around in this fashion in my new surroundings, even when I was at my work detail.

Every morning we had to line up in rows of five men across, and in this formation we marched out of camp to go to work. We quickly learned to vie for one of the spots in the middle of the formation, never on the outside. For, as we left the camp to go to work, we had to pass through the gate at the entrance of the camp, where there always stood a group of SS soldiers and kapos. They developed a routine, that every time we passed through the gate – as when one goes over a toll bridge and has to pay the charge – we had to submit to a barrage of kicks and blows. Obviously, those who were at the edges of the lines marching through got the worst of the beatings. Therefore, we all tried to seize one of the middle positions, but of course, not all of us could succeed in doing so.

It was after we had finished the work at the airfield, and I had resumed working with the commandos who had to perform torturous labor for the Moll and Holtzman Companies, that one day, on our way out to our work detail, I somehow got left standing at the outer edge of a line, close to where the kapos would be standing and waiting. Sure enough, as we moved along, a kapo struck me in the face, and, as fate would have it, on the swollen side. On top of that, he landed another blow directly on my infected ear. This kapo apparently did not appreciate the sight of the makeshift bandage adorning my face. He viciously ripped the towel off my face, screaming that no one was allowed to walk around bandaged with a towel.

The incredible pain that blasted through my head made me grimace and gave me more than a glimpse of those proverbial stars. I grew terribly dizzy and, had it not been for two of my companions who supported me under my arms and led me onward, I would surely have fallen on the spot. This would have spelled certain death, for in this place, one had to keep moving on, whether one was able to or not.

Meanwhile, the accursed SS guards, machine-guns in hand, were prodding us forward with shouts of "Faster! Faster! Run more quickly!"

As I walked on, drained of all strength, I began to feel some moisture oozing out of my ear. This alarmed me immensely, for I could imagine what damage the kapo had done to my ear. As I pushed on, I began to fear that I might even lose my hearing as a result of the wound.

Throughout the day, I barely managed to keep myself from collapsing. I survived the day thanks to my friends, who allowed me to rest every so often by taking over my duties. In my desperation, I resolved to try my luck again at the camp infirmary, and, if need be, allow them to operate on me. I now knew that I had no alternative.

Impatiently, I waited for the workday to end and for our return to the campground. As soon as we received our daily bread ration, I ran straight to the infirmary, almost straight into the arms of the "doctor," to whom I said, "I am willing to be operated on, because I'm scared about what happened to my ear this morning. I'm worried that my ear has been damaged."

Again the doctor inspected my ear, and to my astonishment, he laughed.

"You don't need an operation anymore. You had a large, infected boil inside your ear, which is what I had wanted to cut away. That blow you got this morning on the side of your head burst the boil open, which is what I had in mind to do, anyway, and the infection has been mostly released. But, from now on, come into the infirmary, and we will dab away the remainder of the infection with cotton until it disappears entirely."

He then gave me a piece of cotton to put in my ear in order to avoid further infection from developing or spreading.

From something negative had evolved something positive. I thanked G-d for having converted the evil that had befallen me earlier in the day into something tremendously beneficial. Here again was an example of how Divine Providence worked to keep alive someone whom He wanted alive. Even if badly damaged and beaten, I was meant to survive. It was just as G-d had said to the Satan who slandered Job: "Behold he is in your hand (to do with him what you want, even break his body), but keep his soul (keep him alive)" (*Job* 1:12). Anyone who survived was fated to live by the decree of Divine Providence.

Chapter 19

Disappear!

W e were well into the autumn season when we started to become somewhat accustomed to the backbreaking construction work. The building of massive concrete arch-like structures reinforced with steel girders that were intended to be impenetrable by Allied bombs involved many different jobs that we had to perform. First we had to assemble a huge mound of little round stones, called *kies* in German, which were then piled up, with the use of heavy, enormous machines, into a mold that was about 25 meters high, 80 meters wide and 250 meters long, for the arched structure which we were to erect. Then we had to drag long steel beams and insert them vertically into the stones, after which we needed more of the same in order to tie them

A huge bunker built by us, real slave labor

horizontally to the upright poles. When this was done, we had to lug fifty-kilo bags of cement, and mix the cement with water to form a concrete solution that was then poured over the stones and steel grid. Once the concrete hardened, the machines lifted out the stones from under the newly formed arches so that the space could be used for the manufacturing of the newly invented ME 262 jet fighter planes that the Allied forces did not have yet.

We covered the tops of the arches with a greenish material in order to camouflage them from the view of overhead Allied planes. This was not as laborious a job as carting the heavy bags of cement. At times we were fortunate enough to have a lighter workload, but usually we were overburdened with backbreaking tasks that were meant to kill us, with heavy work and little food.

One day, one of my fellow workers at the site informed me that there was a potato field nearby from which the potatoes had long ago been extracted with special machines, but which could possibly have a few potatoes left in the ground that had been overlooked. We decided that at 10 o'clock, when the guards and kapos would be taking their coffee break, about a dozen of us would venture out to the nearby field and perhaps be fortunate enough to find a few spuds.

As soon as the siren blew, signaling the beginning of the break, we ran to the edge of the field, and began to dig with our hands. This was futile work, however, for the earth was hard, and our fingers were weak. We looked around for any metal implement with which to dig, but by the time we found something usable, three quarters of the ten-minute break had gone by.

We quickly began to dig near the edge of the construction site, but discovered that other, clever people had been ahead of us, cleaning out whatever may have been left in the ground, in that area. So we moved further into the field, until we finally found a couple of potatoes. I went even further, and found a treasure trove of about thirteen potatoes. Just then we heard the whistle shrieking in the distance, summoning us back to work, but we could not resist the temptation to keep on digging, filling our pockets with potatoes, rather than leave those potatoes where we had found them.

Approximately thirty seconds after the siren had blared out, we saw a sizable attachment of SS guards running toward us. With their machine-guns aimed straight at us, they shouted, "Hands up high!"

Paralyzed with fright, we raised our hands. Meanwhile, a few people in our group tried to run back to the construction site. Seconds later, gunshots rang through the air, but we were too frightened to turn around and find out what happened to them. With shouts and blows, the SS guards approached us and ordered us to fall into a single line. While they marched us into the forest, with more yelling and beating, I surreptitiously tried to ditch the potatoes from my pockets, but an SS guard noticed my movements and smacked me with the butt of his rifle, snarling at me that my efforts wouldn't help me at all.

Blindly, we were forced to follow, not knowing whether we would be jailed or shot. Suddenly we saw a large wooden barrack in the forest. The SS guards ordered the seven of us to stand in line again near the door of the building. One guard remained outside to watch us, while the rest went inside the building.

Shortly afterward, the door opened and a guard called in the first person in line. Immediately there were screams of torment and agony that wrenched our souls. After a few, long, painful moments, the door opened again, and out tumbled the body of a bloody, brutally beaten man who could barely move. Then the next member of our group was ordered to go in. He met a similarly horrifying fate, as did the third, and fourth.

Too quickly, my turn came. I stood at the door, trembling with fear as I awaited my fate. As I entered the block, I saw a large room, with a table at the side at which sat a heavy-set officer. He stared at me and then said,

"You stole potatoes!"

I boldly replied that those potatoes would have rotted in the ground and in any case belonged to no one and therefore I could hardly be considered to have stolen them.

Eyeing me coldly, he said, "You did not return to your work post!"

"I was only about half a minute late," I replied, "and I was just about to return to my work."

"How old are you?" he asked me.

"Eighteen years old."

He then declared my sentence to be twenty-five lashes on my backside. Immediately I was grabbed by a couple of SS guards and escorted to a chair in the middle of the room.

"Bend over and lie down on the chair," I was ordered.

Stiff with fear, I was unable to move from my spot.

"Bend over!" one of them yelled.

I just stood there as if congealed. The two SS guards

grabbed me, one by the arms, the other by the feet, and they forced me down on the chair, despite my howling. Nearby stood a third guard, holding an iron rod padded with thick rubber, which he brought down on my bottom swiftly and suddenly. I screamed from the pain. The SS officer who was sitting at the table, apparently enjoying himself, said, "You must be silent. You must endure your blows without shouting. If you shout, the lash will not count toward the twenty-five!"

I bit my lip in an attempt to suppress my shouts, but the second blow was even more vicious than the first, and once again I helplessly screamed in pain.

"Yes," said the SS officer. "You must still receive twenty-five blows, as both of them haven't counted."

Instantly, I received the third blow that was even stronger than the first two. From where I got the strength to do what I did next I can't fathom. I was a mere skeleton, broken and famished from the ghetto, from Auschwitz, and from the present camp where we were overworked and underfed. But suddenly, I sprang off the bench onto my feet, surprising the two SS officers who were holding me down so that they let go of me and fell to the side, embarrassed and outraged. The SS officer sitting at the table was still smiling, even now, in obvious anticipation of the ordeal I was about to experience. Turning to the other men in the room, he said,

"This one is a hard nut. We will soon show him a thing or two. Meanwhile, send him out!" To me, he said, "Go back to the end of the line and stand there. When we finish with the rest, we'll get back to you, and have some entertainment in round two of our game!"

I left the room, and in that moment the *Ribbono Shel Olam* threw a brainstorm into my head. The SS guard who was outside watching the row of men had not, I realized, heard what his commanding officer had ordered me to do. To confirm this, I approached him and asked, "May I go?"

He gave me a swift kick with his boot and said, "*Verschwind*! Disappear!," which I did, very quickly.

I returned to the construction site, but not to my regular detail. This I allowed myself to do since that morning, as I was in the habit of doing, I had given my number to the authorities with a slight change in the numerals, so that their records showed a "96703" had showed up for work, whereas my real number was "97603." I picked up some tools and made myself look busy, remaining with the other workers until the end of the workday. At that point, SS officers led us to the train that would take us back to the camp. Near the train, we waited, and waited, when suddenly brilliant floodlights illuminated the area where the prisoners stood.

A voice bellowing into a loudspeaker announced that number "96703," who had left the SS command block, should stand forward immediately. No one responded. I stayed among the rest of the prisoners, my heart trembling, hoping that my false number would protect me. SS soldiers began to walk about, searching our faces. In our condition, it was hard to distinguish one face from the other, for we all looked like skeletons, almost identical one with the other.

After waiting for a couple of hours, we were all led into the wagons and taken back to camp. No one received any soup that night, but I thanked the A-mighty for saving me from certain agony and torture – possibly death. I did not relate any of these events to anyone, for fear of informers in our midst.

The joy I felt in my salvation was tainted by the fact that I was unable to sit normally for two or three weeks. My backside had become swollen from the three lashes that I had received. But despite the pain and discomfort, I felt as if I had been reborn.

Chapter 20

Life in Camp Four

T here is an abundance of books and films about the Holocaust years, about topics ranging from the Warsaw ghetto uprising, the traumatic arrival of inmates at Auschwitz, and simple descriptions of daily life in the camps, etc. But these days there is a vast decrease of interest in the above.

Nevertheless, one cannot overemphasize the life of suffering that we endured, the starvation, the forced labor, the epidemics of deadly diseases. There resulted from these a tremendous toll of victims, each one of them an unsung hero.

Every day we grappled with the Angel of Death for survival. Every day we witnessed miracles. We clearly saw that those who were destined by Divine Providence to survive did so. We also observed that any efforts made by a human being, any brilliant ideas or intricate plans, could be rendered completely ineffectual, if such was the will of G-d.

Every morning we would be woken up by the deafening ring of the gong – a large metal plate that the kapo would bang on with a hammer. We would quickly get dressed, while the block elder picked a couple of us to go to the kitchen and bring us our morning "coffee" – black water, really, in a pail. This we drank quickly, relishing its warmth but not its flavor. We had to hurry because in a matter of moments we would be rushed out to the *appelplatz*. Here each kapo formed his own work commando to take out to one of the many labor details. In the predawn hour, the sky was still black, although the square was illuminated with electric spotlights. We stood there, frozen and starving, skeletons that were barely alive.

As a child, I had always imagined that hell was a place that burned in a raging fire, where those who had been found guilty by the heavenly tribunal would receive their just punishment. But since my days in the concentration camps, my vision of purgatory is the *appelplatz*. The constant shouts and shrieks of the kapos mingling with the cries of pain and agony of their victims were part of a scene that defies description.

Kapos would grab their victims from other commandos and beat them with sticks or other implements of torture. They became experts at aiming for the parts of the body that would feel the greatest pain. In revenge, one kapo would strike at another kapo's worker, and vice versa, reminiscent of the Polish nobles, who would threaten each other with, "If you hit my Moshke (Jew), I will hit your Moshke."

That is how the kapos fought each other, by hitting at each other's victims.

There were other tortures to which we were subjected in the *appelplatz*, formally called punishment; for example, we would have to crouch with our knees in midair, with arms outstretched, holding a brick in each hand. After a while, our knees, back joints and shoulders would tremble violently with pain. But if one dared to straighten out his body a little bit, his head would get crowned with a stick or a rifle, hard.

One would have to remain in that agonizing position for at least fifteen minutes, sometimes a half-hour or more. Once, I received this punishment for fifteen minutes, but I was fortunate, for the SS guard who was assigned to watch me was called away in the middle, so I ran away in great haste. However, I felt severe pain in my back and my knees for some time afterwards.

We tried to huddle together in order to warm our freezing bodies, but this was not allowed. We were forced to stand like soldiers, five to a row. Every single day we had to replay this scene for an hour or two. Once we started to leave the camp-grounds, we heaved sighs of relief, even knowing that we were facing a day of terrible, backbreaking work, and even while passing through the gantlet of kapos and SS soldiers standing and waiting at the camp entrance. We would consider ourselves especially lucky to have made it through the gantlet in one piece, without receiving any blows or special punishment.

As we marched through the camp gate, the kapos screamed out, "*Heraus!* Get out!" or "Hats off!" and we would have to remove our uniform caps before the camp's chief SS officer in charge of inspecting the inmates as they passed him. Then we trudged on for about a half a mile until we came to the railway line. Here a train would be waiting with a long line of cars, ready to take us to our work.

We marched to the accompaniment of the SS guards shouting, "Left, two, three, four! Left, left, left, left!" We were supposed to lift up our left feet when they shouted, "Left!" Each guard was equipped with a rifle, ready to strike a blow at anyone who so much as dared to walk out of step with the rest. We had to learn how to march in step, the hard way.

Soon we arrived at the place where the train was waiting for us, and we entered the cars, which were uncovered transport wagons. Whenever it rained, we got drenched. In the icy cold, we froze. Most of the time we knew nothing about the sort of work we were being taken to do, especially if a different kapo had snatched us for his commando instead of our regular work detail.

One day we were taken to work with cement. From a huge pile of sacks filled with cement, each weighing about fifty kilograms, we had to load the sacks on our broken and emaciated backs and haul them to the building site. The German overlords supervising us warned us that if we would allow a single sack to fall, it would mean our end. They told us outright that a single sack of cement was worth more than a hundred Jewish lives.

We had to haul these sacks to a construction site quite a distance away, where we would have to drag them up a ramp. My back always felt as if it were about to crack. On occasion, when I felt that I couldn't bear the strain of the heavy labor a moment longer, I would take a chance and escape to a nearby forest. Sometimes I would pick up a wooden plank and drag it back and forth to a wooded area nearby, in the hope that neither kapo nor SS officer would notice that I was merely pretending to work. People who used similar ploys to escape from work reasoned that it was better to be shot and be over with it all in a second than to become crippled and suffer a slow, painful death later on. Death was a redeemer from suffering.

One day I tried to escape from my work detail, but was grabbed by a different kapo to his commando. I was taken to a construction site where I saw a mountain of stones into which iron stakes had been thrust. Our task was to drag more of these steel girders and affix them horizontally to the vertical ones to form a frame onto which concrete would be poured.

We were building hangars in which Luftwaffe airplanes or German rockets would be hidden from view.

We had to drag the weights up a steep embankment that got higher as we built. I, who had a great fear of heights, constantly felt on the verge of panic while carrying the iron rods in my hands and climbing up slippery surfaces to a height of nearly sixty feet. Finally, I felt I could no longer withstand the strain. My arms had grown stiff and they trembled, while with one hand I carried the girders and with the other I groped for something to hold onto in order to maintain my balance. My arms felt like jelly, so I asked an SS guard if I could go to the latrine, which was nothing more than an assigned spot by a tree.

I was too afraid to return to work, so I roamed around the forest, doing various types of work in other commando units, until it grew dark and we all had to return to the camp. Again we were counted, and the number that I had registered with the work bureau each morning was called out. They were on the lookout for me, because I had not come back to my original work detail. But it was not my real number, for I had changed the order of the numerals when I orally registered my number. Once again, my number trick saved my life.

I was fortunate in having a neighbor next to whom I slept and with whom I worked, who had been a *baal agalah*, a coach driver, back in Lodz. Not an intellectual, he was honest and straightforward. Most important, his view of life gave me encouragement, and this helped save my life. The worst danger in the camps was falling into despair and losing all hope. Considering the pitiful conditions we lived in, this was all too easy. In the morning we were awakened to freezing cold, hunger and were hardly able to rise from weakness and exhaustion. I would moan and groan, feeling depressed and dreading the upcoming day, with the work that it brought, the kapos, the SS guards and the *appelplatz* that awaited us outside. But my neighbor would tell me, "You'll see, Srulik. This day will pass. Don't worry so much."

At the *appelplatz,* we would stand together. I would tremble from fear and from cold, feeling that my life was contemptible, and once again my friend would say to me, "You will see. This day will pass. Don't give up hope."

At work the backbreaking labor would ravage our bones. We were unable to relax for a minute, for the kapos and SS guards were watching over us with batons and rifles. Even when we were hard at work, we were still live game for any SS guard or kapo who felt like gifting us with a few blows to the body or head. There could not possibly be any meaning to this sort of life. And again my friend would say, "This day will pass."

When we returned to camp and received our watery soup ration and a piece of moldy bread, my friend would continue his words of encouragement.

"You see? I kept telling you that the day would pass. Well, it has already passed, and we are alive, and a day closer to our liberation."

Before long, the season of heavy rains began, and life became even more difficult. Our clothes would get drenched, our shoes, if one still had leather shoes, would swell from the wetness. Even so, we had to plod through the mud as the cold permeated our bones. Work was never canceled. On the contrary, we would have to work faster as the kapos and the SS shouted at us all the more fiercely, their moods as foul as the weather, causing them to unleash their anger at us full force.

One day, after we had finished our work, the SS told us to march, five to a row, to the place where the trucks usually waited for us to take us back to the camp. It was nighttime already, but the trucks were not there yet, so we waited, while one hour, and then another hour passed, and still we waited, in the cold, wet outdoors. Meanwhile, the rain became a downpour, and we got soaked to the bone. We trembled from the cold, and attempted to draw warmth from each other's bodies by moving closer to each other. This did not please the SS, who immediately began to shout and swing their rifle butts at us. Soon, we were standing again straight as soldiers.

At 10 o'clock at night the trucks finally arrived to take us to camp. It was too late for us to receive our soup rations, as the kitchen had been locked up hours ago. We almost didn't receive our bread rations. Since the other inmates were already lying on the boards, ready to fall asleep, we had to hurry to go to sleep ourselves so as not to disturb them. I hung up my jacket and my camp uniform on a nail over the board where I slept so that they would be dry by morning. I ate a small portion of my bread ration, and then put the remaining larger piece in the pocket of my wet jacket, so I could take it to work with me the next day.

No sooner did the gong sound to awaken us than the block elder was already standing over us with his stick in hand, screaming, "Get up! Get up!" at the top of his lungs. I reached for my clothes that were hanging on a nail, but they were as stiff as cardboard. They had frozen overnight and were like a solid piece of ice, so that I could barely get dressed. Somehow I managed to do so, shivering in the frigidity of the early morning. After putting on my jacket, I stuck my hand hungrily into the pocket to take out my leftover portion of bread, but to my horror, it wasn't there. Someone had stolen it right out of my pocket.

Putting on my shoes turned out to be another dilemma. As they had also been soaked through with rain, I had put them on top of the small stove in the middle of the barracks in order for them to dry, not realizing that leather shrinks when wet and placed on an oven. Now I was barely able to push my feet into my shoes, and with each step that I took, the leather scraped at my skin and bones. My predicament was unbelievably

Inside the barracks where we lived. Note small stove in center.

dreadful. My clothes were frozen, my shoes were painfully squeezing my feet, my stomach was achingly empty, and outside we faced a bone-chilling frost.

A bitterly cold wind blew in our faces as we assumed our places in the *appelplatz*. Immediately, the shouting and beating began, as the kapos ran around grabbing people for their work commandos. Some of us were still exhausted from the previous day, but again we were being forced to confront a traumatic new day, wondering how it would treat us and how it would end.

With every step that I took on our march to the train, which was about half a mile away, my shrunken shoes scraped against my feet, causing sharp pains that were like arrows shooting at my heart. When we reached the construction site, we were given the job of dragging cement from the warehouse to the place where the building was being erected. My co-workers, detecting my agony, allowed me to stay in the warehouse and work there, instead of having to drag the cement bags, as every step I took felt as if it were life threatening.

There were hundreds of sacks of cement piled up in the warehouse. My job, with my partner, was to stand at the loading window, pick up the sacks, one by one, and place them on the backs of the people who had to carry them to the building site. This too was difficult work, but better than having to walk in shoes that were digging into my feet, causing them to bleed, in the freezing cold, carrying the heavy cement sacks. Inside the warehouse, I could remove my shoes, and warm my feet in the thick cement dust. My feet were revitalized, while the cement dust entered my lungs. I had no idea then that it would take a couple of years after the war for my feet and my lungs to be cleaned from all the bits of cement.

I worked in the warehouse for a few hours, loading people's backs with the sacks of cement, when suddenly a kapo came up behind and gave me a smack with his stick across my back. I collapsed, writhing in pain, while the kapo proceeded to treat other inmates in a similar fashion.

I could barely manage to get up again, doing so only with the help of several friends. The pain, which shot through my back, prevented me from straightening it, but I knew that it was too dangerous for me to be standing around idle. My friends carried me close to the building site and placed me with a group of people whose job it was to carry iron posts to the site. They told me to stay off to the side and that they would work for me that day. I had been standing there for only a few minutes when a German company man noticed that I wasn't working. The next thing I felt was a blow across my knees with a heavy stick, after which I once again fell to the ground in immense pain.

This was the last straw. Unable to control myself any longer, I picked up a stone from the ground and with all my might, screamed at the barbaric German, in Yiddish, "You should be a *kapparah*!"

I don't remember what else I screamed, but I had flown into a complete rage. My life at the moment had become so abhorrent to me that I threw all caution to the wind. The German, filled with murderous fury, grabbed me by the neck, and shouted, "What did you bark, you dog, you?!"

His hands squeezed my throat tighter and tighter. I felt almost unable to breathe, when miraculously, another German appeared and pulled him away from me, saying, "Leave the dog alone. He is about to expire, anyway. Let him rot."

He threw me to the ground and in a few seconds I began to breathe again.

This was a typical day in Camp Number Four. Once again, thank G-d, I survived the perils.

For some time afterwards, I was unable to go to work. My knees were swollen, and my back pains were agonizing. I dragged myself to the doctor in the camp clinic, although my friends told me I was wasting my efforts. The doctor was an assimilated Hungarian Jew. If a compatriot came to him for a release from work, he would receive his slip quickly and with no examination. On the other hand, if, for the same reason, a Polish Jew came to him, he would tell him, "You can go to work," even when the Jew was really sick. I said I would go to him anyway, for I had to try out all my options.

When I arrived at the clinic, the doctor came out. I related to him my story of the preceding day. Without letting me speak very long, the doctor gave me a release note for the entire week.

My friends were incredulous, but I merely said again, "One has to try everything, and the *Ribbono Shel Olam* will do what is His will."

In this way, I was able to stay in camp for a week, during which time I regained my strength somewhat.

My friends and I were constantly debating whether it was better for one's health to go to work and eat an extra portion of soup, or to try somehow to remain in camp, eating less but preserving one's energy. We were unable to decide. Most of us felt that besides losing one's strength at work – more energy than one could regain from watery soup – the dangers which abounded at the worksite from the SS guards and kapos were greater than any that threatened us in the camp. This calmed my anxieties about staying behind in camp on sick leave.

I became quite friendly with the Hungarian doctor. He spoke to me in Hungarian, not a word of which I understood. I responded in German. He enjoyed discussing with me a variety of topics, particularly religion. When I felt more at ease with him I told him that I felt that he discriminated against Polish Jews. He smiled, but did not answer. I told him, "You know, I am also a Polish Jew." He told me categorically, "No, you are a Hungarian."

I promised him that I had been born in Poland in the city of Lodz, but he remained unconvinced.

"Your parents must have been born in Hungary."

My arguments to the contrary were futile. He was certain in what he believed, because I "looked Hungarian" in his eyes. I could not but view the situation to my advantage, for as long as the doctor believed himself to be right, I could use any opportunity that came my way to become sick and not have to go to work.

From time to time, epidemics would break out in camp. The worst was dysentery, which caused the victim to dehydrate, losing all his strength, and ultimately, his life. People died like flies. The disease was highly contagious, and entire blocks got wiped out, or else were quarantined, with no one allowed to come in or go out.

Each morning there came a special detail to drag out the dead. All the inmates were stretched out on boards, forty on each side of the block, with a small stove in the center for heat. The burial commando would enter the block and check everyone. If someone did not move, they would pull his body out of line by his feet, the head falling backwards on the ground with a thud. The body would be dragged out of the block, up the wooden steps and out the door onto a wagon in which there were already piled the almost skeletal remains of other victims. These bodies were hauled to a site outside the camp where they were buried in a mass grave.

Day in and day out, blocks slowly emptied out, and new batches of ailing inmates from other camps would be brought in. The sickly air of death hung over us. No one escaped the spreading disease.

At first, despite the high degree of contagion, I remained healthy. I would go about bartering bread for other assorted items, dealing like a businessman. There was no medicine for the sick. There were only two possible cures. One was cheese, which we received from time to time, purchasing it from people who came to the camp. The other was charcoal. We would take either a piece of wood or bread and burn it until it was completely black. This, when eaten, sometimes helped people who were sick, for the diarrhea associated with dysentery would stop.

Those who were sick could not digest the camp bread, which was mixed with various other elements, such as sawdust, I suspect, making it heavy like cement. Camp bread was ideal for plugging up holes in the wall, but for a person as famished as we always were, the bread was as savory as the most delicious cake. One who was sick with dysentery, however, would lose his appetite, and thus could not even contemplate eating the smallest morsel of bread. So there was a lively trade going on, bread for cheese, or bread for potatoes.

It was when the epidemic was over that I became sick. This was the way the Divine Providence directed things. Luckily, I had been able to save up a few cheeses, and after a few weeks, I recovered, although I was barely able to walk on my feet. The sickness robbed a person of all his strength, and with no food getting into my system to build up my strength, it took some time before I could stand and walk on my legs.

Soon afterwards, an epidemic of typhus erupted. The symptoms were an intense fever, spots all over the body, and every limb wrenched with pain. Once again hundreds of people died. And once again, I walked about among the sick in order to barter for bread or water or other goods.

There was plenty of soup to eat. The sick were unable to ingest any food. It was ironic that in the camp there were pots filled with food, and very few people coming to take it. Once again the blocks emptied out, as the epidemic wreaked havoc in the entire camp.

Nor did the epidemic spare the kapos or the block elders, despite the fact that they suffered neither hunger nor hard labor. On the contrary, a well-fed and strong person who contracted typhus perished more quickly. Again, I was walking about, unharmed, while others became sick. My friend Yossel Carmel became ill and was struck with a ragingly high fever. As we both had our sleeping places on the boards in a cold spot near the block door, having intentionally chosen this spot where the lice were less likely to flourish, I decided to drag him to a warmer place in the center of the block, so he would not catch pneumonia because of the cold.

In the morning, I went over to him to check up on how he was doing. He was very weak, so I helped him sit up. Standing behind him, I was horrified to see that his back was as black as tar. I assumed that as a result of the high fever, his skin had become inflamed and discolored. But when I touched the skin of his back, all of a sudden, I saw the entire patch of black "skin" start to move. There was in fact a mass of black lice that had come to settle on the warm skin of my sick friend's back. The vast number of parasites had covered his entire back. This was one of the most nightmarish images that remain with me vividly to this day.

With a bit of straw and my bare hands, I began to clean his back from the vermin. As horrible as the experience was, it was a typical one for the thousands of Jews who were suffering from the dreaded disease. In a steady stream, more sick people arrived from other camps, people who had become afflicted with the epidemics. As more people died, others were brought in to fill their places.

Around the camp there were ditches that became filled with an ever-increasing number of victims. An epidemic would last from three to four weeks. As usual, as soon as the epidemic was over, I became ill, running a high temperature. When we were given our rations, I had no appetite for the lean piece of bread, for my mouth was afire with thirst. Slowly all my strength dissipated.

Within a week I could barely stand on my legs, let alone walk. Suddenly, one day, the head kapo entered and announced, "Today you will all go to an *entlausung,* which means you will wash and clean yourselves in a bathhouse together with your blankets, and the entire block will be disinfected."

In a corner of the camp there stood a barracks in which there were showers, where we would have to wash. By the time our turn came, night had already fallen, and we were rushed out of our block, headed for the bathhouse. It was the middle of January and freezing outside. After we became sick, they took away our clothes, and now we were naked. (Some were able to get clothes by "organizing," i.e., obtaining them through illicit means.) We were expected to go to the showers some distance away with nothing more than a blanket with which to cover ourselves.

With a high fever, and trembling from the cold, even with people helping me, I could barely drag myself to the bathhouse, which was about two hundred meters away. There was no soap, no towels, and the showers were cold. We tried to dry ourselves with our blankets, and then everyone marched back, half running, because of the cold, in order to arrive as quickly as possible back to the block. I remained behind everyone, hardly able to walk, barely able to lift my feet.

Suddenly, I came to a ditch that could not have been more than a foot wide, but as I was unable to lift my legs, I feared I would fall in. Everyone else had already moved far away, so I stood alone in the cold, shivering from the frigidity and from fright, but unable to push on.

All I could do was to stand there and shout, "Help! Help!"

After about a couple of minutes, our block elder came out. He was a Jew who was the epitome of cruelty, who would beat anyone on every possible occasion. I knew then that I would receive my share of blows for having shouted, or perhaps for having remained behind the others. Perhaps he might simply want to get rid of me altogether with his beatings. I trembled both from fright and from the cold, and was totally unprepared for what happened next. Lifting me onto his back, he hauled me into our block, took out a tin can of water and put it on the stove, and then brought me a cup full of steaming hot water. Everyone else stared in disbelief. Such treatment was beyond anyone's imagination. I certainly never expected it, but, of course, it was the will of the Divine Providence.

Several more days passed, and my fever had not yet abated. Burning with thirst, I begged my friend Yossel Carmel to bring me some cold water, but he told me that drinking cold water was very harmful for those struck with typhus, and could even be fatal. Many people had already died, he reminded me, from drinking cold water that was not clean.

But I was parched from the fever. When my friend Yossel went out, I begged another neighbor, a young Hungarian boy, to bring me some cold water, and in return, I would give him my portion of bread. He brought me a full jug. Thinking that I had not much to lose anyway, I began to gulp down the water, downing nearly the entire jugful in one swig. I was almost finished drinking it all when suddenly Yossel returned. He rushed over to me, grabbed the bucket out of my hand, and berated me, "You drank cold water?! You are finished. You have just committed suicide."

I did not answer him. There was only a little bit of water left in the bucket. The strain of my sudden drinking bout had tired me out, and in minutes I grew drowsy and fell asleep. I slept through the entire night, and in the morning when I woke up, I felt that the fever had subsided. I suddenly felt much better.

This was the way the *Ribbono Shel Olam* healed. Just as He had made bitter water sweet with bitter wood (*Exodus* 15: 25), so he cured typhoid fever with cold water which could have been a danger to life. As it is written in *Job* (23:13): "And He is Unique, and who can alter His mind, and that which He desires, He does."

Chapter 21

Chanukah in Camp Four

I will now relate a further experience with my spoon that I had smuggled out of Auschwitz, into Camp Number Eight, where we were quarantined from other camps, ostensibly from fear of our carrying the typhus epidemic. We were about 500 prisoners in the small Camp Number Eight. We were not ordered to go out to work details here, but were kept in the camp in order to help complete its construction.

As I was always willing to experiment, and anxious to discover new things, I often volunteered for work. Having had some experience in the Lodz ghetto as a mechanic, I helped the electrical technician install the lighting in the camp. I worked in a workstation outside the camp, and my supervisor, who wasn't a bad person, would often bring me bread from his house.

I brought to work with me my spoon whose handle had been made into a sharp knife. Thus I could use my spoon both to eat my soup and to cut my bread. This was useful because often we would receive one chunk of bread to divide among two or three people, and without a knife it was difficult to apportion the bread equally. I was often called upon by people who could not agree on the division of their bread portions to use my spoon/knife to cut their bread rations into pieces that were considered fair. This helped to avoid disputes and instill relative peace among us

My spoon was also involved in an additional mitzvah. This occurred when we were already in Kaufering, or Camp Number Four, a camp that was similar to Auschwitz in its horrendous day-to-day lifestyle. As I have already mentioned, we tried whenever possible to remember to do a mitzvah and to each maintain a self-image as a G-d-fearing Jew, despite all the dangers involved in doing this.

I always kept a mental track of the calendar, and soon I knew that Chanukah had arrived. During a free moment while we sat around, we reminisced about how back home our fathers would light their menorahs with fervor and joy. We remembered how we could never get our fill of watching the flames sparkling like stars, with a special warm glow, and how they inspired in us a special sanctity.

Then we got to thinking about the war of the Chashmonaim against their Greek tormentors who were intent on erasing *Yiddishkeit* from Jewish hearts, and we remembered the great heroism of the Jews who risked their lives in order to keep Shabbos, observe *bris milah* and learn Torah. And we remembered how G-d helped them to overthrow the Greeks and chase them out of the land of Israel, enabling all the Jews to freely observe the Torah and the mitzvos.

And here we were, in a camp where not only were our lives constantly in danger, and not only were we considered as low as vermin, but also it was impossible for us to observe such basics of *Yiddishkeit* as Shabbos, *tefillin* and other mitzvos. And, we mused, how happy we would be if we could only light Chanukah candles.

While we were talking and dreaming, we were all suddenly struck simultaneously by the same thought: We simply must discover a way of lighting Chanukah candles. And then, one of our group mentioned that he had set aside a small bit of margarine he had received that day as a ration. This could be our oil. But where to get wicks? Not a problem, for we began to unravel threads from our uniforms, turning them into instant wicks.

But what could be our menorah? I took out my spoon, and within moments, we were lighting the Chanukah "candle," reciting the blessings of "*Lehadlik ner, She'asah nissim* and *Shehecheyanu.*" We all stood around entranced, each immersed in his own thoughts — of Chanukahs gone by — of *latkes,* of *dreidels,* of Chanukah *gelt* which we had all received as children from our parents and family. This singular Chanukah menorah kindled in us a glimmer of hope. As we said "*She'asah nissim,*" telling how G-d performed miracles for our forefathers "in those days," but also "at this time," we understood that the only thing that could save us would be a miracle. "*Nes gadol hayah sham*" was written on the *dreidel,* I realized.

Even the nonreligious Jews stood around with us watching the flame of the Chanukah candle. None of us who survived will ever forget the scene.

This was an episode in the story of the spoon which had involved much self-sacrifice and revealed to us its great benefits. This was one of the most luminous moments in the darkness of our concentration-camp life and our days of suffering.

Dr. Viktor Frankl of Vienna, a famous professor of psychiatry, who incidentally was an inmate himself of Kaufering, wrote in his book, "Man's Search for Meaning," that a person had to have something to live for in order to survive the concentration camps. Someone with a goal had a better chance to remain alive. So we religious Jews, who, even in the camps, lived for our Shabbosos, our Jewish holidays, and our daily recognition of the A-mighty, as much as we could, had better chances of clinging to life than others who, with no purpose or meaning to their lives, sank to the depths of despair and became more vulnerable to the "final solution."

And today, I am overwhelmed at times with gratitude to G-d for my personal miracle, my survival, especially when I am surrounded by the children and grandchildren He has granted me, all of whom are committed to the observance and study of the Torah. And the gratitude comes rushing in as well every winter, when I light my menorah – a real one today – and, as always, I remember my Auschwitz-spoon Chanukah menorah.

Chapter 22

The Last Purim in the Valley of Tears

We were all sitting listlessly on our bunks, waiting impatiently for the high point of our daily existence – the distribution of our meager bread ration.

"Do you know that tomorrow is Purim?" I asked my brothers in suffering, trying to distract them, and myself, from tormented thoughts and painful pangs of hunger.

A few people responded skeptically.

"How do you know that?"

"Who told you that secret?"

"Have you been dreaming?"

"Where did you find a calendar?"

"You are surely mistaken!" some others retorted. "Don't you

realize that this is a leap year? You can see for yourself from the freezing weather that Purim can't be for another month."

"No, no!" Voices protested from all sides. "Srulik doesn't make mistakes like that! We know him from before the war and can guarantee that he has a good memory and knows a lot by heart."

"Crazy chassidim!" others grumbled. "You have nothing else to worry about besides when Purim falls this year? What's the difference any more between Purim and Pesach, Rosh Hashanah and Yom Kippur? Isn't it Tishah B'Av all the time?"

The debate gathered force among the "mussulmen" who occupied the block – eighty human beings reduced to skin and bones, crammed into a hut that was half-buried underground like a wooden tomb overgrown with grass, lying on boards covered with a thin layer of straw, in Death Camp Number Four of Dachau.

It was the hour before nightfall, when the inhabitants of the block, converted into an infirmary, lay tensely on their bunks, eyes riveted to the curtain that separated the block elder's spacious quarters from the rest of the block where eighty men lay packed like sardines, unable to move around.

Suddenly, as if by the wave of a magic wand, a silence descended into the room, a fearful, oppressive silence. The curtain parted, and the block elder appeared with his henchmen, bearing the scanty bread rations that everyone had awaited with great impatience for nearly twenty-four hours. The tension was high. Each inmate, upon receiving his ration, measured it wordlessly with his eyes and compared it to his neighbor's portion, each one convinced that the other had more. Not more than five minutes later, the stingy portions had already been swallowed by the starving, wretched men, their stomachs as empty as before, their gnawing hunger made more intolerable by the realization that they would have to wait a whole day for the next piece of bread.

All the strain and nervous excitement had their effect on me. I had just suffered through a bad bout of typhus and several days of high fever. Falling back on my segment of board, I fell asleep.

When I woke up the next morning, I felt dizzy, and my head felt very heavy. My bones, protruding as they did from my emaciated body, scraped against the wooden plank, stinging painfully as the skin peeled off. But who could pay attention to such trivialities? After six years in the ghetto and in three concentration camps, one's body adjusts, and suffering becomes the norm.

Nevertheless, the hunger pangs were constantly renewing themselves, and since a hungry person can hardly think of anything else but eating, I began to calculate how much time remained until noon, when the "hot soup" would arrive. (This was a lukewarm liquid in which a couple of pieces of potato occasionally would float.)

With my head down on the wooden board, near despair, I began to conjure up images from my past, of my life with my parents and my two sisters, Gittel and Mirel — how I used to learn in the Gerer *shtiebel* and belonged to the circle of young boys. Mostly, I remembered my grandfather, Reb Herschel, who loved me dearly and to whom I was strongly attached, who used to take me, his only grandson, along whenever he went to the Gerer Rebbe. I relived the memory of my entering the room where the Rebbe was, and the deep impression left in my heart by the Rebbe's eyes, eyes that overflowed with wisdom and love, eyes that penetrated the very depths of my soul. While still remembering this brilliant, imposing figure, I thought to myself, "Will I ever have the *zechus* (merit) to press myself into the crowd of chassidim gathering around the Rebbe, to frequent his *beis medrash* and learn from him how to be a chassid and a G-d-fearing person?"

"It's time to *daven*, Srulik."

My friend's voice shook me from my reverie. Immediately, my pleasant memories vanished and once again I found myself in the pit of hell.

Half-dazed, I picked myself up and said, "Yes, of course. Let's wash our hands and *daven*."

A sudden thought struck me.

"But it's Purim today! We have to organize a *minyan* – maybe we'll even remember a few *pesukim* of the *Megillah*!"

And, wonder of wonders! In that instant, I forgot my pain, my suffering, my hunger pangs. Summoning up all my remaining strength, I went to wash my hands and face and then to find some men to complete our *minyan*, and inform any of my acquaintances who would want to *daven betzibbur* (with a quorum). Perhaps I could even find someone else who could still recall a few more verses from the *Megillah*, so that we could fulfill as much as we could of the obligations that are remembered and kept from generation to generation.

And then, as if to show that G-d desires those mitzvos that Jews perform with true *mesiras nefesh* (self-sacrifice), by some miracle a small *Chumash Shemos* was discovered with the complete *Megillas Esther* at the back. (Our friend, Itche Perelman, who was in the burial commando, had discovered it in one of the blocks.) Our elation was immeasurable! Such a find was awesome! It could only be a sign that our prayers had been received in Heaven and the redemption was about to begin. Excitement grew to a feverish pitch. Who remembered the hunger, who remembered the cold, the filth, the degradation? No one gave a thought to the dangers involved in organizing a *minyan* and reading the *Megillah*, if suddenly the Germans or a kapo would decide to drop into our hut. Even the irreligious ones who only yesterday had scoffed at the "crazy chassidim" were filled with excitement at this great event.

"Who will read the *Megillah*?" the question was thrown.

The lot fell on me, for I had learned to become skilled as a *baal korei* (reader of the Torah) from the time I had been locked into the ghetto. Within moments, volunteers managed to locate some clothing for me since, like the other inmates of the infirmary, I had been assigned nothing more than a blanket with which to cover myself. And so, I found myself sitting on the edge of my piece of wooden plank, dressed in a camp uniform, a towel wrapped around my head in place of a yarmulke, reciting with my remaining strength, "and Haman sought to destroy all the Jews …" When I read aloud about Haman's downfall, and that "The Jews had light and happiness, joy and honor," the spark of hope deep inside every Jew's heart ignited into a flaming torch. *"Oy, Ribbono Shel Olam!"* thought each person, "Make a wondrous miracle for us, too, as You did for our forefathers in those days, and we will also see the end of our enemies!"

When I finished, everyone cheered in relief. For a brief instant, the dreadful reality of the SS death camp was forgotten, the hunger and suffering were overlooked. Everyone realized that he was a Jew and a human being, and the savage atmosphere was transformed into a Purim atmosphere. And I, having exerted all my remaining energy in my reading of the *Megillah*, remained sitting almost without breathing, but with my spirit soaring.

When people's actions are pleasing to Hashem, even their enemies are reconciled to them. Even the block elder, who usually strutted in with a cruel, arrogant demeanor and scowling face, allowed a smile to play on his lips as he entered that day, and handed out the soup without shouting or cursing at anyone who did not thrust out his can quickly enough. The ever-present jealousy turned into generosity, since instead of complaining as usual that someone else had received more potatoes, everyone cried out, "Let Srulik get a bigger portion of soup today!"

Instead of dwelling on the past, we began to dream about the future, with the hope that soon the German demon would inherit his own downfall, and that the end of Jewish suffering would arrive. And like a river overflowing its banks, its waters pouring out unchecked, so the festive atmosphere and the vision of redemption burst out of the broken hearts of the camp inmates, and, one mitzvah leading to another, more acts of heroism followed. Someone decided to forgo a small piece of yesterday's bread, and offered it to his comrade instead. Another person donated a piece of potato, and these two "portions," which only yesterday could have caused envy and hatred among friends, now became the means by which the inmates could return to what was written, "to fulfill the mitzvah of *mishloach manos*, one man to another."

These precious *mishloach manos* were passed around from one to the other, until they finally landed on my lap. Everyone decided that I should be the one to keep them as payment for reading the *Megillah*. I thought to myself, "*Ribbono Shel Olam*! Behold Your great nation, that in one second can transform itself from the level of wild animals tearing at one another, to the level of courageous men, faithful Jews. And who is like you, Yisrael, a single nation of the earth?" With great emotion I turned to all present: "*Yidden!* Brothers in suffering! I don't deserve this honor you have given me. We all have but one request from our Heavenly Father: *L'shanah habaah biYerushalayim!* Next year in Jerusalem!"

Chapter 23

Passover in Camp Four Krankenlager

There was never a dull moment in the camps, even in Camp Four Krankenlager. (Dachau satellite Camp Number Four was declared a camp for the sick.) Every day and every night, there was the struggle to survive. In the mornings we waited for our "coffee," in the afternoons for our so-called soup and in the evenings for our bread. We suffered miserably from the cold, as we did not have any flesh to cover our dry bones. In the mornings we awoke, dreading finding out who had not gotten up from his sleep. It might be a friend, an acquaintance or a neighbor. Whoever it was was soon dragged out of the block by the burial commando. Then we would speculate at what the new day would bring us. New orders, or new tribulations? Would it be better than yesterday, or worse? We also antici-

Sign at Kaufering Camp Number Four

pated hearing news or rumors about the progress of the war. The air-raid sirens were shrieking more frequently, and the explosions sounded nearer and nearer. The most we could do was dream and pray that our liberation would come soon.

Even though most of the inmates in Camp Four were sick from the frequent epidemics, some people who had endured the diseases and survived were able to move around more easily in the camp. They "organized" clothes that were taken off dead bodies, and sometimes even a portion of bread that the deceased had left behind, obviously unable to eat it any more. Our friend Itche Perelman, who was working in the burial commando, tried to help us out whenever and however he could. Sometimes, a word of encouragement was worth more than food.

One day we heard a rumor that a transport of parcels from the Red Cross had arrived for the inmates. At first we did not believe that we would get anything from the parcels, even if the rumor were true. Any foodstuff had to pass through a line of higher-ranking personnel who would take for themselves whatever they chose before anything would come into our possession. First there was the camp commandant, then the SS, and then the kapos and block elders, through whose hands the distribution had to pass. Even so, we doubted the truth of the rumor, as there had been many other times when we had believed some good news we had heard and then had been dismally disappointed. Maybe someone was playing a joke on us. We wondered if it could it be possible that the Red Cross that had closed its eyes to Auschwitz,

Maidenek and the other extermination camps would suddenly show an interest in the inmates of Kaufering Camp Number Four.

Two days passed, and then the block elder suddenly showed up with a big box and, after making a grand speech, began to distribute to each of us a tin of sardines, a small bag of sugar and a little can of Swiss condensed milk. Breathless with anticipation, our hearts beat quickly as we awaited our turns. Until we had the goods in our own hands we couldn't be sure they would reach us, as more often than not the block elder would take for himself a large part of the shipment, and then distribute what was left to some of us, while the remaining ten or so unlucky ones were left with nothing. He would then blame the shortage on the rest of us, claiming that somehow we had managed to get double portions. But when we finally did get our shares, our joy was tremendous, not only on account of the food that for us was lifesaving, but also because of the idea that someone outside of the German Reich remembered us.

Many people ate up all their food right away, believing that the safest place for it was in their stomachs. At least for once, they would feel full and satisfied. But my friend Yossel and I decided to eat as little as possible now, so that our portions would last us a longer time. This was a difficult choice to make, since it left us burdened with our hunger pangs that did not leave us for a moment, and also the fear that someone might steal our bounty from us. But once we made our decision, we stuck to it. Whenever I took a small sip from the sweet milk, I felt a renewal of life in me. And Yossel gave me a lecture on the nutritional value of the foods we had received.

At night I sometimes could not sleep, touching my treasure that was under the straw under my head to make sure it was still there. Then my inner struggle would begin: Should I eat a little bit while my friend was sleeping, or wait until the next day so we could eat together? I felt darned if I did, and darned if I didn't. But invariably I would fall into a deep sleep to wake up in the morning to a new day.

Now we began to think about Pesach. We never for a moment entertained the possibility that we could have matzah. It would have been impossible in our situation. Even if we could somehow obtain flour, we could not imagine where we could bake the dough. Our only question was: Could we manage to do without eating bread for eight days? We had no other food that we could depend on to survive the holiday. We constantly discussed this topic among ourselves, but no one had any advice to offer, and we could not make a decision on the matter. Days and weeks passed, and soon it was almost Pesach, in just a few days. I was weak and bedridden, and could not think of going out as my friends did. They tried to exchange their bread for potatoes. Some kapos had contacts in the kitchen, and some members of the burial commando had contacts with German workers. A few of my friends made some sort of deal of exchange for at least a couple of days. But when I asked my friend Yossel to get for me as well some potatoes instead of my bread, he told me outright that I was too weak and sick to forgo my bread even for one day. Since I was unable to go out without the help of my friends, I could not make any deal.

On the night before the first night of Pesach, I ate my portion of bread very late. In the morning I did not eat anything except for the "soup." I was determined that at least on the first night I would not eat any *chametz*. That evening we talked about Passover before the war, and how we all celebrated the holiday with our families. We remembered the *kneidlach* (matzah balls) that our mothers had prepared and all the treats that came with the festival. When the light in our block went out, and everyone turned over on their sides to sleep, I said to my friend Yossel, "Well, we can't fulfill the commandments of eating matzah and bitter herbs – but we really don't need any bitter herbs to remind us of the bitterness the Jews suffered in Egypt. Could theirs have been worse than ours? Impossible! Let us at least say the *Haggadah* (recitation of our ancestors' Exodus from Egypt), whatever we can remember by heart."

So we recited the "*Ma Nishtanah*" and "*Avadim Hayinu*" and anything else that came into our memories. Even though we chanted in very low voices, we seemed to be disturbing our neighbors. "What are you crazy chassidim doing, saying the *Haggadah*? Do you have matzos, do you have wine and all the necessary food to make a *seder*? Sheer stupidity!"

I remember that I answered them, "We aren't doing it just for the fun of it. We are fulfilling the commandment of the A-mighty to relate tonight the story of the Exodus from Egypt. If we don't have all the necessary accompaniments, it's not our fault, and we are not commanded to do the impossible. But we can do what *is* possible. And who knows which *seder* is more welcome in Heaven, our *seder* in the dark and on empty stomachs, in pain and suffering and under duress, or the *seder* of our brothers in the United States and other countries that are not under the Germans' boots, who have matzos, wine, fish and chicken, and have big chandeliers lighting their tables, and are free to do what they want."

At this they became silent, and we felt afterwards that they showed us more respect.

So passed the days of Pesach. I was forced to eat my bread, but I ate it with deep regret, always feeling guilty and disgusted. But I felt vindicated, as I was heeding the commandment, "You shall watch your life and your health," as life must go on. I was following the words of the Torah, "*V'chai bahem!*" Do all the commandments only in order to live and not to die (save for a few transgressions for which one had to die rather than commit them – i.e. murder, illicit relations and idol worship).

On the seventh day of Pesach, my friend Itche Perelman brought me a camp uniform that he had taken from a block that housed people who had just come from other camps where they had camp uniforms. In our camp, which was a sick camp, we were all naked, except for blankets we had to wrap around our bodies. We were all destined to die, so why waste clothes on us? But Itche was able to "organize" a set of clothes for me. I undertook right away to make a *minyan* for praying, making sure that we had at least ten worshipers joining in. As more people began to show us religious Jews respect, they also joined us in prayer. I was chosen to be cantor, and I said out loud what I could remember. Since I was a Kohen (descendant of priests), I recited the blessing of the Kohanim and everyone answered "Amen."

After the prayers, I said to all our comrades in the block in a loud voice, "Fellow Jews! This should be our last holiday as slaves in this camp. May Hashem grant us that on the next holiday we should all be free men!"

And so it happened. But only for some of us, as many died or were killed in the very last days and final hours before our liberation.

Chapter 24

Near Death Again

Three quarters of the victims of the dreaded, contagious diseases — like typhoid fever and tuberculosis — died emaciated, nothing but skin and bones, having become terribly weakened, with no resistance. However, there were also the privileged who were victims of the epidemics, those who were healthier and well fed, such as kapos, block elders and even an occasional SS guard who had been present with us on the construction sites, our "masters," as we called them. These people met their ends even faster than the sick ones who were frail and undernourished.

One of the deadly diseases, dysentery, became an epidemic of vicious intensity, whose victims died like flies. The unfortunate stricken ones would become severely dehydrated, and expire much as a candle being snuffed out. It would happen on occasion, while I was speaking with an acquaintance who was sequestered inside one of the dysentery blocks, that while we were talking, I would watch my afflicted friend drop his head down on the straw where it would lie still — forever. The camp population was constantly being replenished by having more sick inmates brought in from the numerous camps forming the chain around Dachau, only to perish in Camp Number Four, which was nicknamed the "Death Camp." Consequently, one who was fortunate enough to recover from a bout with the disease was very likely to get another attack from being constantly exposed to the highly contagious infection.

Another epidemic arrived – one which was rare and unique. In the course of one week, the entire Camp Number Four had contracted an itching disease. It began with a slight rash on a limb or on the abdomen, but within a few days it spread across the entire body, from head to toe. The rash consisted of blotches that increased in size and spread. Boils soon appeared, oozing pus, and making the whole body sticky. (It was difficult to perform basic natural functions because the openings of the body were sealed shut as if with plastic.)

The itching was fierce, and when one scratched the affected area, there resulted an inflammation of the skin and abscesses with pus in them. The open sores grew rapidly in size, and were extremely painful, at night as well as during the day. I also contracted a large sore beneath my abdomen, near the leg joint, which grew bigger and bigger each day. It soon became difficult for me to walk, for each step that I took caused a painful rubbing against the sore.

One morning it was announced in our block that a doctor would be coming that day to treat us by opening the boils and extracting the pus. I decided to go to him to get treated. When the doctor entered the room, the sick patients began to push to the front towards him. Soon enough, my turn came to stand before the doctor. I saw him standing near the door with a bloodied razor blade in his hand. He looked at us and said, "Who still has to be cut?"

I shrank back, for I was not so keen on being treated after all. First of all, I dreaded the cut itself. And second, if the instrument of choice was that bloodied razor blade, I suspected the infection would only become worse than it already was. (There were no bandages, or disinfectants such as iodine or alcohol, available to us.) So I returned to my place, disappointed and near despair.

My neighbors advised me to apply hot compresses to the big sore in order for it to soften. Then I would be able to cut it open myself. So I took an empty can of preserves and tied it with a wire, filled it up with water (or maybe it was snow), and brought it to a boil inside the little, wood-burning oven in the middle of the block. Using my towel that I had smuggled out of Camp Number Eight, I made a hot compress by dipping it into the hot water, and applying it to the sore. I repeated this treatment often.

After a few days, the boil became soft. I attempted to squeeze it with my finger, but I did not have the capability – or the courage – to puncture it. Then I had an idea. I sat down on the wooden plank where we slept, grabbed my knee with my arms, and with all my remaining strength, lifted it toward my stomach. The boil was squeezed open, and the pus began to run out. I continued to apply pressure with my finger to ensure that all of the pus came out. Now there remained an open sore, and I was afraid it would become infected again. I was particularly concerned that lice not be attracted to it, because there were masses of them all around. So I tore off a piece of the towel, which by then was black from dirt, and stuck it on the open sore.

I did not foresee that this piece of towel would become stuck to my flesh. Following the war I had to receive medical treatment to remove the cloth from my lower abdomen, as the skin around the area had grown over it, making it almost impossible to remove it without an operation. It took about a week of various medicinal treatments in order to reopen the flesh again, and remove the piece of towel. But meanwhile, after I had extracted the pus, the sore began to heal, and I was able to move around again.

I was quite sure that this itching epidemic had not come haphazardly, but with a special intent, courtesy of the German overlords. In the end, the Germans came to our rescue by providing us with a salve, which burned like fire but did cure the rash. I still believe that we were part of an experiment conducted by German doctors regarding the pharmaceutical value of the salve on our bodies.

We would walk about unclothed, except for a blanket with which we tried to cover ourselves. When we were graced with a bit of sunshine, we would recline on the roof and bask in the sun's rays that, together with the fresh air, helped the infections to heal.

Even the strongest could hardly survive the constant sufferings which we had to put up with. Every day we waited for a piece of bread which was more often than not moldy, and then we had to split that piece of bread between two people while everyone looked hawkishly on, anxious that the other might receive a larger piece. (Some people cut out the parts that had green mold on them. I was so hungry that I went around collecting all the moldy pieces and ate them.) At times we would go for arbitration to a third person who would hold the two pieces behind his back while each of the litigants would choose a hand, right or left. What in normal circumstances would be child's play, here was a life-and-death matter. Still, we often felt as if we were hoodwinked. We had the same feelings about the soup, which the block elder would apportion from the large pot. None of us dared remove his hunger-ravaged eyes from the ladle, to see how deeply the block elder dipped it into the cauldron. Near the top there was only water, while at the bottom one could often find a few pieces of potato. When we received our soup portions, we mixed and mixed with a makeshift spoon (usually a piece of wood) to check if there might indeed be a piece of potato swimming around.

Anyone who survived in the camps from the beginning, anyone who had experienced all forms of suffering – such as the forced labor, the *appel* with the SS and kapos always ready to pounce, the extreme hunger, the epidemics – and still remained alive, did so miraculously, through Divine Providence. It had obviously been decided that a particular person was to survive, despite the anguish, the life-threatening situations, and the horrors that could break even the most stalwart and hardy character, pushing him to the brink of death. Inexplicably, Providence kept him alive in the end. I could think of no reason why I should survive, while others who were stronger and healthier should perish, unless for some reason the A-mighty wanted me to survive.

After Dachau satellite Camp Number Four was declared a camp for the sick, and nicknamed "Death Camp," there was not much to do and little to hope for. We languished from the diseases that afflicted us, and were tormented by the lice that attacked us from all sides. All around us there was straw and wood where millions of them thrived. The lice, which ate us up alive, became a problem of epic proportions, and never ceased from the time that we entered the camp. No sooner had an inmate gotten "comfortably" installed than he would feel an itch, and then scratch himself with his fingers on his flesh and pull out a handful of those tiny devils. Some people used to play a different version of the game "odds and evens," just to kill time. They pulled out clumps of lice from their bodies and counted the number to see if it was odd or even.

In our weakened states, we did not do much else than sit or lie around, and we talked. Looking back, I marvel at some of the conversations we inmates often had. The Hungarians, who had been under German rule only since April or May of 1944, could talk all day about the food they had eaten at home, having known little hunger or privation until they had recently entered the camps. We Polish Jews, who were famished since the beginning of 1940, had already forgotten the taste of food.

The religious Jews attempted to remember a bit of *Chumash* (Pentateuch), a chapter of *Tehillim*, or a portion of the *davening*. Sometimes it would happen that a Jew managed to smuggle into the camp a *chumash*, or even a pair of *tefillin*. On such an occasion, we would muster our last energies and drag ourselves over to put on the *tefillin*, or even only to look through the pages of a *siddur* or *chumash*. My friend Yossel Carmel and I would try to recall each *parshah* (weekly Torah-reading) of the week from memory, or perhaps even an occasional pearl of wisdom on the *parshah*. Sometimes we even tried to organize a *minyan* to pray as much as we could remember from the *davening*.

It seemed to be a general rule that once a person allowed himself to sink into despair, losing all hope of remaining alive, he did not stand much of a chance of surviving much longer. By retaining a glimmer of hope that we would yet merit Hashem's salvation, and by still feeling an attachment to the Gerer Rebbe in our daily existence, and holding onto our dreams of a better life after our liberation, we infused ourselves with the courage to fight, and strengthened our determination to live on, despite the pain and agony we suffered. Being religious Jews gave us more faith and hope than the nonreligious had, for, to begin with, we believed that Hashem's salvation could occur in the blink of an eye.

When we used to travel to our work details aboard the railcars, the SS guards would often order us to sing. We would sing, "*Vehi she'amdah* (Hashem's oath stands on our behalf) ... *veHakadosh Baruch Hu matzileinu miyadam* (Hashem will save us from their hand)." Or, at times we would chant, "*Utzu eitzah, vesufar* (Plan your conspiracy, but it will be abolished)." They liked the tunes, but naturally, they did not understand the words. We had the satisfaction of knowing that somehow we could defy them in their presence.

We firmly believed that the *Shechinah*, the Divine Presence, was with us right there in our oppressive situation. "*Imo anochi b'tzarah* – I am with them in their distress." Consequently, we were certain that the *Ribbono Shel Olam* would come to our rescue. We made plans to travel to Eretz Yisrael when the war would end, and to begin new lives there, lives of Torah and Chassidus. In this way, we avoided spending our entire days dwelling on our ever-present hunger or dreaming about a small piece of bread.

Our higher spiritual profile kept many of us from despair. Someone with little or no spirituality in him could think of nothing else but the starvation that wracked his body, and fantasize about little other than food. People used to dream about having an entire loaf of bread, and cutting from it and eating it with no restrictions. My own added wish was to sit at a table and eat like a normal person, without having to keep the bread on my knees. However, since food was a nonexistent entity, many who had nothing else to hunger for, gave up all hope of life and in this way expedited their own ends.

There were times, though, when fate brought little surprises, bringing us brief moments of happiness. One such occasion occurred when I was at work in a forest, and I found a paper bag with apple peels in it. Probably a German, perhaps a guard, had thrown them there. This was a great treat for me, a joyous bit of life itself. The best delicacies that I may be tempted with today can never compare with those apple peels in the forest.

Another time, I found in the woods a piece of bread that was dry and hard as a stone. I tried to bite it, but it was so hard that my teeth could not penetrate it. I pushed it into my coat pocket, and thought to myself that when we returned to the camp I would soak it in water, thus making it edible. During the course of the day, while I worked, I seldom lost touch of the presence of the tidy morsel so close at hand. Occasionally, I would stick my hand into my pocket, and try to break off at least a crust, at first with no success whatsoever. After several attempts, I managed to break off a few crumbs. Later, I tried again for another piece, and then another. By the time we arrived back at camp there was no longer any trace of my treasure. I had eaten the entire piece, hard as it had been. Unfortunately, I remained as hungry as ever.

One day I noticed several youths walking with their bowls into the camp kitchen and exiting with their bowls filled with potatoes. I decided to bring my own bowl to the kitchen and beg for a similar handout.

I knew that the kitchen workers were Jewish girls and women from Hungary. In Auschwitz, the Hungarians had been the last to arrive, and were terribly abused by the kapos and block elders from Poland, who had been interned in Auschwitz years before. (Nevertheless, we Polish Jews didn't get any better treatment from the Polish kapos than the Hungarians did.) Even worse, the newly arrived Hungarian Jews did not know a word of Yiddish, so they were unable to communicate with the others. Here in Camp Number Four the Hungarians had arrived earlier than the Polish Jews and thus the tables were turned. Now the Hungarians had the upper hand, and often tried to get even with us, at our expense, because we were Polish Jews.

I knocked at the kitchen door, and a girl opened it for me. Sticking out my bowl in front of her, I said, in Yiddish, "I beg of you, give me a few potatoes, please."

In reply, she and the others there began to scream at me. One of them brandished a large soup ladle over my head, and shouted, "Get out of here, fast, or I will hit you with this over your head. Or else I will scream for the chief cook."

The chief cook happened to be an SS officer who supervised the kitchen. I knew full well that punishment for unauthorized entry into the kitchen was death. I darted away very quickly, very disappointed, and returned to my block.

Unwilling to give up so easily, I asked one of my neighbors in my block, a Hungarian youth, to teach me how to say in Hungarian, "Give me a few potatoes." This he willingly did, after which I practiced the line over and over again in my head. Then, a couple of days later, I mustered up the courage and made another trip to the kitchen with my bowl. I knocked boldly on the door, but when the kitchen girl opened it I panicked, and forgot the line I had practiced so often. My mind a jumble of words, I did succeed in remembering that the word for "please" in Hungarian was *teshig*, and that potatoes were *crumpli*. I stammered out the two words I knew, interspersed with words muttered under my breath from a garbled, nonsensical language that was neither Hungarian nor Yiddish.

Amazingly enough, she filled my plate with potatoes, and I returned to my block triumphant and happy. I sat down with my friend Yossel, and urged him to partake of my bounty. However, apart from a tiny sample, Yossel refused to take, despite my coaxing, arguing, "You risked your life for these potatoes. You eat them."

It was difficult not to be overcome by the hopelessness of the situation when one lay sick and alone, able to do nothing more than stare blankly at the ceiling. There were a few chassidic young men who would visit us and try to infuse us with courage. Reb Itche Perelman was one of these young men who always made a point of coming to strengthen us and give us a will to live.

At times he was able to procure for us a pair of *tefillin* –
once only a *shel yad*, and another time only a *shel rosh*. But
we were overjoyed to be able to perform any portion of any
mitzvah.

Sometimes he would manage to bring us something to eat.
But the main thing was that he brought us information from
the outside. Since he worked in the burial commando, he had
some contact with Germans. Thus he served as our first harbinger of glad tidings. At any rate, our moods were growing
more optimistic, for at night we could already hear the distant
echo of artillery fire.

Another young boy who became a constant source of
encouragement was a Gerer chassid by the name of Nuta
Eibeshitz, whom I knew from Lodz. Each day he came to talk
with us and recharge us with new hope. We would confide in
each other our expectations for the future and share our rem-
iniscences of home, of the Gerer *shtiebel* and of visits to the
Rebbe. These sessions became for us wellsprings of positive
reinforcement, which actually helped us to survive our terrible
sufferings.

On the day of our liberation, we went to look for him, and
found his lifeless body riddled with bullets. He had been murdered by the accursed Germans a few hours before the liberation.

Chapter 25

Pesach Sheini, 1945

The Nazi beast was trembling with death convulsions as the noose tightened around its neck. From all sides, the Allied powers were pushing deeper and deeper into the heart of the Third Reich.

The end of April was approaching. Day and night we were deafened by the blasts of bombs and the thunder of cannons, as the front was daily getting closer. The nights were ablaze with flares dropped by Allied bombers, which dominated the German skies, and with the fires of buildings burning everywhere. With increasing frequency, air-raid sirens were heard. We sensed that perhaps the end of the war was approaching, but wondered if we could survive until that blessed moment. The quarrel between optimist and pessimist raged on while each of us felt a mixture of hope and fear.

Wednesday, April 25, 1945

The iron discipline to which we had grown accustomed caved in all at once. The SS guards in the watchtowers suddenly disappeared. The kapos and the block supervisors stopped beating and cursing. At once some people broke into the camp kitchen and hauled away potatoes, flour, cabbage and pieces of bread. For lesser "sins" we could have been shot. But our hunger overpowered our fright. It had been several days since we had been given any food. We stuffed both our bellies and our pockets. We were the more fortunate ones, whose legs could still carry us. The majority of the camp inmates lay on hard planks awaiting the Angel of Death. Others stood behind doors looking through the cracks and trembling in fear of the "consequences."

Suddenly the silence was broken by the familiar, murderous voices of the SS criminals. "Everyone in a row! Roll call!" In a flash, the thugs were running about with clubs and revolvers in hand, mercilessly chasing and dragging everyone out of the barracks.

Having already experienced several years together in the ghetto, our small group of young Gerer chassidim from Lodz tried to stick together. We discussed the situation. It was quite clear that the Allied forces were close by. According to reliable rumors that were again circulating, the sources of which were people who had some contact with German officers, there had been an order from the SS command to all camp commanders that upon retreat, all camp inmates must be exterminated, so that no living testimony be present when the Allied armies entered.

Naturally, we did not wish to believe that such a diabolical scheme could be possible. However, six years under Nazi rule taught us that most bleak prophecies did materialize.

We debated our alternatives. Should we follow orders and be evacuated, or should we risk trying to stay behind and await the Allies, and imminent liberation? We decided that our best bet for survival was to stay behind in the camp – risking our lives, which would be worth very little if we were evacuated – and hide out at all costs.

One by one, we stole into the dysentery block, where only the hopelessly ill were lying. People were dying like flies. We reckoned that the guards would choose not to enter the contaminated area for fear of contagion. The sick could not leave, at any rate, so we hoped to be left behind together with them.

But our hopes were soon shattered when the Germans began loading the sick upon wagons. Before long our block door crashed open. In burst an SS officer, his machine-gun crackling, and shouted, "Everyone out!   The camp is to be blown up and destroyed!"

Silence. Not a body stirred, mainly because most were unable to stir. We too lay still, not moving a limb.

As night fell, the line of wagons moved closer to us. Too late, we thought. Now we would have to move on. Our dream of a speedy liberation instantly withered.

Suddenly the air shook with the wailing of sirens. The Allies were bombing the German defenses. As the ground trembled with thunderous explosions, we prayed that they would go on forever. In an instant, the Germans disappeared. That night we fell asleep listening to the melodious sound of bombs blasting, music to our ears.

Thursday, April 26, 1945

The next morning we awoke late. In the ominous silence around us, only the moans and dying breaths of the ill could be heard.

We arose cautiously and went outside the block. Desolation was all around us, not a living soul anywhere. The watchtowers in which we had always seen those murderous eyes and the black holes of machine-guns had been abandoned. In the barbed wire, a gaping hole had been torn open by the Germans to shorten their way. Could it be true? Were we actually free? It was hard to believe, but — where were the Germans?

We went to the other barracks, and found ghastly, frightened faces. We told them of our discovery, and slowly, reluctantly, they made their way outside, those "musselmen," skeletons of men.

Free at last! We could not believe our eyes. Remembering our hunger, we began a search for food. We found a stack of potatoes someone in a hurry had left behind. We stuffed them into our pockets and into every conceivable place in our clothing. Some we ate then and there, raw.

Then we started to discuss the future. We decided that it was safer to wait inside the camp until the Americans came. With the Nazis gone and the Americans not there yet, we figured that we were in no man's land. Were we to leave, we could take a wrong turn, and end up back with the Germans. It would be safest for us to stay in camp.

While we were sitting and making plans for the future, we heard the rumbling engines of a convoy approaching. As the long line of trucks drew near, we wondered who they were. We waited, fear and excitement in our hearts. Our disappointment was acute when the all-too-familiar SS uniforms came into view. They brought with them an entire detachment of prisoners from other camps to help them finish their "work."

Once again a fiendish atmosphere pervaded the camp – screams, obscenities and the rasping voices of the SS sending shivers down our spines.

We hurriedly hid in one of the blocks near the SS barracks, for we had no time to run further and we thought that the SS wouldn't search under their very noses. We covered ourselves with straw and rags and lay still, our hearts pounding with terror.

Soon we heard footsteps in the block. I felt a hand on my head. We had been discovered, by commandos, non-Jewish inmates of other labor and POW camps. We entreated and pleaded with them that they just ignore us, offering them our potatoes. Just as they agreed, an SS officer came stomping in, swinging his club that he used on our heads efficiently and heartlessly. A boot on the behind, and we were on our way to the trucks, accompanied by the commandos and the SS. We were picked up by our arms and legs and thrown onto a pile of several humanlike bodies lying one on top of the other. Now the silence of the dead replaced the moaning of the sick.

I was able to make eye contact with my friend Yossel Carmel. By a stroke of luck, while the guards were busy with another wagon, we managed to roll out of the truck. (We were incapable of jumping.) For a while we hid in a nearby toilet. Our hearts had already turned to stone, but our stomachs were convulsing. But we couldn't remain long in this hiding place, for any minute someone could come in. So, with our skin burning, we crept back into the block we had been in earlier.

No sooner had we climbed down from the window into the block, then the door opened and in walked another SS officer, revolver in hand. "*Schnell!* Fast! To the wagons!" Another whack on the behind, and again we found ourselves on the loading platform. Our plight seemed hopeless. Then we noticed our guard running forward into another block. Instinctively, and without looking back, we made our way as quickly as we could to our old block.

This time we weren't noticed. I tore down the light hanging from the ceiling, and in seconds we once again assumed our previous positions, posturing as corpses. We waited there for what seemed like hours, although time seemed to stand still. Every so often the door would open, and we would hear a shout of "Everyone out!" Darkness had already fallen. Perhaps the guards were too scared to come in. Our minds almost paralyzed, we were incapable of thinking, but our ears were pitched to hear every noise outside.

Finally, a gong clanged. A shout called in all the commandos, "Everyone in line!" There was counting, and then, the sound of motors grumbling away. Then — quiet.

More time passed, but we remained hidden, afraid to stir. Overcome with numbness, we tried to move from our places, but this was very difficult. Some others, who had escaped being moved out earlier, began to peek out of the windows. Slowly we crawled out and began talking, in hushed tones, to pass the time. Some tried to sleep, but with nerves overstrained as they were, did not manage to do so.

Friday, April 27, 1945

It was a cold morning outside. White clouds chased each other across the blue sky. A frigid wind blew into the barracks and chilled our bones. Periodically, the earth trembled with explosions that sounded increasingly closer, almost as if the bombs were flying overhead. In the deserted camp, we sat each engrossed in his own thoughts.

Suddenly, we heard motorcycles rumbling and dogs barking. One of our group who had been standing guard outside came running in with a half-swallowed yell: "Bad news, brothers. The Germans are back!"

Within a few seconds we were back in our hiding places. Outside there resounded the familiar heavy steps of the SS boots marching through the camp. Minutes later, several shots rang out and the rat-tat-tat of automatic fire pierced the air.

Peering out from under the rags concealing me, I noticed that one of my friends let his curiosity get the better of him and picked his head up toward the window. I wanted to call to him to hide, but the call just stuck in my throat. At that moment, I saw a pair of black boots marching past the window. I held my breath. A few seconds later, I heard footsteps in the block, and then a frenzied voice, "Swine! You are waiting for the Americans? Come with me!"

There followed a commotion, the sound of running, the shattering of glass, and then, a burst of machine-gun fire. I peeked and saw that the group that had been hiding near the window had tried to escape. My friend Yossel and I were stationed further away near the door opposite the window, paralyzed with fright.

A few minutes later, we again heard footsteps approaching our barracks. Then they came inside and we heard the rustling of straw. Our terrified souls almost departed. Then the piles in which we hid were tapped. We held our breath in fear of being detected by the sound of our breathing. A moment later, the footsteps moved away, and we heard them outside. I made myself a hole to look out of only to find smoke billowing in my eyes. Ripping off the piles and rags, we were faced with flames everywhere eating their way from the window to the door, coming closer and closer to us.

I whispered to Yossel, "We have to get out." But there was only one exit now, the door. Hand in hand, we fumbled toward the door, almost suffocating from the smoke, our heads spinning. With great effort, we kept ourselves from falling. In a mere moment that seemed like an eternity, we found ourselves outside.

We scarcely had time to look around. Just a few yards from us stood the German murderers, fortunately, with their backs to us. The entire camp was ablaze. We threw ourselves on the first pile of corpses that we saw. Lying still, we did not move a muscle. In any case, we had death written all over our faces. We heard only heavy footsteps and screams from victims and moaning from the fatally wounded. It was blood, fire and clouds of smoke – hell on earth with devils incarnate.

I do not know how long we lay there like that. We lost all sense of time, with seconds seeming like eternities. Again there was silence, save for the moaning, the incessant moaning. I mumbled to Yossel that we ought to say *Vidui* (Confession), for all hope appeared to be lost. He, however, tried to encourage me with these words: "Remember what you told me when we came to Auschwitz. When I despaired, you reminded me that the Sages said, 'Even if a sharpened sword is placed on your neck, you should not despair of Hashem's mercy.' We must not lose hope now. Remember that the Sages also said that Jews should renew their commitment specifically in times of great tragedy and danger."

I looked around. All the barracks were succumbing to the flames, and piles of dead were strewn everywhere. We crawled to a nearby pit, shivering with cold. Through my smoke-filled eyes and fear-ridden senses, I saw SS guards everywhere, standing with weapons poised. My friend, however, finally managed to convince me that there was no one in sight.

For an hour or more we lay in that pit. Every few minutes we heard bombs whistling overhead, accompanied by fearsome explosions nearby. The earth shook, but each blast pumped new hope into our hearts. Slowly, we crept out of the pit and made our way to the only building still standing – the camp kitchen.

There we found a few more frightened faces. Together we located a fresh hiding place – just in case. We sat down, hearts pounding. After discovering a sack of flour, we started the ovens and baked matzos. I remarked that ironically that day was Pesach Sheni. Would our deliverance come on that day too?

We sat there talking, when suddenly the door flew open. A Jewish inmate came running in breathlessly, crying out: "*Yidden*! The Americans are here!"

We were free! We wanted to cry, sing, dance, but our hearts had turned to stone. I wanted to rush outside, but my strength had left me altogether. I could not comprehend how I had managed until then.

With great pain and effort, I struggled to move outside, and found a long convoy of tanks and jeeps roaring through the camp. A handful of soldiers were dropped off, and they approached the barracks. One of them, an officer, looked around him, tears streaming down his face. Only then did I grasp the horror around us. The barracks were nearly completely burnt down. In front of each block lay a pile of burnt-up, blackened skeletons. We, a group of ghouls, living corpses, stood around the American soldiers, and together we all wept.

Then more American soldiers filed in. At once, we saw a pile of chocolate bars and jars and cans of preserves lying on the ground. One of us found a bottle of wine and said aloud, "For years I have not recited the *Kiddush*. Today, I feel that I must." He said it aloud, together with the *Shehecheyanu*. I stood and thought of loved ones and friends and countless others who had not survived to reach this moment. Spontaneously, our lips formed an oath, which our innermost hearts felt: "Remember what Amalek has done to you." NEVER FORGET!

At the annual Seudas Hodaah, on Pesach Sheini, of the survivors of Kaufering Camp Four, who were liberated by the American Army on Pesach Sheini, April 27, 1945. Seated, facing forward, left to right: Israel Cohen, Yossel Karmel, Chaim Kempinski. Standing is Itche Perelman.

After liberation; Israel Cohen is first on right

Ninety percent of the approximately 5,000 prisoners in Kaufering Camp Number Four were ill with dysentery, typhus, dehydration and/or malnourishment. When on April 25 the SS called on all the inmates to assemble, only about 300 gathered together, mostly kapos and block elders who were strong and fit, as they habitually stole from the sick people part of their meager rations, and never did any hard manual labor. They were marched off into Alach, a concentration camp situated near the railroad, to be shipped to Tirol, in the southern end of Germany, where the Germans thought they could hold out against the Allies because of the mountainous terrain of the Alps. Most of the prisoners survived, as the American army overran the Germans before they could transport them anywhere.

The rest of us were either too sick to march, or were hiding. The Germans dragged out all the people who could still walk a little, and shoved them into wagons to bring them to the railroad station. There they waited for the train to transport them to wherever they were supposed to be taken. Some were placed in the cattle cars; others simply died before they could be placed on the train. As the train left, there arrived another train on a parallel rail full of SS and German soldiers carrying weapons, mainly anti-air cannons. Suddenly, there were American fliers overhead, bombing both trains, killing many prisoners. Some Germans were able to dodge the bombers by running and hiding – they were always terrified of the airplanes and hid like mice in mouse holes. Some of the inmates were also able to run and hide in a nearby forest, and stayed there until the Americans came. But more than half of them died in the train or were killed by the bombs.

The rest of us were all on the brink of death, as we were sick, and nothing but skin and bones. The slightest exertion could make one's heart stop. Some of the inmates ventured out to the closest village to beg for food and shelter, but most Germans still believed in Goebbels' propaganda machine that claimed the Americans might still be pushed back, and so they delivered the people seeking refuge to the SS, who immediately shot them.

The next day, which was Thursday, April 26, the Germans did the same thing to the remaining inmates, heaving them into trucks that transported them to the railroad, where they shared the same fate as the first group had on the previous day – death by bombing of the U.S. Air Force. The Germans, though, did manage to transport a number of the prisoners to Tirol, where some were shot, some died of starvation and some were liberated by the Americans, as the Germans capitulated. Some SS still kept on fighting, but were wiped out by the American army.

In Kaufering Camp Number Four, there now remained only those who were hiding. That Thursday night, when the SS and the trucks left, some of the inmates came out of their hiding places, certain that the SS had gone and the Americans were very near.

There were French prisoners in one of the blocks who on Friday morning were singing as they boiled potatoes that they had acquired on Wednesday when the mob had plundered the kitchen. Since they were at the very end of the camp, they could not hear the SS returning with their motorcycles and dogs, in search of any hiding inmates. They took the French by surprise, and marched them out of the block, lined them up against the wall and shot them, point blank.

Among the French prisoners, there were also some Jews, one of them by the name of Leibel Verleger. He was born in Germany, and spoke a perfect German. While attempting to talk to the murderers in their language, and to attempt to reason with them to let the people live, they shot him in the head. The bullet went straight through his cheeks, and he fell to the ground, feigning death. As he kept his mouth open, one of the SS noticed that he had golden crowns on some of his teeth. He shouted to his colleagues, "Look! This swine had gold in his teeth!"

No sooner was this said, than he and his cronies got a pair of pliers and tore out the teeth with the gold, ripping out part of the gums. Despite the terrible pain he suffered, Leibel did not move, and lay among the dead until the American army entered Kaufering Camp Four.

He was an unforgettably shocking sight. The picture is still horribly vivid in my mind's eye. I remember him standing before the troops, bleeding profusely from his cheeks and gums, with some parts of his teeth and gums hanging down from his mouth.

Later, when I was myself in the hospital, I heard that the Americans had taken him to a German hospital, assembled all the doctors, and ordered them to operate on his mouth and make sure that he survived, or else they would all be shot. When I saw him a few years later, the scars on his face were still visible. He married and had children, but, unfortunately, his body and mind had been broken, and he did not live a long life.

Chapter 26

Liberation From Camp Number Four

The few of us who were survivors at the time of our liberation from Camp Number Four were mostly living skeletons. The American soldiers who had liberated us had to march on with the American army deeper into the crumbling German Reich, so they were not available to care for our immediate needs. But as we were only one or two dozen survivors from Lager Four, they did make arrangements for us to be taken care of by nearby farmers and villagers.

The Germans who lived closest to the camp, who in fact knew what took place there, were afraid that the American soldiers would exact revenge from them, and punish them or even imprison them. For lack of choice, they welcomed us with proverbial open arms. They even assumed that in the eyes of the American soldiers we were celebrated heroes. Goebbel's propaganda had brainwashed them into believing that the entire war had been fought because of the Jews, and that the entire U.S. government consisted of Jewish politicians.

Our hosts began to pander to our every whim, making sure to provide us with whatever we asked for. My friend Yossel and I stayed with a farmer who lived not far from the camp. American soldiers accompanied him with his horse and buggy to take us to his farm. The first thing we thought of doing when we got there was to eat to the point of satiety, something we hadn't done in a number of years.

Yet the first thing I did when we got there was to take a hot bath. Not only had it been years since I had bathed properly, but our clothes and our bodies were infested with lice, which bit us all over even if we were literally only skin and bones. Despite our overwhelming hunger, the idea of eating while our bodies were crawling with the creatures disgusted us. So we told the farmer that the first thing we wanted was a hot bath and clean clothes. He immediately provided us with our request.

The bathtub was in a shed near the barn. After the farmer's wife heated up a large cauldron of water, she poured it into the tub. We bathed one at a time. While I was immersed in the hot water, my open wounds stung fiercely, but the idea of being able to soak in a hot tub, and to wash myself with soap, outweighed the sharp pains I felt, and the hunger pangs.

After my bath, the farmer brought me undergarments, a shirt, a pair of trousers and a hat, and I felt like a new person. In all the years since our liberation, I give thanks to Hashem that I have never again seen a single louse. It would be a shocking feeling if I did, understandable only to someone who has experienced the vileness of one's body being overrun with vermin.

Once I was clean again, I sat down at the table and ate some bread that was white like *challah*, and drank milk. My friend Yossel advised me not to eat too much, citing for me a *gemara* in *Gittin,* concerning the destruction of the *Beis HaMikdash.* At that time, the Tanna Reb Tzadok had fasted for forty years in order that the *Beis HaMikdash* not be destroyed, and consequently his stomach had shrunk. Vespasian, the Roman general, sent Reb Yochanan ben Zakkai a doctor to cure Reb Tzadok. The *gemara* relates that Reb Tzadok started off by eating lighter foods, such as watery soups, in small amounts, until his intestines expanded.

Our stomachs had also shrunk, and it would have been extremely dangerous for us to eat too much at once, so we in fact controlled ourselves, hiding some bread under our pillows just in case there would be none left the next day. It took us a long time to get rid of the haunting fears that had been our constant companions throughout our camp lives.

That night we fell asleep in minutes, despite the inner, nagging dread that our German host might choose the quick and simple method of getting rid of unwanted guests – and kill us.

After about an hour of sleep, I awoke with a start and a terrible pain in my abdomen. I headed straight for the bedpan in the room, and shortly after I had finished using it, my friend Yossel woke up with the same distress. We took turns using the portable facility, realizing that we had contracted dysentery, the dreaded disease that robbed its victims of all their strength, and which very often led to their deaths.

Now we were once again laden with fears and anxieties, as we worried that in this isolated spot, no one knew of us. If we were to die, as we were already certain that we would, we would not even get a proper Jewish burial. The irony of having survived the camps only to die after our liberation was too agonizing to imagine.

As we struggled through the night, our strength waned, and by morning we were both exhausted. Suddenly, the door opened, and as if from nowhere a blessed angel came into our room. It was our friend, Itche Perelman, who had been looking for us and had tracked us down to this farm. As soon as he realized our predicament, he ran out, returning a short time later with an ambulance, which promptly transported us to a hospital in a nearby town, Kloster Lechfeld.

What kind of arrangements he had made, and how he had communicated with and convinced the American soldiers – without any common language – who were now marching deeper and deeper into German territory, to send us that ambulance, I still don't know. I do know that Itche served as a messenger of Hashem by saving us from certain death, and, it is surely known that Hashem sends His blessings through the agency of worthy people. Again, here was a certain indication of the Heavenly Providence that constantly manifested itself in our lives.

Chapter 27

Kloster Lechfeld

T he hospital at Kloster Lechfeld, originally a convent that had been converted into a hospital, had initially been established for wounded German soldiers. Now, however, the American army had ordered that an entire floor of the facility be prepared in order to serve concentration-camp survivors who were very sick and needed treatment.

At least we were not alone, at the mercy of some German farmer.

We were together with approximately fifty other Jews from neighboring camps. The treatment that we received there in the hospital was exemplary. Day and night, there were nurses who indulged us. We merely had to press a button to summon her and a nurse would come right away to ask us what we needed. During the night they brought us hot tea with medicines. To use the toilets we did not even have to leave our beds, for we were provided with bedpans.

The food we received was very solid and rich, fatty and with meat in it, suitable for wounded soldiers, but not for patients with severe dysentery. We needed a diet of liquids and toast, devoid of fat, to cure our illness. As my stomach could not contain and digest the food we received, my sickness became even worse. With each day's passing I felt my body growing weaker, until I had to call a nurse every time I wanted to turn my thin, bony frame over, because of the pain I felt from lying too long on one side. I could never have managed doing this alone.

One day I asked a nurse to bring me a mirror, so I could take a look at my appearance. However, she refused to grant me this request. A while later, I saw an orderly cleaning the room, and as she bent over to clean underneath the beds, a mirror fell out of her pocket. I watched her, hoping that she would not notice what happened. Indeed, after her work was done, she left the room, unaware that she had left her mirror behind her.

After she had gone, I called a nurse and begged her to pick up "my" mirror, which had "fallen out of my hands." She complied, and handed me the mirror. I looked at my reflection, and nearly fainted. I saw my reflection not as I remembered myself, but as a caricature of the angel of death, similar to the skull and crossbones that usually adorn bottles of poison. The eyes bulged out of their sockets, the cheekbones protruded in a ghastly way, making the face as gaunt as a stick. This could not be me, I thought. I looked behind me to see whose reflection was in the mirror. But as I looked in the mirror, opening my mouth, closing it, touching my face with my hand, the image mimicked my movements exactly. There was no question that this was I, and this was the way I now appeared.

I wondered, "Oh, *Ribbono Shel Olam*, is it possible that I shall still continue to live and be healthy again? According to the laws of nature, it should be simply impossible. *Ribbono Shel Olam, shelach refuah sheleimah lecholei amecha.* Please send a complete recovery to those of Your nation who are ill."

Thus immersed in my prayer, I became drowsy and fell asleep, clutching the mirror in my hands.

As good as the service was in the hospital, the doctors did not seem to have any idea of the proper treatment for us, causing us, instead, to become sicker. All patients received the same foods – the fatty soups, the fresh bread – regardless of the special dietary needs of the dysentery cases. My own sickness grew worse daily. None of the food I ate could be contained in my stomach. As I grew weaker and weaker, I became more and more helpless, until I was barely able to move a limb.

One day a commotion erupted suddenly in our wing. I soon found out that a patient in our wing had died, and almost at once, all the Jewish patients began to shout that the Germans were poisoning them. Amid the pandemonium of shrieking and screaming, people flew into a panic from fear of becoming the next victim.

Soon American and Russian doctors and nurses arrived in order to sift through the mess to determine what in fact had happened, and what should be done next. The German doctors and nurses suddenly became most friendly and cooperative with their American and Russian colleagues.

After a while they determined that the sickest among us should be transported to Landsberg, where the Americans had set up a DP (displaced persons) camp and had opened up a hospital. They selected five of the most critically ill patients, in order to avoid the outbreak of another riot, which would surely have erupted if another patient were to die.

I was one of the five chosen patients. Now I had to be separated from my friend Yossel Carmel, and be transported in an ambulance to Landsberg. We got no food on that day. Furthermore, the ambulance, which was supposed to arrive at 10 a.m., ended up arriving at 2 o'clock in the afternoon. But this was only the beginning of our ordeal.

The trip itself took about a half-hour. I was the only one lying on a stretcher, while the four others were dressed and sat on a bench inside the ambulance. When we finally arrived at the DP camp in Landsberg, we saw that the camp was comprised of military buildings that had been inhabited by German soldiers. The ambulance parked in front of one of the barracks that had been converted into a hospital for Jews who had been liberated from the camps. There it remained, with us inside it, the driver having abandoned us, while half an hour passed, then an hour, then two. We waited and watched as hospital workers wandered about inside and outside of the building, yet everyone seemed to be ignoring us. Finally, we deduced that we had been forgotten, and we began to shout, for none of us was able to go out of the vehicle to find out what was going on. After ten minutes of yelling, some people who were in charge came out of the building and explained to us that there was no place for us yet inside the hospital. At the moment they were cleaning out the fourth floor and readying it for dysentery patients and others afflicted with contagious diseases. We would just have to be patient, and, as soon as they could, they would return to bring us into our ward. We had to wait an additional hour and a half until they came back to escort the sick into the building.

The four others who were dressed were taken in first, each with two orderlies to help him in and support him while he was being admitted. I was left alone, lying on the stretcher, unable to get up, while minutes turned into an hour, the sun gradually making its way below the horizon.

Suddenly I was terrified that I would be left lying there the entire night, alone in the ambulance. I began to scream and shout and bang on the metal walls of the vehicle. In a little while, two orderlies carrying a stretcher arrived, removed me from the ambulance, and brought me into the hospital. However, my troubles were far from over.

I was left lying on the stretcher in the entranceway near the stairs, and was told that I would soon be carried up to the fourth floor. Slightly reassured, I lay there helplessly until another two hours had elapsed. By this time a stillness had pervaded the building. Not a soul was in sight. Nighttime had arrived, and I realized that I had been forgotten, or had intentionally been left to lie there through the night.

Once again, I resorted to the only device that I had at my disposal, and which had already proved to be effective. I began to shout at the top of my lungs. Within minutes, two workers came and brought me upstairs, still lying on the stretcher, to the fourth floor.

Because it had only recently been converted into a hospital, there was a real lack of organization in the facility. The administration was unstructured and the employees were not yet experienced in hospital service.

As the room I was deposited in had no electricity, I could barely make out my new surroundings. There were nine beds, one of them still empty, with no linen on it – a bare mattress. The orderlies placed me on the hard floor of the dark room and left, supposedly to bring me bedsheets and blankets. To my chagrin, they did not return.

There on the floor I lay, cold, helpless, unable to move – and I began to cry. The other patients pitied me in my sorrowful predicament, but they frankly told me that no one would arrive during the night – no doctor, no nurse, no caregiver. I felt totally abandoned.

But after a few minutes, a young man sat up in his bed and called his neighbor. They both got up and lifted me off the floor, putting me into the young man's bed. He said that for one night we could manage to both sleep in the narrow cot. I did not know how to thank him.

However, despite his supreme kindness, I still felt rather distressed. I was not receiving the care that I needed. There was no one to give me medicine or even tea, or to bring me a bedpan, as there had been in Kloster Lechfeld. What could I do if nature compelled me to follow its bidding during the night? Since I could not move, this was a matter of great concern. However, fatigue overcame my worries, and I fell into a deep slumber.

Sure enough, during the night, I began to feel painful cramps in my stomach, signaling to me that I needed to relieve myself. My pains were compounded with my fearful feelings of anxiety that I would soil my rescuer's bed, an obnoxious way to repay him for his kindness. Everything was pitch black, but I remembered having noticed that in the middle of the room there was a big garbage can to be used as a portable toilet for the dysentery patients.

That very morning I had been unable to move at all from where I lay. However, necessity empowers a person to do the impossible. Mustering any remaining energy or strength that I had, I succeeded in getting up and out of bed, and then dragging myself over to the can. Afterwards, I barely managed to push myself back to where the bed was, but there was no way I could lift myself back onto the bed. Thus I fell asleep on the floor.

It was morning when I awoke. I looked around and saw the room I had entered last night in the dark, with nine beds, eight of which were occupied, one still empty, no nurse, no electricity, and no bell to summon any caregiver in case of need. The young man who had shared his bed with me the previous night now helped me up once again back into his bed. At this point I was half-frozen. The one remaining empty bed still had no linens or blankets. By 9 o'clock we were still waiting for a doctor to show up, or even someone to bring us some form of breakfast.

In order to pass the time, we each related to the others our wartime experiences. All of us were sick, depressed and left with no family or relatives. To make matters worse, we were all in this abandoned hospital room, nothing remotely like a place of healing.

It appeared as if we had once again been left to our own devices. Finally, at a little after 11 o'clock, an orderly came into the ward with our breakfast, which consisted of a piece of bread, black and sticky like tar, and a bit of hot, black coffee, really just colored water.

We asked the orderly when a doctor might be coming to examine us and suggested that perhaps we needed medicines for our ailments. No clear answer was given on either matter. Maybe in two, three days, no one could know for sure.

The entire hospital, if it could be called a hospital, appeared to be highly disorganized. No doctors or nurses were to be found; there were only a few workers who were helping to prepare the facility for future use.

At about 4 o'clock in the afternoon, we received dinner, which was a bit of rice, a soup resembling cream of wheat, and a boiled potato. Nothing more. Here there was no comparison to the special treatment we had received in the hospital in Kloster Lechfeld.

However, looking back now, it would seem that it was precisely the lack of food, and the fact that I was receiving no help in my unenviable predicament, that forced me to help myself, to sit up and turn over and move about as much as I could. That night the situation became even more desperate, as the orderlies decided to remove the "portable toilet" from the room. Their reasoning was that since not all of the patients had dysentery, its presence was not necessary, and therefore, we would have to use the bathroom in the corridor outside of our room, more than a few doors away.

I was terrified. What would I do if I could not make it to the bathroom? I knew from past experience that due to my sickness, I would need to use the facilities during the night. But how would I manage to reach the bathroom on time, if at all, in my state of extreme weakness? While I kept dreaming that I could have my own bed, my prayers remained unanswered, and the nightmare of having to soil my neighbor's bed loomed in front of me.

Yet when the *Ribbono Shel Olam* wants to help, He can have you do things that you were sure you could not do. In the middle of the night, while everyone else was asleep, I awoke with the sensation that I had fully expected, that my intestines were strongly urging my body to relieve itself. I sat up, and set my feet down next to the bed. My head was spinning, but I knew that I had to try to support myself on my legs. Holding on to the bedpost with my arms' every strength, I moved to the next bed, and then the next, until I reached the last bed in the row, the last haven in my treacherous journey. Now I groped for the wall, and holding onto it for dear life, I inched my way toward the washroom, shuffling my feet carefully until I reached my destination.

Then I had to face the challenge of the same journey back to bed. It took a very long time, but somehow I managed to throw myself onto the bed again, and for several minutes I just lay there gratefully trying to catch my breath.

With the A-mighty's help, I had succeeded in traveling to and from the bathroom, which I had thought was an impossible feat. This gave me the courage to attempt the procedure again, with more confidence. Once I started to accomplish more, I began to feel that I was once again a human being, with my strength returning, slowly but surely.

Thus you can see the hand of the A-mighty in everything. A person alone often does not know what his potential is, or what he can achieve in the face of the seemingly insurmountable. With sheer will and determination alone, one can accomplish what appears to be impossible. Not only in physical matters, but also in the spiritual does this hold true, for if someone wants to attain a high spiritual goal, no matter how he has failed in the past, then the *Ribbono Shel Olam* helps him, and he finds that he can realize his desires. If one's will is the will of G-d, nothing is impossible.

Chapter 28

After the Liberation: Part One

When my dysentery had passed and I no longer suffered from diarrhea, I finally got my own bed with sheets and blankets. On our fifth day in the hospital, the doctor finally came, and put me on a strict diet of sweet rice and sweet cream of wheat. Now I complained to him that I felt as if there were a heavy object in my stomach, as if the raw potatoes I had eaten in the last few days before the liberation were still there, undigested.

The "hospital" we were in had just been converted from a barracks for German soldiers in order to house the sick survivors. It was not equipped with facilities or instruments for medical exams; there were no laboratories, no x-ray machines, nor even any qualified medical staff.

Now, despite the fact that I had suffered hunger and deprivation for over five years, and was only skin and bones, weighing only about thirty-five kilograms, I had no appetite for my daily food. I constantly felt nauseated, and feared that any food I ate would come out of the same place that it went in.

I spent most of my days lying in bed, having difficulty getting up and down. I was getting bored of just staring at the ceiling, when I noticed one of my neighbors handling an army periscope which he had found in one of the other rooms. I begged him to let me use it for a little while. As my bed was near the windows, I could, while lying in bed, put the viewer through the window and look down at the street below. I could see people walking in the street, mostly young men and women, Jews who had survived the concentration camps and had ended up in Landsberg, an American DP camp. It was rare to find an elderly person, for most had been sent to the gas chambers.

As I started to feel a little stronger, and could already walk without help, or without holding on to the wall, I began to move about a little, making new friends or looking out the window.

Once I witnessed a scene in the street below that was all too common in those days. I saw people walking, and then suddenly one survivor was shouting, "Here is a kapo!" People rushed over from all sides and began to beat up the man with fists, shoes and stones. As he fell, they kicked him until he could no longer scream. He was then taken away to the hospital. With their suffering still fresh in their memories, the survivors, who had recognized a former enemy, a kapo who had beaten and tortured many of them, could not help but release their pent-up anger and succumb to the temptation of meting out their own justice.

Most of the day I stayed in bed. Stairs were still too hard for me to handle, as my knees could not hold the weight of my meager frame.

One day we received a parcel from the Red Cross, containing chocolates, cigarettes, sardines and candies. A friend asked me why I did not seem very happy with the package, so I told him,

"I can't look at any sweets. The sweet rice and cream of wheat that they feed me here make me sick. Cigarettes are of no use to me, so there really is nothing in here for me."

Later in the afternoon, my friend returned to me with the suggestion that we trade some of the chocolate and cigarettes for other food. Finally we made a deal, and we received a salami and canned fat for our cigarettes. I made myself a sandwich with the forbidden food, and then ate with such an enthusiasm that when I finished I was totally exhausted and fell into a deep sleep.

About two hours later, I woke up with terrible cramps. I ran to the bathroom, and it seemed as if the dysentery had returned with a vengeance. After fifteen minutes I returned to bed to rest, but five minutes later I had to go back to the toilet. After repeating this pattern many times, I decided not to return to my bed. I sat on that toilet for a good few hours, as the cramps increased and then subsided. Finally, at about 2 o'clock in the morning, I went back to bed and managed to fall asleep.

When I awoke it was already 11 o'clock in the morning. The sun shone brightly through the window. I felt weak and fatigued, as if I had fought a heavy battle the night before. But strangely enough, I felt that for the first time my stomach was empty, freed by last night's escapade from those raw potatoes that had allegedly been lying there until this morning. I now made up my mind to start a new diet as I saw fit. I put some of the claylike bread on the windowsill so that it would dry out in the sun and become like toast. From this I ate only one slice, and also drank some hot water. I gave my daily dose of sweet rice to my neighbors. The next day I added another slice of bread to my diet. I was actually starting to feel hungry, longing for food for the first time during my stay in the "hospital." Every day I started to eat more of my "toast," and every day I became more famished than I was the day before. Craving solid food, I traded all my extras — such as butter, eggs, jam and cheese — for bread, which at least filled up my stomach more than the little supplements. Despite my wheeling and dealing, my hunger pangs did not let up.

One day, a young man came into our room and asked for Cohen. After being shown to my bed, he approached me with a jar of richly mixed fresh cottage cheese and sour cream. He also handed me a letter from my friend Yossel Karmel and others who were still staying with the farmers with whom the Americans had assigned them to live on the day of our liberation. They had been searching for my whereabouts until they found out that I was in the DP camp hospital in Landsberg. Now they were asking how I was doing, and if there was anything they could do to help. Sure, I thought, they can help me by getting me out of this camp.

I greedily gulped down their gift of the cheese mixture, and then I wrote them a letter, as follows:

"If you do not sometime in the near future take me out of this place where I am starving, you will have me on your conscience for the rest of your life."

The man looked at me sympathetically as he promised that he would deliver the letter to my friends as soon as possible. That night I dreamed that I saw my comrades, especially my friend and mentor, Yossel Karmel, whom I had not seen for a long time, and that I had enough food to eat to my satisfaction.

The very next morning, three of my friends came to visit me. They told me that it was not so easy to enter the camp, and it would be much harder for me to leave the hospital, the reason being that there were patients in the hospital with contagious diseases, and the American governor had declared the entire area of the DP camp off limits to outsiders. We were quarantined for twenty-one days. My friends, though, had received a special permit from the administration to visit close relatives. They came with a well-designed scheme. One of the three was to exit the camp by climbing over the wall, allowing for one extra person to go out with the remaining two, legally, with the permit, through the gate. I dressed quickly in the one pair of pants, shirt and shoes I had, given to me by the farmer. My two friends helped me walk down the stairs, and then, as I could hardly walk normally, we pretended that we were taking a leisurely walk, for pleasure, in slow motion.

Soon we came to the camp gate. The American guard stationed there stopped us, and questioned the permit that my friends had obtained. One of them had to go back to the command office to straighten out the difficulty. While we were being detained, I began to feel tense and uneasy, fearing that I would not be able to leave the DP camp. After about half an hour, my friend returned with the corrected document, and we walked away from the gate. I dared not look behind me as we strolled along, nonchalantly. Soon we turned into a side street where another friend was already waiting with a horse and buggy. I was lifted onto a seat, and speedily we took off. My friends had brought with them a sponge cake and milk, which I devoured on the way to the farm.

About a half-hour later, we arrived at the farm at which my friends had arranged for me to stay, in their neighborhood. At this time, the German farmers were still afraid of the American army that was then in charge of the occupation. These were the soldiers who had seen with their own eyes the horrors of the Holocaust and the concentration camps, the mounds of dead skeletons, and the near dead whom they had just liberated. The German people were afraid that with the help of the Americans, we would try to take revenge for all the atrocities that had been done to us. That is why they were very friendly to us. This farmer provided me with a private room, a soft, clean bed, and the most important item for me: food. At night before I went to sleep I received cake and milk. In the morning there was a breakfast of bread and butter, cottage cheese, eggs, coffee and cream. Then at 10 o'clock I had a snack of cake, cottage cheese and sour cream. Afterwards, I went to visit my friends and say my prayers. As they were already satiated with food, having been at the farm for a few weeks, one of them said to me, "I have a cake in my room. You go eat it."

In a matter of minutes I finished the entire cake. Then another friend offered me a piece of chicken, which I promptly gorged down. For lunch I went back to my farmer, or rather, for "dinner," as the middle meal of the day — the main one — is called in Europe. Later, I went back to my friends and ate more food, and then I had supper. After staying at the farm for three weeks, I gained about fifteen kilograms or more. The flesh returned to my bones, but I was still a long way from having regained my strength. I still had to walk slowly, and I had difficulty climbing and going down stairs. I had to rest a lot as I tired easily and often.

Meanwhile the American government replaced the Seventh Army, that had fought in all the battles, with an occupation army that had to cooperate with the German civilian administration. One day we heard a rumor that the farmers had complained to the military governor that they did not feel it was their obligation to feed the survivors. We were to be sent to the Landsberg DP camp, with all the other survivors from the neighborhood camps. This relocation would take place the following afternoon. But I told my friend Yossel Carmel that I would definitely not go to any camp, for I had had enough of camp life already. So the next day we put our scanty belongings in a small briefcase and set out on foot to the highway that overlooked the farms, and waited there to see what would happen.

We waited for maybe an hour, and sure enough some military trucks arrived. Out jumped some American soldiers with machine-guns in hand, who started to round up the survivors and push them up onto the trucks. Happy that we had left earlier, on our own, we began to walk away along the highway. When we reached a point where the farmers could not see us, we stuck out our thumbs in order to try to hitchhike to any other place. After a while a jeep stopped, and the driver, an American soldier, asked us where we wanted to go. We answered that we would go wherever he was going, so he shouldn't have to go out of his way. He said that he was going to the city of Augsburg. We did not know the city, nor anyone living there, but we told him that that was exactly where we wanted to go. After all, our main goal was to leave the farm and not end up in a DP camp. We arrived in Augsburg after about an hour of driving. We thanked our benefactor and then started to walk the streets, worrying about finding a place where we could sleep that night.

As we walked down a street, looking at the buildings, I was awe struck at the sight of a building that looked like a synagogue. Holding my breath, I looked more attentively, making out a big Star of David on the front. I was shocked to find in a German city a synagogue that had not been destroyed by the Nazis. Was it real, or just a mirage? Then I looked further and spotted on the next building a sign that was barely legible. We managed to make out the words, "Juedische Kultus Gemeinde," meaning Jewish Confederation Building. Thinking that perhaps we could sleep there overnight, we knocked on the door, our hearts beating. Out came a young man with a little beard who looked very Jewish. Timidly, we asked him if we might possibly sleep somewhere in the building. Grinning, he said, "Come in and join our group and everything will be taken care of for you." Inside we saw that there were more survivors like us there. We were served supper, and despite the fact that the food did not compare to what we had had at the farm, we were extremely happy to be among our own, religious Jews, and to be part of a group of people who cared about each other. We slept in a room with several young men, and exchanged stories of our adventures with each other.

The next morning when we awoke, we went to the synagogue for our morning prayers. The man who welcomed us inside was Rabbi Abraham David Horowitz, also a survivor, later the Chief Rabbi of Strasbourg, France, and today living in Jerusalem, Israel, a member of the *Badatz*, or rabbinical court. He was older than all of us and became the leader of our group; also, he knew how to organize things. One of our group was a *shochet,* a ritual slaughterer of cattle. Every week he would slaughter a calf for us at a local butcher. The meat would be stamped, and put away in a separate place. Another one of our group was a cook, and from this time on we started to eat only kosher food. The rabbi gave us lectures daily in Talmud and *halachah* (Jewish laws). We also did some studying on our own. Slowly we started to remember the subject matter that we had studied before the war, when our learning had been brutally interrupted by the German occupation and our slave work. Now my strength improved daily, and I began to feel much better both physically and mentally.

Every Friday night was a memorable event. We lit the Sabbath candles and recited the evening prayers in the synagogue. Afterwards, we made *Kiddush* (benediction over wine), washed for *challah*, and sat down to an enjoyable meal at which we sang Sabbath songs and listened to the rabbi speak on many different subjects. Very often he would be overcome with emotion and start to cry, and we cried with him as we remembered our parents, and brothers and sisters who had perished, and the murdered children of those of us who had been married before the war. I was thankful that we were free people, not having to live in a DP camp, and not having to be subject to the orders of the camp administration, or any other overseers.

On the Sabbath morning we returned to the synagogue for our morning prayers. Then truckloads of American Jewish military personnel arrived in the synagogue for services, led by the army chaplain, who also preached to the soldiers. After the sermon, they all returned to their quarters, except for one soldier who stayed behind. When we asked him why he had not left with the others, he replied that he was an observant Jew, and had walked all the way from his base, a trip that took about four hours. He planned to stay until dark and then return to his station. Naturally we invited him to join us at our Sabbath table. As he spoke German, we could converse with him. He told us that his name was Henry P. Cohen, he lived in Baltimore, in the United States, and his family had been Sabbath observant for generations.

1945, Augsburg, Germany. Henry Cohen of Baltimore is in center, and Israel Cohen (wearing German military cap) is at right.

Summer 1945, Augsburg, Germany —
Israel Cohen

The next day he came to us in his jeep and brought us many things that we needed. I received from him his army sweater and some underwear. He took pictures of us, and, as postal service had not yet been restored in Germany at that time, he took letters from members of our group, who had relatives in the U.S., to send by military mail.

So we passed a very satisfactory three months. Unfortunately, I became sick again and had to leave Augsburg for a few weeks to go to a hospital in St. Ottilien. But I returned again to our group in Augsburg when I recovered.

Every day people came to the congregational office to register as members. Hardly any of them were full Jews. One who had only a Jewish father was only half-Jewish, by Hitler's standards. (According to Jewish law, he was not at all Jewish.) Another had a Jewish grandmother, so he was a quarter-Jew. Each one had a different background. But the congregation grew with all these supposedly Jewish members, who did not know much about Judaism and were not at all observant. Our religious group became a minority, and a thorn in their eyes.

One day the chaplain had to go to another city, so he asked our rabbi to give a sermon to his army men. Since he could not speak English, the rabbi spoke in German, which they could hardly understand. Among other things, he said, "In Hungary, Poland and most of Eastern Europe, the majority of Jews were strict in their religious observance, and did not try to hide or deny their Jewishness. They remained a distinct group of people, sincere in their religious beliefs. On the other hand, in Germany, most of the Jews became assimilated, intermarried, and were more patriotic than the Germans themselves. These assimilated German Jews who intermarried and had German wives and children thought that they would be safe, as the Germans wouldn't harm their own grandchildren. And yet this was the place where Hitler rose to power, and this is where the Holocaust started, which almost annihilated all of European Jewry. Any German with the slightest trace of Jewish ancestry, even from many generations before him, was sent to Auschwitz and exterminated together with all the true Jews.

"It is clear then that the Jews must keep their distance from and remain different from the gentiles. We must hold on to our religion, and not let go of it."

Present at the sermon were many of the old "half-Jews" and "quarter-Jews" who had registered themselves as members of the Jewish congregation in order to regain the property of the synagogue from the government, and to benefit from the good will of the American military. The following week, we received a letter from the American authority stating that the majority of the "Jewish" congregation did not want an Orthodox rabbi, but would prefer a Reform one instead. In other words, we were not welcome there, and were advised that by a certain date we had to leave the premises and move elsewhere. That was the end of our Talmudical yeshivah in Augsburg.

In a way we were almost happy to be leaving Augsburg. Here we were just thirty to forty young Jewish men in a sea of Germans. The high holidays were approaching, and we were starting to feel that we needed a larger Jewish environment.

The DP camp in Landsberg was developing into a young, vibrant and dynamic Jewish community. It was no longer the closed-off camp that it had been when I was there in the hospital. Rapid growth was apparent as the survivors began to get back on their feet. Schools and even a yeshivah were started, many Jewish organizations were formed, and Jewish activities flourished. Since we had many friends living there, we decided to move to Landsberg, in order to stay together. Our rabbi arranged for us to take over a house outside the camp as a Talmudical yeshivah, where we would continue our studies. It was a large house, quite comfortable, and soon we were joined by more students and rabbis.

When the high holidays arrived, it was a very emotional time for everyone. We had to face the stark realization that we were alone, having lost our families. Some of us remembered how wives and children, siblings and parents, were murdered before our very eyes. On Rosh Hashanah, before the blowing of the shofar, the rabbi, Reb Hillel Lichtenstein, the Krasner Rav, gave a very heartfelt, emotional speech, saying, "Why does it say in the Torah that G-d tested Abraham when he was about to sacrifice his son Isaac to the A-mighty? Was it not also a great test for Isaac to allow himself to be sacrificed? The answer is, that to give away one's own life takes courage for only a short time. But to sacrifice one's only son and then to have to go on to live a lonely life of pain and anguish, that takes much more strength and true faith in G-d."

Tears flowed freely, as people remembered their own children who had perished together with their families, while they survived with great suffering and grief in their hearts. But we knew that no matter how bitter and distressing the feelings were, life had to go on.

Immediately after the holidays, we started to look for our relatives who might have survived the war, and were now possibly in different DP camps. We heard that many Jewish women had survived Bergen-Belsen, an infamous concentration camp on the north side of Germany. We set out to travel to this camp from Bavaria, where we were, on the south side of Germany.

At this time travel was not easy, for the railroad bridges were in a sad state of disrepair after having been bombed by the Allies, or by the retreating German army. Trains were scarce, and for each train that did arrive at the station, there were hundreds of people waiting on the platform. Order was nonexistent, and in order to get on, one had to push and push, through the door or through the window.

Fortunately, we managed to bulldoze our way into the train, but we got separated by a human wall. We were traveling at night, and we could neither see the names of the stations where we stopped, nor hear the conductor calling out the names. I knew that we would have to change trains in Kassel, which was about halfway to our destination, and I knew that we would be traveling all night, but I was not sure when exactly we were supposed to arrive there. At one of the stations, I heard someone calling out a name that sounded like Kassel, so, using all my energy and brute force, I pushed myself out of the train. Outside, and out of breath, I realized that I was one station short of Kassel. Here I was, alone, in the middle of the night, in a strange German city, with no money and no friends. I was desperate. I tried with all my might to push myself back onto the train, but there was no way to go in, as people were hanging out of the doors and windows. After a few torturous minutes passed, the train slowly started to move. Helplessly, I watched the cars passing by, one after the other, until at the end I saw the caboose, a freight car that was hitched to the rear of the train for the use of trainmen and train mechanics. At the tail end of this car there was a ladder attached, and, while the train was moving, I grabbed for the ladder and held on tightly, so that I would be able to join my friends in Kassel.

It was already the end of October and the night was a cold one. My hands started to become numb and I was afraid that I would not be able to hold on. While clutching on with one hand, I pulled out my belt with the other and affixed myself to the ladder. We were now approaching a skeleton of a bridge that had been bombed and then provisionally repaired just in order for the trains to pass. There was a terrifying drop of about a hundred feet to the river below. I felt dizzy, and nausea gripped me as the train very slowly inched its way over the bridge. The minutes seemed like hours, while I held on to the iron bars as tightly as I could, fighting my inherent fear of heights and the cold wind that froze my face and legs and entire body. Finally, after two hours of this nightmarish train ride, we came to a stop in Kassel, and I joined my friends who emerged from the train.

I made sure to make it onto the next train with my friends. They were somewhat stronger than I was, and they managed to push themselves in through the door. I succeeded in getting in with my head through the window. But even with my feet still hanging out, I was glad to know that I was not alone. Later I was pulled into the car in my entirety. We decided to get off at a city named Celle, which was very close to the DP Camp. The rabbi of the city, Rabbi Yisroel Moshe Olewski, was a friend of ours, and he would be most qualified to give us the advice and information we were sure to need.

The rabbi welcomed us with open arms. He told us how to get to the Bergen-Belsen camp, and where we could view the lists of all the survivors residing in the camp. He insisted that we stay with him over Shabbos, an invitation that we gladly accepted. We stayed with him for a few days, I myself being very glad for the rest after my ordeal during the train ride. Some of our group were longtime friends of Rabbi Olewski from before the war. My friend Yossel had been with him in the same yeshivah, the famous Yeshivas Chachmei Lublin. At that time, we were all single, most of us still teenagers, while others had lost their wives and children in the camps. After a very pleasant Shabbos, and a good rest, we left on the following day for the camp.

Chapter 29

After the Liberation: Part Two

I n the afternoon we arrived in Bergen-Belsen, a large camp full of people. Some of the people had been interned there, and some, like ourselves, came from other DP camps in order to look for lost relatives; some just wanted to be in a bigger camp, which was better organized than the smaller places. As we walked in the streets, looking at the faces, hoping to recognize a family member, or friend, or neighbor, I heard someone calling my name. He was a distant relative of mine from Lodz who had come from Poland where he had been liberated by the Russians. He said to me excitedly, "You know, I saw your sister Mirel in Lodz, and she is looking for you."

I became exhilarated with the knowledge that I was blessed with the good fortune of having a surviving sister, and that soon we would be reunited. Unfortunately, there was no communication between those in the American zone and those in countries under Russian control. I was extremely anxious to get back to Landsberg, and from there to find a way to get to Poland, ignoring the fact that I had no money or identity papers, but simply hoping that somehow, with G-d's help, I would make it. There was actually no way for the train conductors or inspectors to check if people had tickets or permits. What we needed was sheer perseverance and tenacity to push with all our might to get inside the trains.

I was impatient, but I had to wait until my friends were ready to go back to Landsberg. Although I wasn't feeling well and had a bad cold, I did not hesitate to return with our group. When we arrived back in Landsberg after another torturous journey, I fell ill with pneumonia, most likely a result of my ride on the ladder of the train on that frosty night. Since my body was still weak from the years of affliction, and medical care and drugs were not readily available, I took longer than the usual time to recover from my illness. When I finally felt better, I was so weak that there was no way I could undertake such a voyage by myself. At last, in January 1946, I decided to take my scanty belongings and set out for Lodz, Poland. My friends tried everything to discourage me from going ahead with my plans, pleading with me, begging me to stay, but my will to be reunited with my surviving sister outweighed all their logical talk.

My first goal was to cross over the border into Czechoslovakia, which was then under Russian occupation. I contacted some people who were smuggling American cigarettes and selling them to the Russians. They consented to allow me to cross over the border with them on the next Saturday night. Their plans were to leave Landsberg on Thursday morning, and stay with a friend in Regensburg, which is close to the Czech border. We would stay there over the Sabbath and then on Saturday night we would take a train to a station that was right next to the border, and from there we would walk over the border to Czechoslovakia. Then we would stay overnight at the house of another of their friends, and from there, the next day, I would take a train to Prague, and then another train to Lodz.

Ignoring my friends' protests, I packed all my "belongings" in a briefcase and set out for the train station. Just as I was about to get onto the train, I noticed someone running towards me. I recognized him as a new arrival in Landsberg, Shmuel Charash, who was obviously playing the role of the wandering Jew, as many survivors were wont to do. When he reached me, he told me grimly that it was true that my sister was in Lodz after her liberation by the Russian army early in March. She had come to Lodz in search of surviving family members. Then, in July or thereabouts, she was murdered by Polish anti-Semites, who were resentful of any Jew coming back alive. Even before the war they had wanted to get rid of the Jews. Now they were afraid that the Jews would try to reclaim their property that they, the Polish, had appropriated, and were unwilling to give up to the rightful owners. At any given opportunity, they murdered Jews who returned to Poland. One of their victims was my sister. Now, he said, my proposed adventure of going to Poland in search of my sister was both dangerous and futile. At first I was numb with shock from hearing this incredible story. Then I became very upset, for I began to suspect that my friends were scheming to make me change my mind about going to Poland, but I found it hard to believe that our group members who always cared for each other would devise such a cruel plan to have me return to them. So I told him firmly that I made my decision, and I was not going to change my mind under any circumstances. I was not about to leave the train and return to Landsberg. Shmuel left me then, but fifteen minutes later, he came back with a small suitcase, and said, "I am not letting you go alone. If you go, then I am coming with you." I felt powerless to argue with my new friend, and so we left together for Regensburg.

We spent our Shabbos there at the home of Mr. Mottel Finkelstein, a Polish Jew, a survivor, who had settled in Regensburg and started a business there. Although he made us feel at home and we spent a pleasant Shabbos in his house, I could not remove from my mind what Shmuel had told me about my sister. I could not believe that it was true. My relative had told me explicitly that he had seen my sister in Lodz. He would surely have known if something had happened to her. Doubts and worries persisted in my mind and tormented me whenever I had a free moment. In the end, I just could not believe what I had been told about my sister, and I maintained my resolve to continue with my travels. That Saturday night, we set out with our two guides to cross over the Czech border.

Anyone who has ever crossed over the border into another country illegally knows the dangers involved. At the last train station where we disembarked, we had to be extremely careful and try to look relaxed and natural, so as not to arouse the suspicion of the special police and border guards stationed there. The border we were about to traverse was not only a border between two countries, but also a border between two different occupation-army zones. We were now in the American zone of occupation; our destination was Chep, a city on the border of Czechoslovakia which was under the jurisdiction of Communist Russia. To make matters worse, we had no official identification papers.

As we walked out of the German village, our guides told us to keep our distance from them so as not to be seen as a group. The ground was covered with snow and that made us more visible, in the darkness of the night. Suddenly, the entire area was illuminated with floodlights moving back and forth and in circles. Our guides hit the ground, and we followed suit, until the lights went out and we were once again enveloped in darkness.

All at once, we heard from the distance the noise of dogs barking. We could make out from afar the silhouettes of German border guards on patrol. We did not dare move. Fortunately, they did not notice us. We now entered a forest where we began to feel a little more secure. As we silently moved between the trees, the guides suddenly stopped, and without uttering a word, indicated to us a trip wire near the ground at about ankle height. We proceeded carefully, lifting our feet to avoid touching the wire that would have surely sounded an alarm at the border and resulted in a subsequent search. After treading carefully on the snowy ground, we were again forewarned of another trip wire, this time at chest level. We went under it, making sure not to touch it.

At the end of the forest, we came upon a little river that we had to cross. The water was frozen, but the ice was very thin in places, and our feet broke through into muddy water. It was scary, to say the least. Then finally we reached another small forest, and at the end we could see the tracks of the railroad that was the first outpost and official border of the Czech Republic and their Russian masters.

As we stood between the trees at the edge of the forest, our guides told us that they would now cross over the rails, but we should still wait at least a half-hour to make sure that they would have safely disposed of their merchandise by that time. They were to drop off their goods with their partners and friends who lived not far from the railroad, and these men would take the cigarettes and sell them to Russian officers, in return for gold or jewels that they had taken from German houses. After waiting the half-hour, we were to cross over the rails ourselves and head for the city, take the first few blocks to the right, then make a left to the spot where they would meet us, so they could take us to the place where we would stay with them overnight. The next day we were to take the train to Prague, and from there to Poland.

We watched them as they crossed over the railroad. Then we heard loud voices in Czech shouting, "Stop! Raise your hands!"

In the darkness, we could make out a group of Czech policemen or soldiers leading them away, presumably to a police station.

We reckoned now that we were on our own. We didn't know their friends' address, and no one was going to wait for us. But we could not stay in the forest, for if a search were conducted, we would surely be discovered. After much deliberation, we decided to cross over the border and head for the railway station that we could see down the tracks, far away, in the direction of the city. There we would stay overnight, and then take the next train to Prague.

Our hearts pounding, we started to walk towards the tracks. Fortunately, we were not noticed as we ventured across the border and then proceeded towards the city.

The streets were empty. There was no person in sight. After walking for a few blocks, and then turning towards the train station, we bumped into a Russian military patrol unit.

"Hey! Where are you going now? Don't you know that there is a curfew here every night at 9 o'clock?"

We tried to explain that we were Jews originally from Poland and trying to go back there. Could they please just let us go to the train station nearby?

"No," they said, "you must come with us to the military post so that our captain can interrogate you and find out who you really are, and what should be done with you."

We found ourselves back at the railroad. The soldiers led us to a small building that was their post. The room was full of other soldiers talking loudly, eating and drinking. We were told to wait in a corner, while the soldiers who had brought us in went to get the captain.

After a while, they returned and said to us, "Sorry, fellows, the captain has left for the night. You will have to stay here until the morning when the captain will be back."

Bad luck, we thought, after we had already rejoiced in having crossed the border without a mishap.

We were about to resign ourselves to having to stay in the army depot overnight, when I had an idea. I remembered that my father had told me stories of how he had been in danger several times, and had managed to bribe his way out. Russians and Poles, he said, were always eager to accept bribes. We had with us about twenty packages of American cigarettes that we had hidden under our shirts. We had no money, certainly not Czech money, so we figured that cigarettes might be a good substitute for cash.

I approached a soldier who seemed to be friendly, and asked him if he smoked.

"Sure," he answered, "whenever I can get some cigarettes."

I took out a package of cigarettes, handed it to him, and said, "Americanskie," showing him the picture on the package. His eyes lit up as he took the cigarettes, and then he motioned to his friend standing near him, saying, "For him too." My friend took out a package and handed it to his friend.

Then the soldier said, "I will take you outside to the street, and you can go to the train station. We know that you have illegally crossed the German border to Czechoslovakia. But if you get caught by another patrol, tell them that you want to go to Germany, so that you will be allowed to go to the train station."

We thanked him, and soon thereafter we arrived at the train station without a hitch.

The part of Czechoslovakia that we were in, near the German border, had been called Sudetenland before World War Two, and had been inhabited by ethnic Germans. This gave Hitler his excuse to annex this region to the Third Reich, and then take over the whole country. Once the Germans lost the war, the Czechoslovakian government decided to expel all the ethnic Germans and send them back to Germany. Thus, the train station, when we arrived there, was full of German men, women and children, with their belongings packed in bags, sleeping on the benches and even on the floor.

We proceeded to the stationmaster's office, and asked at what time the train for Prague was due to depart. He told us it was scheduled for 4 o'clock the next afternoon. We were in a state of shock. We had no idea where we would stay and sleep overnight, for here there was certainly no room for us. Besides, we were repelled by the thought of having to stay all night with the Germans.

My friend said that he needed to go outside for a few minutes and think over what we should do. I was afraid that he might be caught by a patrol guard for violating the curfew. However, he soon returned and said to me, "Let's get out of here. With G-d's help, we'll find a place to stay."

We picked a building at random, and my friend Shmuel pulled a wire which activated a bell in one of the apartments. A boy of about 13 came down the stairs and opened the door for us.

"What do you want?" he asked.

Shmuel pulled out a flashlight from his pocket, shoved it in the boy's face, and said in German, "You were a member of the Hitler youth."

The boy trembled, and said, "We were forced to do it."

"All right, then. Take us to your apartment," Shmuel replied.

A middle-aged woman opened the door. We entered without any hesitation.

"Where is your husband?" my friend asked.

She replied, "He was in the German army and is probably a prisoner of war."

He took out a little notebook, and looked inside as if he were examining an official record. Then he looked up at her and said, point blank, "Your husband was serving in the SS."

The woman turned pale, and in a shaky voice asserted that he was only in the Waffen SS (the fighting SS army), not the real SS (Himmler's elite storm-troopers).

We ignored her, and began to look around the apartment for a room suitable for us to sleep in. We found a bedroom with two beds in it and a key in the door.

My friend said in broken German, "We are intelligence men, we are here on a secret mission, and we need to stay here overnight, in this room. Please make the beds for us now, and we will leave in the morning."

The woman protested that this was her children's room, and where were they to sleep?

"No problem," Shmuel snapped back. "For one night they can sleep with you."

When the beds were made, we entered the room, locked the door and immediately went to lie down. It was fascinating to us how the snow-white sheets turned a murky brown as we lay down in bed, our feet still soiled from the muddy river. However, we remained unperturbed, and quickly feel into a deep sleep.

In the morning the woman offered to make coffee for us, but we thanked her and said we had to leave right away for an important meeting.

As we walked the streets of the city, we realized that we had not a penny to our name. We returned to the train station that was empty at that time, and asked how much a ticket to Prague would cost. We found out it was about 180 crowns. We passed some stores, but were afraid to go into any of the big stores to sell our cigarettes, as they might call the police if they suspected us of smuggling. Then we noticed a small shoe-repair shop, so we went in and inquired about shoes.

Shortly after, seeing that the shopkeeper seemed friendly, we changed the topic of conversation to cigarettes, asking the owner if he would be interested in buying some American ones. We sold him half the packages we had in our possession, and now we had money to pay our train fare to Prague.

We traveled all night, sleeping only a little bit, and the next morning we arrived in Prague. Immediately we inquired about the train to Lodz, only to discover that we did not have enough money to buy our tickets. All we could think of doing was to go out in the street and look at all the people in the hope that we could maybe find a Jew who would help us. Prague was a beautiful city and the people seemed friendly, but I was very anxious to get to Lodz as soon as possible to find out about my sister. We decided to go to the Polish consulate, and there we were told that the Polish government had set up a mission in Prague to help repatriate Polish citizens. So we went to the mission, and began to fill out some forms, all the while noticing in the eyes of the officials that we were not quite welcome to return to Poland. However, as it was under communist rule, officially anti-Semitism was banned, and we received our train tickets to Lodz, which we immediately made use of.

The train compartment in which we were seated was full of Poles. As long as we were in Czechoslovakian territory, everyone behaved correctly. As soon as the train rolled onto Polish soil, and many more Poles entered the train, which was now packed with people, the situation changed. We heard people talking derogatorily about Jews, in nasty tones. Now we remembered stories we had heard about Jews who had returned to Poland and were murdered on the trains or in the towns where they had previously lived. Frightened that we might be recognized as Jews, we pulled our caps down over our eyes, pretending to sleep. But we did not dare to sleep, and remained tense and on guard for the duration of this nightmarish trip. When we finally arrived in Lodz, we gratefully breathed a sigh of relief.

Kibbutz Poalei Agudah in Lodz, 1948.
Israel Cohen is in top row, third from left.

In Germany we had been told that there was a religious kibbutz in Lodz. As we were both natives of the city, we had no problem with the language or orientation. We simply felt intimidated by the looks of unspoken hatred of our Polish compatriots. In the kibbutz, which was called Poalei Agudah (Agudah workers; under communist rule, only workers could have a club or organization), we found many friends and were welcomed with open arms. We had no problem with food and lodging. The people of the kibbutz worked on different projects with the goal of immigrating to Palestine – as it was known then – but which we always referred to as Eretz Yisrael.

I began to ask people who had been there since after their liberation about my sister Mirel, but everyone seemed to avoid answering my questions directly. I found out her address and went to the apartment where she lived with a few friends. Identifying myself as Mirka's brother, I asked them where she was. They all seemed to have lost the power of language, looking down at the floor, avoiding looking me in the eye.

Finally, after I pleaded with them incessantly, they told me the bitter truth.

At around the end of June or the beginning of July, five girls, my sister among them, went to the cemetery to visit the burial site of their parents who had died in the ghetto, and to find a place to put up a tombstone. Before going off in different directions, they agreed to meet in a half-hour at the gate. They all met at the designated time and place, except for my sister. They waited for a while, and then, when she still did not show up, they began to look for her. When night began to fall, they decided to return home, thinking that perhaps she had gone on home by herself. But when they did not find her there, nor did she show up after another period of waiting, they started to worry. The following morning they went to the police station, and reported her as a missing person, and expressed their worry that perhaps something terrible had happened to her. The answer they received from the Polish police was, "What is your worry? So there will be one Jewess less in Poland."

Lodz, Poland, 1946. Funeral for three young men and one girl from a Kibbutz who were murdered by the Poles.

Unfortunately, this was the attitude of the majority of the Polish population. For example, when I boarded a streetcar, an old woman exclaimed, "Look! Another Jew returned. A great pity that Hitler didn't kill them all!"

Even though some people volunteered to search for my sister, they could not find her. Her friends thought that maybe she had escaped from Poland, as most Jews wanted to leave this hated country. It was two weeks later that her body was discovered under some bushes, identifiable only by her belt and some clothes.

Upon hearing this I was so shocked and dumbfounded that I almost collapsed. Mirka's friends gave me some water and made me sit down. I asked them if they had anything that belonged to her. They gave me two pages of poems that she had written in the camps (see appendix for their translation from Yiddish to English), and offered to show me her gravesite. I strongly felt the need to put up a tombstone for her, as well as for my father, who had starved to death in the ghetto in 1942. My friends in the kibbutz helped me find a tombstone maker and also helped in paying the fees, for I had no money. When the tombstones were erected, I became so depressed that I sat down on the ground in the cemetery, feeling almost suicidal. My whole world had collapsed; all my dreams for the future had been crushed. Here I had been so happy to find a sister who had survived hell, only to suddenly discover that she had been murdered by the Poles. Now it finally hit me – I was alone in the world. The idea that my mother had actually been sent to the gas chambers had never really sunk in, for I still wanted to believe that somehow she had survived, but then gradually I began to realize that any chance of her reappearance in my life was remote and farfetched. But here, after my liberation, I had first learned that my sister Mirel had survived, and then suddenly, another disaster came crashing down upon me – a tremendously fierce blow to take.

My friends went to search for me and found me at the gravesite. They had to literally drag me away and practically carry me back to the kibbutz. For some time afterward, they kept an eye on me and would not let me go out by myself. During this interval, I heard some more bad news. I met a girl, originally from Brezezin, who used to visit my grandfather when he was sick in the Lodz ghetto, and had helped take care of him and clean his apartment. She told me that she had been with my older sister, Gittel, in the same camp, and that Gittel had died in an epidemic in the winter of 1944.

⁕

I set my mind on the learning that I had always practiced, resuming the studying that had been brutally interrupted by the war, the ghetto and concentration camps. I engrossed myself in my Talmudic and other Jewish studies so that I would not have time to think about what happened to my sisters. And so, life went on.

Chapter 30

After the Liberation: Part Three

T he kibbutz I had joined was composed of people who had been liberated in Poland by the Russian army. There were also some people who had returned from exile in Russia. What they had in common was that they were all religious, and their parents had been members of Agudath Israel. However, as I mentioned before, since the Communists who ruled Poland did not allow the existence of any religious organization, the kibbutz was registered as Poalei Agudah, or Workers' Organization. All the members had one common goal. We all wanted to leave Poland as soon as possible and get by any means to Eretz Yisrael, then called Palestine. The problem was that the Russians had closed all the borders so that no one could leave the country. Therefore, legally, it was impossible for us to leave Poland as a group. We needed a way to get out in spite of the closed borders.

Mrs. Recha Sternbuch, a member of the Sternbuch family who, during the war years, had been very active in trying to save Jews from the Nazis, lived in Montreux, Switzerland. If I were to elaborate here on the heroics and benevolence of the noble Sternbuch family, I would have to add a few chapters to this book. There is, in fact, a book called "Heroine of Rescue," which is about Recha, the wife of Isaac Sternbuch. I had the privilege to write a chapter in that book about my own encounter with Recha. The Sternbuch families, especially Recha, worked tirelessly day and night during the Second World War rescuing Jews from the deathtrap of the Nazi regime. Recha's deeds and self-sacrifice were indeed outstanding. She was the contact between the Vaad Hatzalah of America — an American-Jewish organization formed to save Jews from the German occupation — and European Jewry. After the war, she put her efforts into extricating Jewish people from under the Communist rule in Eastern Europe and helping them to reach their longed-for destination, Eretz Yisrael, or Palestine, as it was called then. We were the beneficiaries of her courageous actions.

Mrs. Sternbuch conceived of a plan for us. In the concentration camps that the Germans had set up all over Poland there had been many people from all over Europe, brought in as slaves, prisoners and hostages. The Russian army, hot on the tracks of the retreating Germans, liberated many of the prisoners before they could be taken to Germany by the Germans on the run. Since not everyone could be repatriated to his country of origin right away, and many were too sick to travel, there were many displaced Europeans in Poland in February 1946, still in the process of repatriation. Mrs. Sternbuch concocted a daring scheme to extricate us from Poland by having us pose as foreign residents. Phony Greek identity cards were provided for us so that we could leave the country as Greek citizens who had been interned in Poland. As additional insurance, a little bribery money was added to supplement the efficacy of the identity cards.

One evening we all took separate routes to the train that would take us to Katowice, where more young people from Agudah kibbutzim would join us in our journey. We were advised to go to the station only about five minutes before the train would depart, so as not to arouse the suspicions of the Polish militia and Russian soldiers who were guarding the station. I personally had an unfortunate encounter with a militiaman, who wanted to take me to his army post because I had not registered for the army after my "repatriation." In desperation, I offered to give him a donation for the Red Cross, which was the standard way of bribing an official. Thank Heaven he accepted the money, and I ran to catch the train that had already started to move.

In Katowice, we spent a few days in the local kibbutz. It took a few days to assemble the young people from different cities and towns in Poland and ready them for the adventurous voyage out of Poland. Understandably, we were more than anxious to leave the country as soon as possible. We did not dare walk about in the streets for fear that the NKVD (Russian intelligence) and the Polish authorities would suspect what was going on. Finally, on Thursday night we boarded the international train to take us to Czechoslovakia.

Anxiously and tensely, we awaited the moment of truth when we would know if we would succeed in getting out of Poland, or if we would go to prison, or even get sent to Siberia. We felt somewhat secure in knowing that Mrs. Sternbuch was traveling with us. When the train finally stopped at the border, the Polish customs officers, emigration and army personnel mounted the train and entered our cars. They asked questions in Polish, but we pretended not to understand the language, and talked to them very quickly in Aramaic, such as we say in our daily prayers, "*Yekum purkon min shemaya ...*" After an agonizing hour, our train started to move again, and in a little while we could read Czech names at the stations that we passed. We all breathed sighs of relief, and since we were exhausted, fell asleep readily in our seats.

We arrived in Prague late Friday afternoon, at candlelighting time. The train conductors urged us to disembark, as the train was scheduled to continue on its run momentarily. We refused to get off, as it was already the Sabbath, and we could not move our belongings. The train authority officials were very polite, but they could not allow the train to stay in its place for twenty-five hours. Once again, Mrs. Sternbuch, who was traveling with us, came to the rescue. After she conferred with the stationmaster, our cars were disconnected from the train and pushed to a side railing until the Sabbath was over. Only then did we leave the train and board buses to take us to our destination.

We were then set up in a transit camp. Free to come and go as we pleased, we wandered the streets of Prague, marveling at the politeness of the people, who always greeted us nicely and with smiles, in sharp contrast to the Poles, whose blatant anti-Semitism was apparent wherever we went. For the first time we felt free and secure in the streets that were bright and clean. There were no hatred-filled looks directed at us as there had been in Lodz. We visited many historical places, such as the old Maharal synagogue, and the cemetery where many famous Jewish scholars were buried. As it was just a few weeks before Passover, my friend Shmuel Charash traveled to Bratislava, where there was a strictly religious congregation, and brought back with him a big bag of *shemurah* (watched) flour with which to bake matzos. We stayed in Prague for about six pleasant weeks, and then once again resumed our travels, this time to France. There was an Agudah kibbutz in

Hennoville, a city not far from Paris, which was set up as a transit point for people on their way to Israel. Here we were to stay until it would be our turn to travel to Marseilles, a port city in southern France, where we were to board a boat that would take us to Eretz Yisrael.

When we arrived in Hennoville, we were given our lodgings, and the following day began our training for agricultural work in the fields. However, my friend Shmuel Charash and I wanted to continue our studying and learning, which had been interrupted by the German occupation. We intended to study in Yeshivas Sfas Emes, which the Gerer Rebbe had established in Jerusalem, and to remain close to the Gerer Rebbe, who had been our spiritual leader since our youth, and that of our fathers and grandfathers. We approached Rabbi Binyamin Mintz, who was the head of the Agudah kibbutz movement, and told him of our problem. He understood our situation and told us, "I am also a Gerer chassid, and I can find a way to fulfill your wishes. You will be sent to Aix-les-Bains where there is a yeshivah, and you can study there until we get the authorization to make *aliyah* (travel to Israel). Then we will contact you and you will go with our group to Eretz Yisrael."

We arrived in Aix-les-Bains the day before Passover. We were welcomed with open arms by the *rosh yeshivah*, Rav Chaikin. Everyone else was happy with the flour that we had brought with us. Right away an outside oven was built, and we started to bake matzos. Much to our surprise, we met Mrs. Sternbuch there. She was about to return to Montreux, Switzerland, which is not far from Aix-les-Bains. We thanked her again for all that she had done for us, and we gave her some of the matzos that we had baked to take home for her family for the *seder*. We were looking forward to having a wonderful environment for our *seder* such as we had not had for six years, since the war had started in 1939.

On our train from Paris to Aix, there were also fifty Jewish children, ranging in age from 5 years to 17, who were on their way to an orphanage in Aix. They had also gotten out of Poland with the help of Mrs. Sternbuch, and they were the reason she was in Aix on the day before Passover. Most of these orphans were from different backgrounds. Some had lived with partisan groups that had hidden in the forests and fought the Germans. Some had been taken out of Polish monasteries, where they had been sent by Poles who had been entrusted with their care by Jewish parents who feared for their lives. There they were raised as Christians by the nuns. Some had been in communist boarding schools, undergoing indoctrination as communists. Some had parents who had returned from the Russian gulag, and wanted their children out from behind the iron curtain as soon as possible. All had been saved by members of a Jewish organization in Poland who risked their lives in order to save Jewish children and bring them to Israel to ensure the maintenance of their identity as Jews, their awareness of their roots, and their continuity as part of the Jewish nation.

The children were wild and unruly, dirty and infested with vermin. They were placed in a big house, once a nobleman's castle, in the city, which was to be their home. There was definitely a staff shortage; the only adult who had come with them was the cook. I pondered on how we could help them, wondering how we could enjoy our own Passover *seder*, when those precious Jewish souls, remnants of the million Jewish children killed by the Germans, would not have any *seder*, especially since many had never had the opportunity to celebrate one.

I discussed with my friends the possibility of volunteering to make a *seder* with the children. At first they were reluctant, understandably so, for, as refugees of the Holocaust, none of us had had a proper *seder* for many years. But I argued repeatedly about self-sacrifice, how we could help those unfortunate children, and what a difference our effort would make to them. My perseverance finally succeeded in winning them over, and we set off for the children's home to prepare for Passover evening.

To say that things went smoothly and that there were no difficulties would be misrepresenting the facts. There was no way that we could make the childeren sit in an orderly fashion at the table. They snatched at the food like vultures, stealing the matzos from the table and hoarding the soup they received in a container under the table and hiding the bowls, so that the cook complained that she was serving more bowls of soup than there were children and yet there were still those who did not receive any. Any bottle of wine that was left unattended at the table for more than a few seconds would vanish. These children were starving, had grown accustomed to scavenging for food for many years, and were still uncertain of what tomorrow would bring. But somehow we succeeded in maintaining a festive atmosphere, and most of them were very happy.

The next day my friend Shmuel Charash and I returned to the orphan home to bring the children to the synagogue morning services. We took with us as many as were willing to come. We kept our eyes on them so that they would remain quiet and not run around. The members of the congregation were astonished to see so many children. One elderly person inquired about them, and then asked why their pockets were all bulging. I called over one of the boys and asked him to show me what he had in his pockets. He took out a mishmash of bread and matzah and other edibles.

"Why do you need to carry all this food in your pockets when you know that there will be plenty more at home?" I asked him, puzzled.

He explained that for many years they had gone hungry. When finally, one day, they received some food, there was a

Delegation of Rabbis from Eretz Yisrael visiting Kibbutz Poalei Agudah in Hennoville, near Paris, March-April 1946: Rabbi Wohlgelerenter, Rabbi Gold, Rabbi S.Y. Rubinstein, Rabbi Herzog, Reb Binyamin Mintz, Rabbi Munk

long wait until they got food again. Consequently, they formed a habit of hiding the food that they received, and storing it for the days ahead when food would be sparse.

It broke my heart to see how these young children had suffered for so long. When we returned to the home, I assembled all the children and explained to them that those evil times had passed. From now on they need not worry about food, as they would never be hungry again. We spent the rest of the Passover holiday with the children, and, despite their misgivings and distrust of strangers, we finally succeeded in gaining their confidence. After all, we ourselves had been in the same boat, and we understood each other.

After Passover, a delegation of rabbis and representatives of religious organizations in Israel came to check up on the survivors in France. We had already made some headway with the children and some order had been established. We grew as dependent on the children as they were on us. We became like one big family, the orphans taking the places of the brothers and sisters and even children some of us had lost in the Holocaust. To them I was like a father, even though I was not much older than many of them. As there was a shortage of teachers and educators even in Israel, the visiting rabbis urged us to stay with the children and help guide them along the right path of Judaism. They said it would be a mitzvah, a good deed that did not come frequently, and was like saving fifty worlds, for safeguarding one person's return to the Torah way of life is akin to preserving many generations of Jews. We, however, contended that we wanted to further our own Talmudic education, for we had lost our best years of study during our ghetto and camp lives.

In the end, we agreed to stay with the children until we would all be able to legally enter Eretz Yisrael. (Since 1918, at the end of World War One, Palestine had been under the rule of the English, who, in order to please the Arabs, did not allow a large Jewish presence there.) Dr. Lebel was the administrator of all the refugee children in Aix, appointed by the Vaad Hatzalah, a religious organization in the United States that funded this project. The arrangement we made with him was as follows: We would stay and take care of the home completely, until we would bring the children with G-d's help to Eretz Yisrael. We did not want to get paid for our work with money, but we would eat the same food the children received, and get clothes from the Joint, another American organization which helped refugees. Our goal was still to join the Gerer Yeshivas Sfas Emes in Jerusalem. Meanwhile, we would stay here and care for the orphans, on the one condition that we were given complete control of the children's education, with no outside interference. We were infused with the ideal of turning all the children into Gerer chassidim. With great eagerness, our condition was agreed upon, and we were now in charge of the home.

Aix-les-Bains, Israel Cohen (top, center) teaching the children in his charges

Aix-les-Bains, 1946. Israel Cohen (r.) with Naftali Feigenbaum, who is now a rav in Kiryat Harim in Tel Aviv

The children performing a play written by Israel Cohen (about a German raid on a secret minyan)

Aix-les-Bains, 1946, Israel Cohen (top right) with his co-worker, Shmuel Charash

Aix-les-Bains, 1946; Israel Cohen's charges

Ours was not an easy job. We had no medical help and had to apply ointment ourselves on the bodies of the children who had boils – a nearly impossible task, for they refused to be treated as the ointment caused their wounds to sting. Very often we would have to wake them up at midnight, when they were half asleep, and put them in a tub with hot water, wash them, and administer the ointment. Then there were the children who were infested with lice. It was with great difficulty that we managed to persuade them to part with their dirty verminous clothing, or to take a shower. We had to be nurses, mechanics, teachers and peacemakers when there were disturbances. After about four weeks, we noticed a remarkable improvement in their attitude and behavior. Some of them were still wild and unruly, but we could overlook their minor aberrations from decorum for the sake of education and cooperation.

Without any exception, each and every child received our utmost dedication. There was one 12-year-old boy who was very hostile to some of the other children. His temper was such that when he quarreled with another boy, he could lift up a chair and hit his adversary over the head. He was also constantly clashing with the cook, stealing food from the kitchen and continuously arguing with her; he was the strongest defender of his own rights.

One day the cook approached me and informed me that this boy must be expelled as he was uncontrollable. I replied that we could not afford to lose even one child, and we needed to do whatever we could in order to remedy any of their faults.

My answer did not satisfy her. She went straight to the director, Dr. Lebel, who came to me the following day and requested that the boy be expelled. I gave him the same response that I gave the cook, "It doesn't even come into question that I would expel any child, no matter what he did."

He gave me all sorts of arguments. Then he finally said, "What do you, a 20-year-old young man, know about education? Have you ever studied psychology or teaching skills? I am older than you, and I know better. When there is a rotten apple in the basket, we need to throw it out before it infects the other apples."

I remained firm in my position, and did not budge. I said to him, "We made an agreement that we would have no interference in all matters relating to education."

He said, "This case is an exception, and we need to take action."

"If this is your final decision, we have no alternative but to resign," I told him very calmly. "We will go back to Hennoville from where we will leave for Eretz Yisrael as soon as possible."

"All right. Fine," he said, so my friend and I went to prepare for our voyage to Paris and then on to the kibbutz.

They brought in a famous educator from Switzerland, a neat, elegant man who asked Dr. Lebel, "Why did you engage two young men with no experience in education? If the children are wild, in a few weeks they will be entirely changed. My experience is excellent as are my qualifications. Just wait and see."

It was with mixed feelings that we left the place. On the one hand, we were happy that we would be leaving for Israel much sooner. This was our dream when we were in the camps and even before the war. On the other hand, we had grown deeply attached to the children, who had become to us like family. We could not help but wonder how they would fare now, and if they would be happy, without us to guide them. Thinking these thoughts, we arrived at the kibbutz, and tried to forget the four weeks we had spent in Aix-les-Bains with those precious Jewish children who were so rare and unique, whom we had tried so hard to help.

We had not even been three days in our new environment, when we were urgently summoned to the office. The administrator in Aix was on the phone, telling us that we could have our way, and the unruly boy could stay in the home if we wanted. All the conditions that had been agreed upon the first time would from now on be fully honored, just as long as we returned and resumed our roles as educators and leaders. Now, again, we were in a dilemma. Should our own personal welfare come first, to realize our dreams of going to the Holy Land, or should we consider first the interests of those fifty youngsters whom we had undertaken to care for and raise in the true Jewish spirit as if they were our brothers and sisters? Our hearts won out, and once again we were on the train to Aix-les-Bains.

We could not have foreseen what an eventful journey we would have. We missed the 8 o'clock train to Aix that Thursday evening, for we were unfamiliar with the streets of Paris and the transportation. The next train was supposed to leave at about 8 a.m. on Friday morning, and, as according to the schedule it was supposed to arrive in Aix about four hours before the Sabbath, we took that train.

I don't know whether the blame lay with the train, or with lack of order in France after the war, but we ended up being delayed in one section for about two hours. We sat on pins and needles wondering if we would still arrive on time before the Sabbath. When we arrived in Lyon, we were told that the train would not go any further, and we would have to take another train to Aix-les-Bains. Upon checking the schedule, however, we discovered that the other train would arrive precisely at candlelighting time, at the start of the Sabbath. As we had already lost all confidence in the French trains and their schedules, we decided to stay in Lyon for the Sabbath, and leave for Aix on Sunday morning.

Now, at this time, France was not interested in acquiring immigrants. In order for us to enter France as a transit point to Israel, Mrs. Sternbuch had procured for us false papers for going to Venezuela, or some other South American country, thus enabling us to obtain temporary French transit visas. We did not dare show our papers to the police or any other French government official for fear that they would uncover the scheme used by many Jewish organizations to bring Jewish people to Israel through the port of Marseilles.

With our meager belongings fitting into an ordinary brief-case, we set out to find a Jewish person or place where we could stay for two nights. It was the time of *sefirah,* days between Pesach and Shavuos, when certain customs of mourning are kept, and our unshaved faces must have caught the attention of two police officers patrolling the streets on their bicycles. They stopped us and asked us for our identification papers. Not understanding a word of French, all the while knowing full well what they were asking, we just mumbled some words in Yiddish. After a couple of minutes, a pedestrian, a Jewish man, stopped by and offered to be an interpreter. While he was talking to the officers, a streetcar stopped right in front of us, opened its doors, and let us hop on, leaving the officers and the Jew behind us. We got out when we passed a hotel, and we arranged to get a room for two nights. Then we went out again to look for a Jew who could show us or take us to a synagogue.

We walked the distance of one short block when we again came face to face with the same police officers on their bicy-cles. This time they insisted that we go with them to the police station. With our hands we tried to explain to them that we were religious Jews in search of a synagogue, but to no avail. When we arrived at the station, the officers began to speak with different personnel while we waited. Finally, an officer at the desk told us in broken German that we would have to wait until morning when the station head would arrive, as he knew German well, and we would be able to discuss matters with him. We were told that we could sit or lie down on one of the benches in the station until the next morning.

Fortunately, we had our prayer books with us, and some bread. We made ourselves comfortable, and began to pray, as if we were in a synagogue, singing some Gerer songs that we used to sing at home. Afterwards we asked if we could wash our hands, and we made *Kiddush* on the bread. The officer at the desk watched us and scratched his head, as if to say: What kind of strange animals are these two guys? But there is freedom of expression in France, and he was resigned to our *shtick*. For our part, we defiantly continued to sing, quite loudly, all the *zemiros* (Shabbos songs). When he put down his head on the desk in order to take a nap, we came forward with the only French word that we knew, *salle de bains,* which means bathroom. Naturally, he could not let us go alone, and needed to watch us. All this took up a big part of the night, until we got tired and lay down on benches for a few hours of sleep.

In the morning the police captain arrived, and we explained to him our situation, without showing him our papers. We showed him pictures of us with the children in Aix-les-Bains. Obviously moved, he apologized warmly for the officers who arrested us. He explained that with our shaven heads and unshaven beards, we looked like German prisoners of war who had escaped from custody. Then he told one of the officers who had brought us in to take us to a synagogue. We finally found a chassidic *shtiebel* where we were welcomed with open arms. We were then invited for the meal by Rabbi Shapiro, a brother of the famous Rabbi Meir Shapiro, founder of Yeshivas Chachmei Lublin.

Early Sunday morning we took the train to Aix. As we walked down the hill on the way to the home, the children spotted us from a distance. We heard shrieks of delight, and in a matter of moments we were down on the ground with the children climbing on top of us and all over each other. They were singing and dancing around us as we walked down to our residence.

I asked the cook what had happened to the educator from Switzerland. She told me that the gentleman had been used to Swiss children who came from normal, disciplined homes. In his institute in Bex-les-Bains, near Lausanne, he had children who had been raised with more restraint and obedience, as befitted citizens of Switzerland. He was unable to bring himself down to the level of these refugee children, to empathize and identify with children who had neither homes nor parents, who had been raised in the forests and in the camps where fighting for one's food and one's rights was the norm. It was no wonder that they were unruly and restive, but for him they were unmanageable and uncontrollable, and he could not tolerate their resourcefulness in mischief making. So he left. We, on the other hand, understood the children well, and they understood us, because we were on their level, and could share their feelings since our experiences were similar to theirs. We never gave them orders, but we motivated them to do on their own what we thought they should be doing. Ours was an exemplary family relationship, for they trusted us, and our primary concern was for their well-being. Whatever we lacked in experience and psychological know-how, we made up for with our hearts.

Epilogue

The boy whom the administrator and the cook wanted to expel became very friendly with me and I gained his confidence. When I was talking privately with him, I learned that when he had been in a kibbutz in Poland, his teacher, who probably did not want to put in any extra effort in his education, had told him that he was a *shmatte kop* (dunce), giving him the message that he had no ability to learn, no matter how hard he would try. So why should he try now?

I asked him to try once more with me. I would test him and assess his capabilities. Starting with learning to read a line in a prayer book, he made quite a few mistakes. However, I stretched the truth a bit, and told him that he had read it perfectly. More than once I would tell him that I found him to be highly intelligent. Gradually he regained his self-confidence. In a month, he reached the same level as the others.

This boy, whom we fought to keep in the children's home, is now living in Israel and has raised his children and grandchildren to be deeply religious and fine, highly respected citizens of the country. In 1962, I made my first visit to Israel, and when I reunited with my former student, he embraced me and said, "What would have become of me, if not for you!?"

Teachers and educators can learn a lesson from this. It may be the simplest solution for a teacher to rid himself of a problematic student, who might cause him trouble and extra work. But what about the child in question? Should he be abandoned and sacrificed in order that the teacher should have a stress-free job? A teacher must care for each and every child, and give him the love and dedication that he deserves, despite his misbehavior. For every child is precious, and with a bit of extra effort and resolve, one can do wonders.

❧❦❧

The ways of G-d are undecipherable by the human psyche. One can make plans that will lead him in one direction, and G–d's Providence will take him in another direction. After I had been at the children's home for almost a year, waiting to go with them to Israel, my health – which had been weakened from the years of hunger, hard work and beatings in the ghetto and the camps – failed again. I contracted pneumonia and tuberculosis. My benefactors were once again from the wonderful Sternbuch family. Eli and Guta Sternbuch, together with her mother, Mrs. Aisencwaig from Warsaw, took care of me and brought me to a sanatorium in Davos, Switzerland. I was not alone there. Hundreds of survivors, young men and women, wound up in hospitals in Davos. My education did not come to a standstill, for there were volunteers, patients them-

Reb Eli Sternbuch and his wife Guta with their children in the 1950's

Seated (left to right): Mr. Newman (son-in-law of the Sternbuchs), Reb Eli Sternbuch, Guta Sternbuch. Standing (left to right): Mrs. Newman, her son, Israel Cohen, Perle Cohen. Picture was taken in 1994.

Davos, Switzerland, 1948, sanatorium for treatment of TB. (Right to left): Israel Cohen, Joseph Rinski, Mottel Stern, Mayer Peses, Moshe Gefen, Menachem Haberman

Davos, 1948. Resting after a walk in the mountains. Israel Cohen is on top, middle

selves, or outsiders paid by the Swiss Jewish community, who instructed us in our schooling.

After two years in the sanatorium in Davos, we were transferred to a convalescent home in Montana, in the French part of Switzerland. There we were able to learn a trade, and also languages, mathematics and other subjects that we had missed learning because of the years we had spent in the camps.

Now Providence once again revealed its profound involvement in my life. G-d wanted me to meet a visitor there, a bright, cheerful, lovely young woman from the prominent Sternberg family in Geneva, a unique chassidic family that helped Jewish refugees who were interned in special camps by the Swiss authorities during the war. They would bring them kosher food and stay in touch with them in order to cater to their needs.

This young woman, who was gifted with both brains and beauty, was to achieve a momentous difference in my life. She agreed to become my wife. To her I owe the most in my efforts to become a sane and healthy person. Any survivor of the Holocaust has undergone enough trauma and upheaval to provide a lifetime of negative effects on his sanity and health. The right lifetime companion could help to partially heal one's physical injuries and battered nerves that resulted from the years in the ghetto and camps. Although the harmful aftereffects could never be totally erased, I am deeply grateful to my wife for helping me to lead a somewhat normal existence.

I still wanted to go to live in Israel, which by now was an independent country, but because of the uncertain situation there, I was advised by the Israeli government to wait for better times. The rest of Europe was closed to me, as I was still a refugee. We immigrated to Canada in 1951. I continued to teach as my first career. Thanks to the A-mighty, we have raised a fine family of five children — three daughters and two

1988, at the wedding of my youngest son. Left to right: Itche Perelman, Yossel Karmel, Henry Cohen (formerly U.S. Army), Israel Cohen

sons — who are now all married and bringing us *nachas* (pleasure) from our grandchildren.

My book has often emphasized the point that a person is not the master of his destiny. The A–mighty's guiding hand leads us to the places where He wants us to be. As I did in the camps, I still now feel that there are angels at my side protecting me and escorting me along the right path. Anyone contemplating his roots and his past must soon recognize that faith in G-d is an absolute necessity in order to traverse life's vicissitudes. Both in joy and in sorrow we trust in the A–mighty, as it says in *Tehillim* (116:3,4,13): "In suffering and sorrow ... I call the Name of G-d ... I raise the cup of salvations and call the Name of G-d."

Afterword

I chose "Destined to Survive" as the title of my book, because I believe that any person who survived the Holocaust did so only on account of Divine Providence, absolutely not by chance or luck. We have to admit that we do not know why so many perished and why some survived. The question of why a righteous person should be doomed and a bad person saved was already asked by Moshe Rabbeinu, and the answer from Hashem, according to the Talmud, was: "I will be gracious to whom I want, and I will show mercy to whom I want, without regard to whether the person deserves it or not" (*Berachos* 7a). It is futile for us humans to attempt to understand the ways of the A-mighty, the Creator. How can we understand that a highly cultured nation like Germany – that had in its ranks so many people who excelled in medicine, science, music and writing – should suddenly reveal themselves to be the most barbaric and savage nation, a nation of murderers, who slaughtered, without mercy, women, children and innocent civilians, just because they were Jews? They tortured millions with starvation and deleterious work, and – like Haman – tried to eradicate the Jewish nation so that any remembrance of them would remain only in the museums that they planned to erect. They almost succeeded in their endeavor, with their diabolical methods and meticulous procedures.

So how could there be any survivors? I have seen the smartest and the most intelligent people trying to escape death – to no avail. The healthiest and the strongest could perish, while some of the weakest and most sickly survived. From my own experience and from observing others, I came to the only possible conclusion: Divine Providence determined that certain people would live to tell the tale. How often was I in situations in which there was no way out? Logically, I should have been gassed, shot, or succumbed to epidemics, hunger and cold. How many times was I at the gates of death, only to be saved at the last minute? It could not be otherwise than that somehow G-d wanted me to continue to exist, and sent His guardian angels to save my life. I was destined by Heaven to survive against all odds. Nor am I alone in this perception of wartime experiences. I have heard from many people incredible tales of their endurance in the face of incredible odds. Here are only a few examples:

This is the saga of my friend Mendel Przityk, now living in Jerusalem, Israel:

As the Allies closed in on the German empire, the Germans were forced to retreat, and they did not want to leave any witnesses to their crimes. Wherever they could, they dismantled the concentration camps and gas chambers and crematoriums, and forced the remaining prisoners to march with them deeper into the Reich. These were the infamous death marches, and the prisoners who were already frail, without warm clothes and shoes, died like flies on the journey that lasted for weeks. The SS guards who pressed them on had a special unit in the rear watching out for people lying on the road, many of whom were already dead, and shooting each one of them in the head to make sure that no one would survive.

Mendel Przityk was a participant in one of these marches. He had survived five years in the Lodz ghetto, Auschwitz and other camps where he had been taken, and now was mustering up his last strength to keep up with the rest. After a few days of marching, feeling that his feet could not carry him any longer, after barely managing to trudge in the cold and snow without adequate clothing and shoes, and not having eaten for days, he told his friends that he was giving up, as he could not continue to march. His companions urged him to persevere and not give up, as the Allies were on their tail and might overtake them at any time. He tried again for a few hours, but finally, he could not continue one more step, and fell to the ground, helpless. As he lay there in the dark, painfully aware of people stepping on his body, he could only hope to escape his misery by being shot by the SS unit. Suddenly, he heard one of the guards cry out, "Here's another one! Put a bullet through his head!"

Then another voice, in German, spoke. "Hey, this guy is a faker. He wants to be shot to get out of his suffering. We are not going to oblige him by fulfilling his wish. Let him suffer some more!"

Mendel felt a gun jam into his ribs, and the same voice ordered, "Swindler! Get up immediately!"

Mendel did not open his eyes and did not budge.

The guard shouted out to the marchers to stop moving,

then called out to two people who were obviously stronger, "You! Take him by the arms, pick him up and hold him between the two of you! You are responsible with your lives that he marches on!"

Mendel survived. Clearly, destined to survive.

Rabbi Y. Denebeim, of Palm Springs, California, told me this story:

He was sitting in the synagogue at the third Shabbos meal. Many people were sitting around the table, singing Shabbos songs. One man sitting near the rabbi asked him quietly, "Who is the man sitting across the table from us?"

The rabbi said, "He is Mr. Kornwasser of Los Angeles."

Mr. Kornwasser, sensing that the man across the table was looking at him, asked him, "What is your name? Your face is somehow familiar to me."

"My name is Leiserowitz," answered the man across the table.

"And what city are you originally from?"

It turned out that they were both from Sosnovic (Sosnovitz in Yiddish). Meanwhile, there were another two men at the table who said that they were also from Sosnovitz. One was Mr. Kornwasser's brother and the other was a Mr. Korn. They asked each other particulars about the city, and the people they knew, and about the last time they had been in Sosnovitz. There emerged a tale from this exchange that was mind-boggling.

In September 1939, when the Germans invaded Poland, they arrived in Sosnovitz after only a few days of marching, as it was not far from the German border. Here they left a small occupational army detail, then continued to march on deeper into Poland. The person in command of this detail, wanting to show the people that the Germans were now in power and would not allow any opposition or rebellion, ordered all the people of the city into the marketplace, Jews on one side, gentiles on the other. Then he picked out ten chassidic teenaged boys, set them up against the wall and ordered a dozen German soldiers to act as a firing squad.

Suddenly, the ground in the marketplace trembled, as a number of German officers on motorcycles roared into the square. The highest-ranking officer demanded to know what was going on. The detail captain replied that someone had fired a shot from a window at a German soldier and therefore, he had picked out these ten people at random to show the populace that no resistance against the Germans would be tolerated. The head officer of the motorcycle crew said, "Why do you need ten people to be shot? Let nine of them go, and shoot only one."

Now, at the table in Rabbi Denebeim's shul, the incredible story arrived at a new conclusion, as the four men from Sosnovitz realized that each of them had been one of the nine teenagers who had been miraculously saved from certain death on that day. Destined to survive by Divine Providence, they were also astoundingly destined to be reunited at one table in Palm Springs, California, in 1985, after not having seen each other since 1939, each one of them amazed to find his friends alive after all those years.

❧

This is the story of Moshe Gefen, now living in Lugano, Switzerland:

As a young boy, he was interned in one of the camps in Poland, one of the "good" camps, where the inmates worked in a factory and had contact with Polish workers. As these workers came in from outside the camp, there developed a kind of black market, a smuggling operation of goods in exchange for money – Deutsche marks, American dollars (very rarely), with gold pieces more available. They did not deal in large amounts, maybe a hundred marks, or a couple of gold pieces. Naturally, possession of marks or gold was a capital offense, punishable by death. Soon, an informer started to blackmail Mr. Gefen, and when he did not get what he wanted, denounced him to the camp commandant. At first, Mr. Gefen denied having anything valuable, but after a good beating, he was forced to confess and showed the camp heads his hiding place where he kept a couple of gold pieces. The next day, his number was called out at the *appelplatz*, where a gallows had been erected. He was ordered to remove his shirt and was taken to the gallows. Just as the SS person in command was reading out his sentence, the air-raid sirens started to wail, indicating that an air raid was about to occur. The Germans, fearing for their lives, ran away like terrified mice into the underground bunkers. Our hero also ran away and hid, but, as soon as the air raid ended, a manhunt was conducted for poor Mr. Gefen. Again, he was led to the gallows, and before all the inmates, the sentence for his "crime" was pronounced. Once more, the screaming sirens interrupted the procedure, signaling another air raid. This time, the SS guards, fearing that the Russian army was rapidly approaching, ran away to the west, where the German army was retreating. Thus, our Mr. Gefen was saved from certain death at the last minute. Once could be called luck, but twice was certain evidence that Divine Providence had decreed him "destined to survive," for which Moshe Gefen is undeniably grateful to the A-mighty.

The last story was told to me by Mr. Stanford, my friend and neighbor in Toronto, Canada, who died two years ago at the age of 93.

Mr. Stanford had been married before the Second World War, and had a wife and five children. He lived before the war in Krakow, Poland, and was a successful businessman. When the war broke out, the Germans sent all the Jews to the ghetto. Later, the ghetto was liquidated and all the Jews were sent to Plashow, a camp near Krakow, made famous by the film, "Shindler's List." The camp was run by the infamous Nazi commander, Goeth, featured in the film as a psychopath who killed people in order to satisfy his thirst for blood. When they entered the camp, there was a *selektzia*, in which Goeth sent the men fit for work to one side, and the women and children to the other side. Mr. Stanford saw this SS commander Goeth walk around with his gun among the women and children who were made to sit on the ground. He witnessed the beast shoot each of his children, and then his wife. Mr. Stanford was sent to Auschwitz, where he worked for many months. There, there were *selektzias* almost daily. People were taken away whenever there was a need to keep the gas chambers working incessantly. One day, he was selected with a group of forty men, ordered to undress, and led to the gas chambers. As the commandos were busy removing the gassed bodies from the chambers, the forty men were told to sit on the ground and wait until the gas chambers were ready and until more people would be brought in to be gassed. While they were waiting, an SS officer passed by and asked them what they were doing there. They told him that they were waiting to be gassed. The officer, probably needing some workers, told them to get dressed and come with him. Thus, Mr. Stanford lived – because he was destined to survive.

I can tell everyone, survivors, or children of survivors, and anyone else: Just open your eyes and try to see that there is a guiding hand that causes us to make the right decisions (or the wrong ones). If you try hard to think objectively, you will see the meaning of the verse in the book of *Proverbs* (19:21): "Many are the plans in a man's heart, but it is the design of G-d that shall stand." I am sometimes amazed at how Providence works for me up to the present time. I could write another book relating these stories. I thank the A-mighty for allowing me to live to tell the world my tale and the tales of the ones who did not survive. I am just one small cog among the millions of people who passed through hell, as are the other people who suffered as I did, some more, some less. At least, as one destined to survive, I can be a messenger for those who cannot speak. Remember the words of King David, that are mentioned earlier, from the Talmud, Tractate *Berachos* 10: "Even if a sharpened sword is placed on your neck, you should not despair of Hashem's mercy." Do not give up hope, but pray to the A-mighty Who can save you against all odds.

Appendix

Buchgraben KZ, February 1945
By Mirka Cohen

I

Oh! You beautiful years of young age
How miserably do you pass me by.
Inside a fenced barbed-wire cage
From ceaseless crying my eyes are dry.

In the darkness of the night
On my bunk bed I ponder –
Oh G-d! Why don't You show us
All Your wonders?

I cannot stand on my feet
My blood freezes in my veins.
I feel dejected and beaten
By life, which from my body drains.

I feel that I am about to expire.
I am almost dead in the mire.
I am ready to be put on the pyre.

And help is nowhere in sight.
The future seems as dark as the night.

Oh, why? I still remember a different life.
You could go your own way
With no obstacle, without strife
You could sing, dance, play.

Life was so lovely, so fair
So cheerful and so sweet.
Now where has everything gone, oh where?
The sound is as faint as a heartbeat.

I lie on my bunk bed nearly dead
In the misery of hunger and cold.
I have almost forgotten the taste of bread
What I eat is mostly mold.

My sorrow keeps growing
Day and night,
To see my young sisters
Swallowed by death's might.

Oh no! How can human life be so cruel?
I would like to live like a squirrel
In a tree, or like a worm or bee
Or like a bird soaring free
If only the harsh world not to see.

No father, no mother,
No friend, no brother dear.
What hope is there for the future
When the present is so severe?

II

In the darkness of the night
A troubling thought passes my mind –
Oh G-d! Why don't You show Your might
Against Amalek, Haman and their kind?
You gave our enemies the right
To make us vanish from Your sight.

In a stormy fire we are caught.
For three days and three nights
The bombs are falling
On the huts of the slaves.
I crawl down from my bunk bed
To the ground below.
I passed the window and almost at the door
Suddenly a bomb blasted in our midst.
It shattered some of my sisters
To pieces and bits.
Those of us who survived
Began to scream and to yell
With all of our strength –
SHEMA YISRAEL!

This volume is part of
THE ARTSCROLL SERIES®
an ongoing project of
translations, commentaries and expositions
on Scripture, Mishnah, Talmud, Halachah,
liturgy, history, the classic Rabbinic writings,
biographies and thought.

For a brochure of current publications
visit your local Hebrew bookseller
or contact the publisher:

Mesorah Publications, ltd

4401 Second Avenue
Brooklyn, New York 11232
(718) 921-9000
www.artscroll.com